CW00495184

EXCEL 2023

No More Secrets with The Updated Crash Course to Become a True Excel Master in Less than 7 Minutes a Day, From Basic to Expert User, with Formulas, Tutorial, Tips and Tricks

By

THOMAS HARRETT

Table of Contents

INTRODUCTION

The most widely used program today is Microsoft Excel, which is pre-installed with other Microsoft Office packages. Worksheets are the main use for them due to their adaptability and flexibility. The use of Microsoft Excel has increased in large businesses across the globe. It can do various technical, financial, and computational activities that would be ineffective if conducted manually. Using Microsoft Excel 2023 for more productive work saves time and energy. Businesses are searching for staff that is not just familiar with the internet but also have a solid grasp of Microsoft Excel because of how the world is changing. You know how to utilize Microsoft Excel; hence, you do not want to miss a job chance as an entrepreneur.

Major organizations and department leaders should teach their staff how to use Microsoft Excel 2023 as one of the programs to guarantee that a company runs smoothly and, more significantly, to boost employee productivity both within and outside the firm. What is the big deal? Microsoft Excel 2023 is a challenging technology to understand and use, so what is the big deal? This user manual will teach Microsoft Excel 2023 in an approachable and useful way. After reading this guide, you may quickly master the excellent talent of excel. If you set up some time each day to learn Excel in one week, it will assist.

We hope your journey to learn more about this book will be enjoyable.

CHAPTER 1

WHY EXCEL AND THE HISTORY OF EXCEL

Data may be stored, organized, and analyzed with the help of Microsoft Excel. It is a globally used computer application in offices, despite its short lifespan (1985 release date). Excel experts may be useful in any company activity, regardless of industry.

Excel has become an integral part of corporate procedures throughout the globe, evaluating stock or issuers, financing, or maintaining client sales lists. Using Microsoft Excel, you may edit data entered into a spreadsheet. Excel's sophisticated analytical and computational capabilities make it a popular choice among financial and accounting professionals.

Trends may be found, and relevant categories can be created in Microsoft Excel.

Human resources services, such as categorizing hours worked and arranging employee profiles and costs, are also performed by Excel, which aids organizations in better understanding their workforce's structure and activities. Data from the worksheet is summarized into a graph using pivot tables.

1.1 YOU CAN DO ANYTHING WITH A SPREADSHEET

Excel's commercial uses are almost limitless. Here are a few instances:

- For a baseball team excursion, you may use Excel to keep track of RSVPs and expenditures.
- For the latest items, Excel produces revenue growth projections based on estimates from new customers.
- You may use a spreadsheet to plan out your website's editorial schedule.
- Budgeting for small products may be as simple as putting all the costs into a spreadsheet, which you can then keep up to date every month, and then generating a graph to indicate how close your product is to stay within its allocated budget in every category.
- According to a customer's monthly purchase volume, discounts may be calculated for them.
- Customers' revenue may be summarized by product so that users can identify areas where they can create deeper ties with their customers.

Make use of sophisticated formulas, such as Sharpe ratios.

The toolbar was initially introduced in Excel.

1.2 EXCEL IS NOT GOING ANYWHERE

Excel will remain a mainstay if organizations use it for various tasks and purposes, including IT projects and workplace picnics. Excel proficiency is now a requirement for many office workers, and those who have honed their Excel abilities may be better positioned to advance in their careers and take on more responsibility.

The power of Excel is undeniable, yet it can't do everything by itself. Excel can only be used to its full potential by an experienced computer user who knows how to get the most of its features.

1.3 WHAT IS MICROSOFT EXCEL AND HOW IS IT USED IN BUSINESS?

Excel is a spreadsheet tool for organizing and analyzing data. Excel is used by businesses for budgeting, recognizing patterns, forecasting, reporting, and more.

1.4 HOW CAN YOU CREATE A BUSINESS BUDGET IN EXCEL?

Templates for both personal and corporate users are available in Excel. A budget spreadsheet tailored to your company's needs is the quickest and easiest way to establish a business budget.

Input labels, analysis algorithms, and other spreadsheets with the most well-known budgeting variables, such as revenue, staff costs, and operational expenditures, are common in most of these budgeting packages.

Manual budget creation is also an option in which the user enters their labels, tables, & calculations.

1.5 HOW DO YOU TRACK BUSINESS EXPENSES IN EXCEL?

Templates for keeping track of expenditures are available in Excel. The Expense Management template is most often used, containing areas for various business-related costs. A user may edit or remove column labels or headers to better suit his or her own needs. The template has been designed to make it as simple as possible for the user to enter data into the appropriate cells. Manually creating expenditure reports is also possible for users.

1.6 THE HISTORY OF MICROSOFT EXCEL

As Multiplan, a widely used CP/M (Control Programs for Microcomputers), Excel has been available since 1982, although it was overtaken by Lotus 1-2-3 on MS-DOS systems. Microsoft launched the Windows version of Excel v2.0 in 1987 and started to outcompete Lotus 1-2-3 & the then-new QuatroPro in 1988. VBA (Visual Basics for Applications), often known as Macros, was first introduced in Microsoft Excel v5.0 for Windows in 1993. This has made no limits to number crunching, data presentation, and process automation possible.

1.7 PRESENT DAY MICROSOFT EXCEL

Now that you've reached the current day, Microsoft Excel has become the most extensively used business program in the world since it can be utilized for every company function. Little can't be accomplished with the help of Microsoft Office products such as Word, Outlook, PowerPoint, etc.

As far as Excel and Office Suite go, there are almost no limits. As an example, below are the ten most used and effective built-in Excel features:

- The ability to model and analyze almost any kind of data
- Focus on the most critical information as fast as possible.
- Use one cell to create graphs of data
- Utilize your spreadsheets from any location that has internet access.
- When people collaborate, they can do more.
- Utilize more dynamic and engaging PivotCharts.
- Your data presentations should be more visually appealing. Do things quicker and more efficiently.
- Build larger and more sophisticated spreadsheets with greater power.
- Publication and distribution of workbooks using Excel Services

A powerful BI (Business Intelligences) platform that can be easily customized and automated using Visual Basic for Applications (VBA) is now even more valuable. Do you want to use Microsoft Excel to solve your business problems? Count on this guide. You've collaborated with companies of various sizes and in a variety of industries. Whether a large corporation or a small business, this guide can help you get the most out of Microsoft Excel.

CHAPTER 2

BASICS FOR BEGINNERS

With Excel, you can do anything. It can manage anything from simple data management chores to more complicated mathematical procedures for business or technical applications. The program's vocabulary might be a little confusing, but it's not difficult to grasp the fundamentals. Excel utilizes a variety of terminology to describe its core capabilities, and this chapter examines a few of them.

2.1 LIST OF TERMS COVERED

Term	Quick Explanation
Workbook	An Excel file.
Worksheet	A worksheet within an Excel file.
Ribbon	The menu bar at the top of Excel.
Cell	A rectangular box in a worksheet that contains data.
Name Box	Shows the cell/table selected; also used to rename cells/tables.
Cell Reference	The cell/table selected.
Formula Bar	Shows the data/formula/phrase in the cell selected.
Formula	A set of instructions for Excel to carry out.
Functions	Formulas built into Excel.
Array/Range	A group of cells or tables denoted by a colon between th 1st and last cell.

Workbook

Simply described, an Excel file is a workbook. Regardless of how many worksheets are included, all Excel documents are workbooks. Book 1 is the title of the workbook seen in the illustration. If the file name is not altered, it will be stored with this name. Think of it like a ledger book for bookkeeping. Exactly. The whole thing. Worksheets are individual pages.

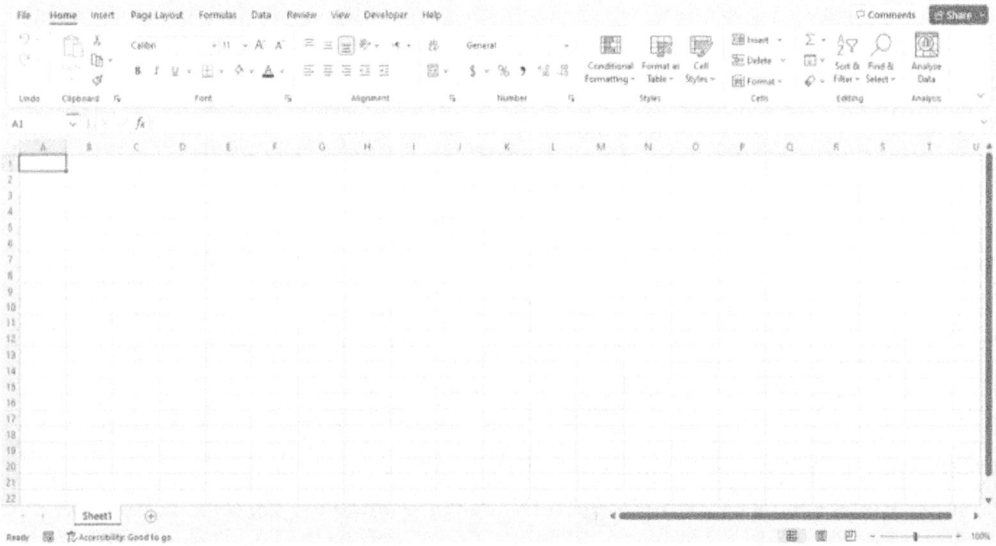

Worksheet

Each worksheet is a stand-alone document that may include one or more data tables (we'll get into that further in a minute). You may think of it as a single page in a much larger tome of financial records.

There are usually three worksheets at the beginning of a new workbook. To remove any, right-click just on the worksheet and choose Delete from the context menu. Click on the Add Worksheet button to begin adding new worksheets (A green box is highlighted).

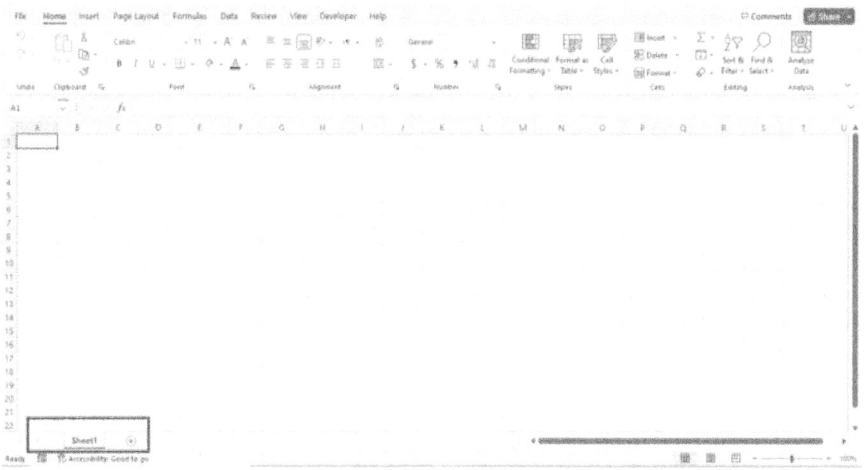

There are no worksheets that are related to each other in any way. Worksheets may be referenced in a formula. The following will provide detailed explanations of each formula.

Ribbon

The line of buttons that runs down the top of the work area is known as the Ribbon. A ribbon is just available in Excel 2007 and subsequent editions. The previous versions' menus & toolbars have been removed.

In addition to the Home, Insert, & Page Layout tabs, there are many more on the Ribbon. When you click on a tab, the relevant choices on the Ribbon will be shown.

Cell

Any worksheet's rectangular cells are referred to as "cells." Data or algorithms may be stored in them.

The presently chosen cell is known as the current cell or active cell. Using a strong black outline, it's easy to spot.

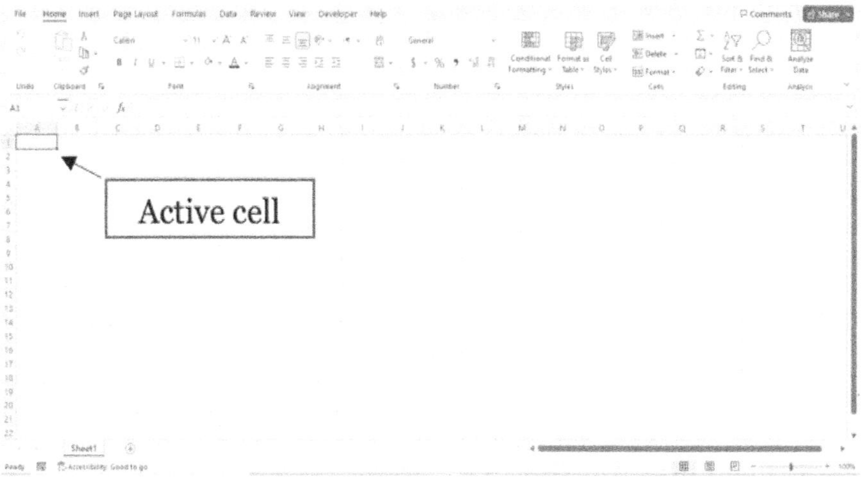

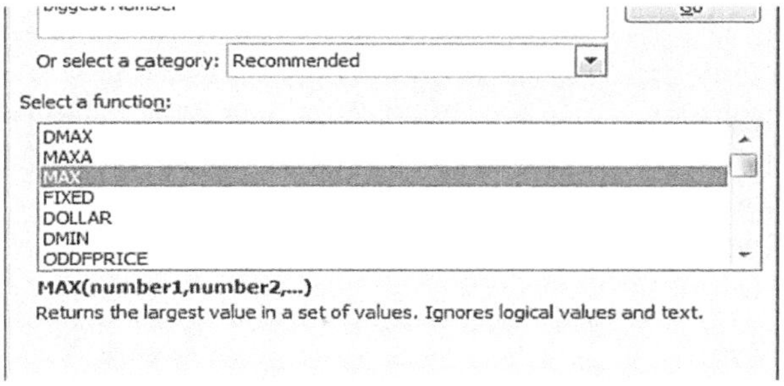

Name Box

Using the Name Box, you may see the current/active cell's name or even the title of a specified range of tables or cells. If a cell is selected, you may change its name within the Name Box by clicking and dragging it to a new location. Each worksheet can only have one cell/table with the same name.

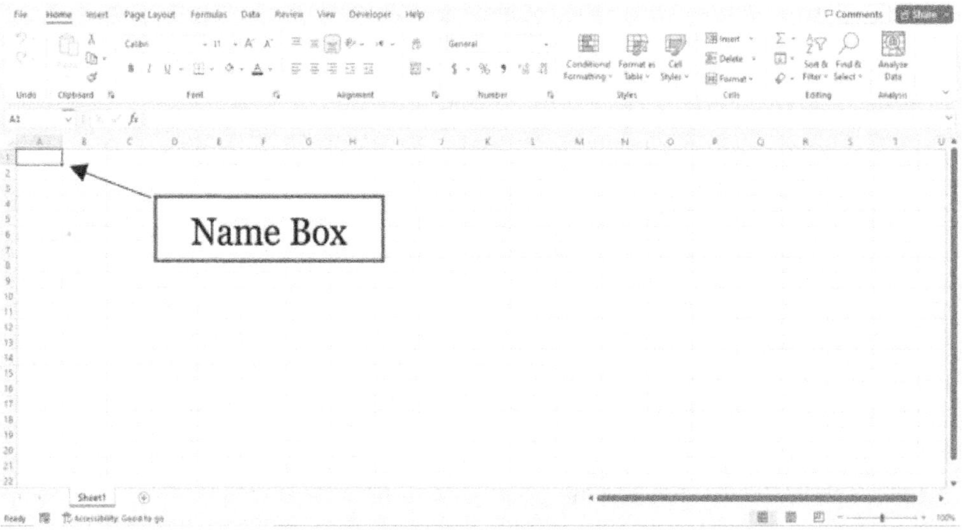

Cell Reference

The name of the chosen cell or table appears in the Cell Reference, indicating that it is the active or current table or cell.

The Name Box displays cell references.

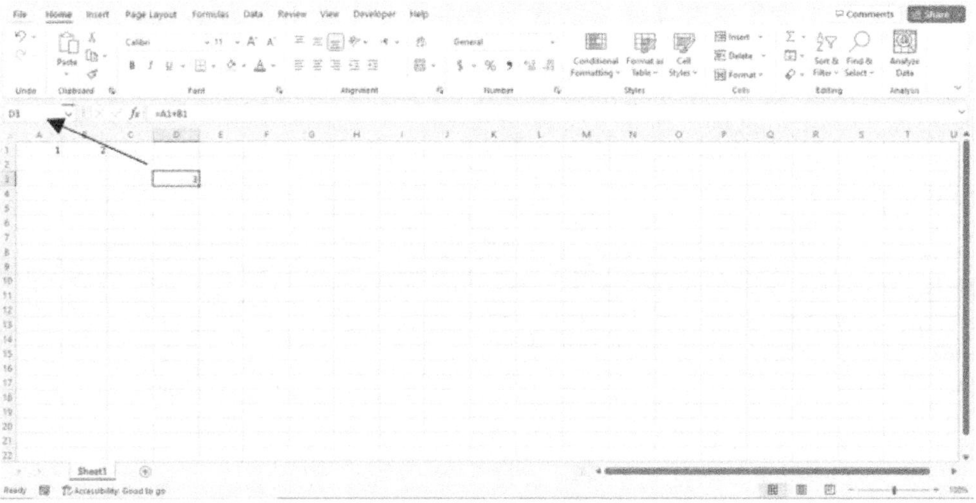

Formula Bar

A Formula Bar displays the current cell's contents.

On the other hand, a formula in the current/active cell displays the computed result in the current/active cell rather than the formula itself (which can be a phrase or number).

Formula

Formulas are an extremely useful feature of Excel. Using formulas, you may do automatic computations inside and between spreadsheets.

Enter the equal (=) symbol in the formula bar to begin a formula. A formula may include any of the four fundamental mathematical operators (subtract, add, divide or multiply), brackets to state the order in which the formula is solved, or Excel's built-in functions to perform any of these operations.

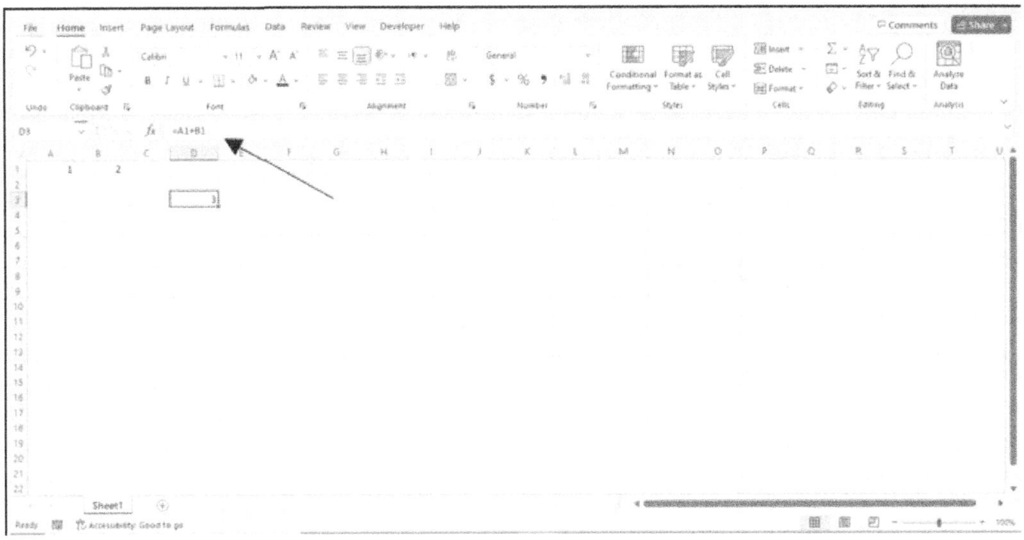

Functions

Excel's built-in functions are formulae. Formulas may be simplified by using functions.

For instance, the sum of A1 and B1 in the figure above is what we're looking for. The formula would be written as follows: =A1+B1.

Formula =SUM; using the SUM function would be more accurate (A 1: B 1).

It's possible that adding both cells would be more convenient. The SUM functions would involve writing your formula much simpler if you had to perform it for several cells or across several tables. Excel has over 400 built-in functions.

Extra reading might help you understand how to make the most of functions. This book will help you better grasp Excel's many functions, which are explained in detail.

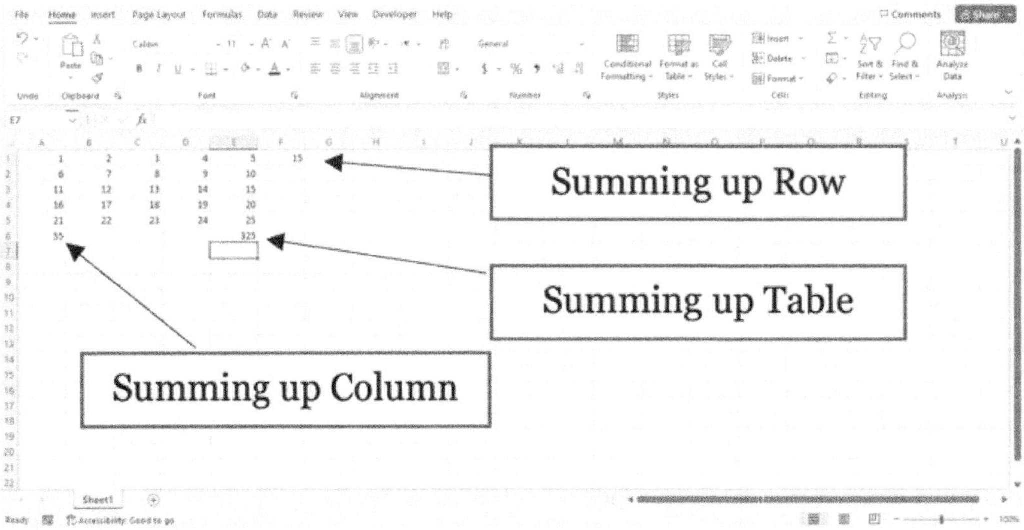

Array/Range

Finally, you'll discuss the array, or range, which is a data collection. In computing, an array or range is just a collection of related cells. The SUM formula, for example, uses an array/range of A1:B1 to go from A1 through B1.

To identify a range/array, the start and final cells of the range/array are separated by the colon (:). To access the cells in:

- Rows (e.g., A 1: E 1, shown within the red box)
- Tables (e.g., A 1: E 5, shown within the blue box)
- Columns (e.g., A 1: A 5, shown within the green box)

As can be seen, including these items in the formula significantly helps to shorten it, particularly in situations where many cells are being referred to.

2.2 UNDERSTANDING SPREADSHEET BASICS

A computer application that records, displays, and modifies data in columns and rows is called a spreadsheet. Excel spreadsheets are among the most widely used programs with personal computers. A spreadsheet's primary use is to store numerical data and a few text characters at a time. Spreadsheet cells are the individual areas inside a spreadsheet application that store individual data elements. Their names may be changed to more accurately represent the information they store, and their rows and columns can be cross-referenced using numbers and letters.

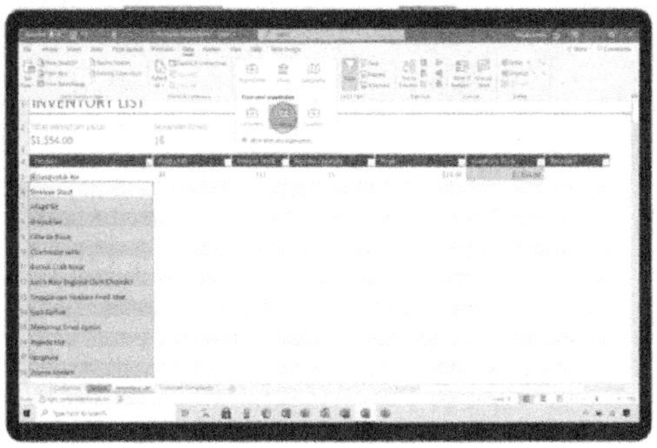

To organize and gather data for a specific purpose, a single spreadsheet may serve as a worksheet, or numerous sheets can be integrated into a single workbook. Each cell in every row and column refers to a value and is labeled according to its position (for example, A 1, A 2, A 3). The data may be saved as an a.csv file and then exported to be loaded into another program or vice versa.

Let's look at some of the capabilities available on spreadsheets.

What are some aspects of a spreadsheet that are often used?
The next is a brief list of spreadsheet software's capabilities.

Cell formatting
Different numeric values may be represented in the spreadsheet by formatting cells. For instance, accounting formatting may be used in financial data to depict dollars & cents with decimal places & commas.

Formulas
Using the formula bar, people may compare one cell's contents to another and do computations. For example, when users use the spreadsheet to balance transactions, they might mark all the cells that need to be implemented and enter a sum function.

Pivot tables
Customers may use the toolbar to the group, total, sort, or average data with the pivot table.
User has access to various tools and functions, and there are certain things about them that they should be aware of.

Common spreadsheet applications
The first spreadsheet program, VisiCalc, was designed by Daniel Bricklin & Bob Frankston. Just Apple II, among the first commercial computers, was quite popular.
After overtaking VisiCalc in popularity in the late 1980s and early 1990s, Lotus 1-2-3 became the most widely used personal computer application in business. IBM purchased Lotus around 1995 and sold Lotus 1-2-3 until 2013, when it abandoned the spreadsheet program, which had slipped behind Excel Spreadsheets in the 1990s and never regained. IBM bought Lotus in 1995.

Today's most popular spreadsheet applications include the following:

- In addition to Microsoft Office and the subscription service Microsoft 365, Excel is a component of the Microsoft Office suite (formally Office 365). Windows, Android, Mac, & iOS are all supported.

- Google Sheets is a component of Google Workspace, a collection of web-based apps from Google. Google Sheets is a free desktop and mobile application access for various operating systems, including Chrome Browser OS, iOS, and android.

- Ports of the free software suite Apache Open Office too, are accessible for operating systems than Linux, macOS, and Windows. One of them is Apache Open Office Calc. It wasn't until 2012 that it was made available to the public, although its conception dates to 2002.

- The freeware LibreOffice suite includes an application known as LibreOffice Calc, which is a fully functional spreadsheet program. Apache Open Office and LibreOffice can trace their origins to the same codebase, which is why both of their spreadsheet applications have the same name.

- Thinkfree Office is a free comprehensive productivity suite with a spreadsheet developed to provide a reliable system across various devices. A version may be accessed online and stored in the cloud.

At a glance: Google Sheets vs. Microsoft Excel

	Google Sheets	Microsoft Excel
PRICE	Free	Requires Office 365 subscription
TYPE OF APPLICATION	Cloud-based	Full-featured application is not cloud-based
COLLABORATION	Preferred for collaboration	Less favorable for collaboration
DATA PROCESSING	Weaker; storage is limited to 5 million cells	Stronger; storage is limited to 17 million cells
FEATURES	Basic spreadsheet features	Larger offering of advanced features
INTEGRATION	Integrates with Google apps and Microsoft files	Integrates with Microsoft apps
SUPPORT	Help articles and an interactive community	Community help forum and an Excel learning hub

Although Lotus 1-2-3 would be the first spreadsheet program to feature cell names & macros, Excel Spreadsheets were the first to integrate graphical user interfaces and the capability to point & select using a mouse.

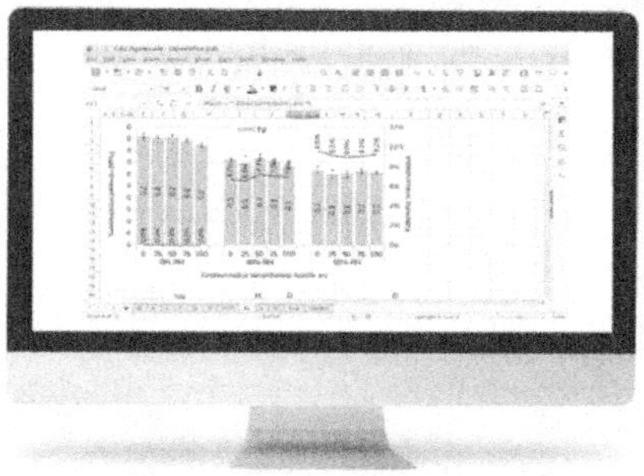

Most professional spreadsheet apps provide users with lessons and template documents to assist them in becoming proficient with the tool.

2.3 WHAT ARE SPREADSHEET CONTROLS?

Spreadsheet controls are methods that an organization's accounting staff utilizes to preserve the integrity & accuracy of the company's bookkeeping operations and the records of its financial transactions using spreadsheets. A continual effort is being made to quickly identify and correct mistakes, as well as to preserve the safety of the data. Spreadsheet control programs cannot be considered successful without first undergoing extensive training.

Included in the features of the software that controls spreadsheets should be:

- Control of access (usernames, passwords, biometrics)
- List of approved users that are always up to date.
- Cells that conduct essential calculations are restricted from being accessed.
- Secure ciphering
- Accuracy checks before data are sent out.
- Verification of the correctness of incoming data
- maintenance of network gear regularly
- Cross-referencing checksum techniques help prevent data loss and corruption.

- The most recent spreadsheet functions and features have been thoroughly assessed.
- Archiving and incremental backup regularly
- Off-site storage is available.
- Multiple media formats and redundant backup and archiving methods
- measures in place for data recovery
- Efficacy and adaptability

You'll enter data into cells for most of your work using Excel. Worksheets consist of a series of cells. To compute, analyze, and organize data in Excel, you'll need to grasp the fundamentals of cells and the material inside them.

2.4 UNDERSTANDING CELLS

Cells are rectangles that make up a worksheet's rows and columns. In a cell, the rows and columns meet. In which a row or a column intersect is called a cross-column. An alphabetical system is used to designate columns (A, B, C), whereas a numerical system is used to designate rows (1, 2, 3). Row and column determine each cell's name (or "address"). Column C & row 5 cross within the example below; thus, the cell value is C 5.

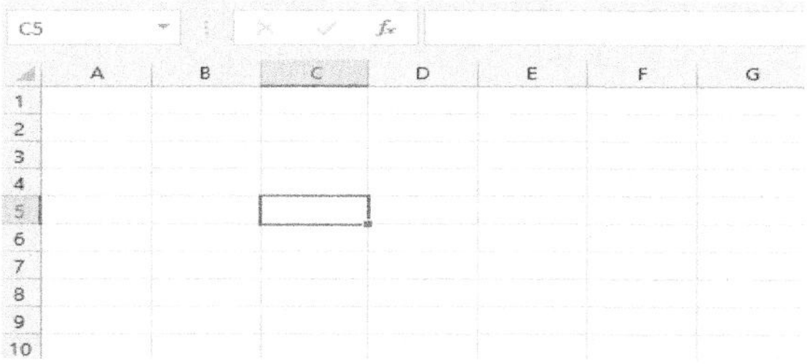

When a cell is chosen, the cell's column & row headers are highlighted in the Name box at the top-left corner. Selecting many cells at once is also possible. The term "cell range" refers to a collection of cells. Instead of utilizing an individual cell address, each cell range is defined by the colon-separated addresses with the first and final cells in the range. Using the example of a range of cells that includes A 1: A 5, you might write the following: Cell ranges are shown in the table below.

- Cell range A 1: A 8

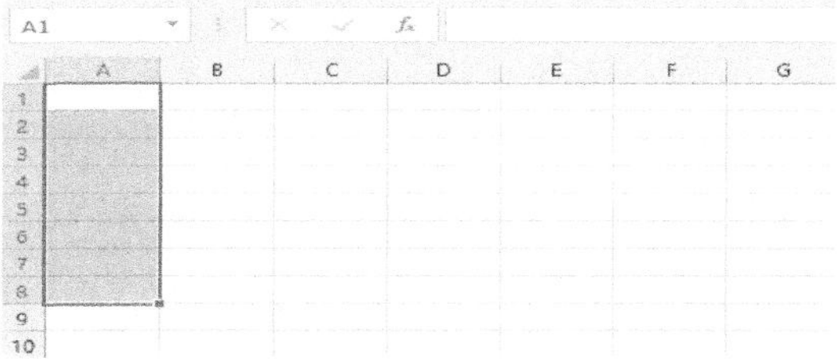

- Cell range A 1: F 1

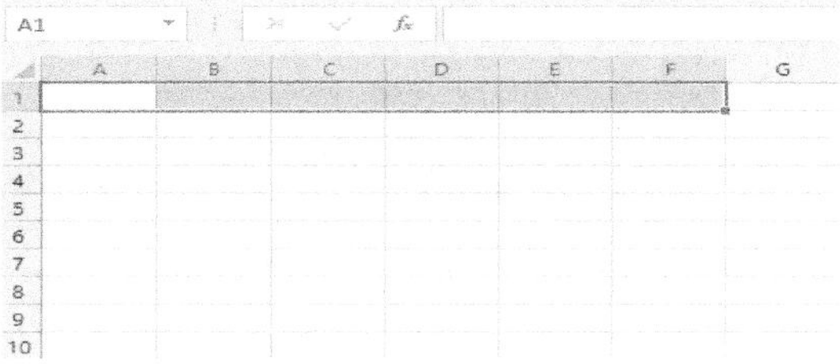

- Cell range A 1: F 8

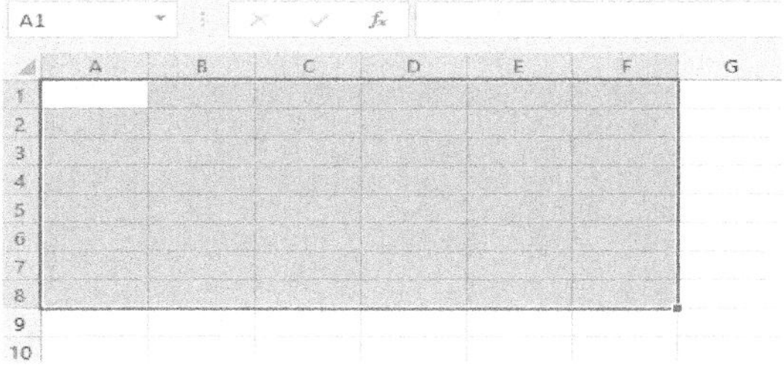

If your spreadsheet columns are labeled with numbers, modify Excel's reference style.

To select the cell:

You must first pick the cell to enter or modify cell content.

- To choose a cell, click on it. Cell D9 will be used as an example in this case.
- The chosen cell will have a border around it, and the column & row headings will be highlighted as well. Unless you click on another cell within a worksheet, the currently chosen cell will stay selected.

4	Department	First Name	Last Name	User Name	Part 1	Part 2
5	*Sales*	Walter	Rivera	wrivera	X	X
6	*Sales*	Heidi	Lee		X	X
7	*Claims*	Josie	Gates		X	X
8	*Accounting*	Wendy	Crocker		X	X
9	*Accounting*	Loretta	Johnson		X	
10	*Sales*	Walter	Rivera		X	
11	*Claims*	Misty	Whitfield		X	
12	*Marketing*	Matilda	Lewis		X	
13	*Accounting*	Elizabeth	Hicks		X	
14	*HR*	Alvin	Rios		X	
15	*HR*	Brian	Gaines		X	
16	*Sales*	Megan	Bosworth		X	
17	*Claims*	Maria	Menzies		X	
18	*Claims*	Micheal	Russell		X	
19						

You may also use your keyboard's arrow keys to pick cells.

To select the cell range:

A cell range or a bigger group of cells may be useful in certain situations.

- To select all adjacent cells, click & drag your mouse until they are highlighted. Cells B 5: C 18 will be used in this example.
- To choose a cell range, just release the mouse button. When you pick a cell, it will stay chosen until you click on a different cell inside the worksheet.

4	Department	First Name	Last Name	User Name	Part 1	Part 2
5	*Sales*	Walter	Rivera	wrivera	X	X
6	*Sales*	Heidi	Lee		X	X
7	*Claims*	Josie	Gates		X	X
8	*Accounting*	Wendy	Crocker		X	X
9	*Accounting*	Loretta	Johnson		X	
10	*Sales*	Walter	Rivera		X	
11	*Claims*	Misty	Whitfield		X	
12	*Marketing*	Matilda	Lewis		X	
13	*Accounting*	Elizabeth	Hicks		X	
14	*HR*	Alvin	Rios		X	
15	*HR*	Brian	Gaines		X	
16	*Sales*	Megan	Bosworth		X	
17	*Claims*	Maria	Menzies		X	
18	*Claims*	Micheal	Russell		X	
19						

2.5 CELL CONTENT

Each cell in the spreadsheet stores the data you input. Text, formatting, formulae, and functions may all be included in a single cell.

Text: Text, including characters, numbers, & dates, may be stored in cells.

	A	B	C	D	E
1	Date	Sales	Percentage of Total		
2	4/4/16	93	0.71		
3	4/5/16	42	0.78		
4	4/6/16	46	0.86		
5	4/7/16	73	0.28		
6	4/8/16	12	0.49		
7	4/9/16	24	0.65		
8	4/10/16	19	0.57		
9					
10					

Cells may have formatting elements that alter characters' appearance, such as letters, numbers, and dates. Percentages, for example, may be expressed as 0.15% or 15%. Even the color of a cell's content or background may be changed.

	A	B	C	D	E
1	Date	Sales	Percentage of Total		
2	April 4, 2016	$93.00	71%		
3	April 5, 2016	$42.00	78%		
4	April 6, 2016	$46.00	86%		
5	April 7, 2016	$73.00	28%		
6	April 8, 2016	$12.00	49%		
7	April 9, 2016	$24.00	65%		
8	April 10, 2016	$19.00	57%		
9					
10					

Calculation functions: Cell values may be calculated by using formulae & functions. Adding the values of every cell within range B 2: B 8 to cell B 9 is done using SUM (B 2: B 8).

B9 =SUM(B2:B8)

	A	B	C	D	E
1	Date	Sales	Percentage of Total		
2	April 4, 2016	$93.00	71%		
3	April 5, 2016	$42.00	78%		
4	April 6, 2016	$46.00	86%		
5	April 7, 2016	$73.00	28%		
6	April 8, 2016	$12.00	49%		
7	April 9, 2016	$24.00	65%		
8	April 10, 2016	$19.00	57%		
9	Weekly Sales	$309.00			
10					

To insert the content:

To choose a cell, click on it. Cell F 9 will be used in this example.

4	Department	First Name	Last Name	User Name	Part 1	Part 2		Part 3
5	*Sales*	Walter	Rivera	wrivera	X	X	On hold	X
6	*Sales*	Heidi	Lee		X	X	On hold	
7	*Claims*	Josie	Gates		X	X		X
8	*Accounting*	Wendy	Crocker		X	X		
9	*Accounting*	Loretta	Johnson		X			X
10	*Sales*	Walter	Rivera		X			X
11	*Claims*	Misty	Whitfield		X			

Press the Enter key once you've typed anything into the currently selected cell. The cell & formula bar will display the content. Within the formula bar, you may also enter and change data for individual cells.

4	Department	First Name	Last Name	User Name	Part 1	Part 2		Part 3
5	*Sales*	Walter	Rivera	wrivera	X	X	On hold	X
6	*Sales*	Heidi	Lee		X	X	On hold	
7	*Claims*	Josie	Gates		X	X		X
8	*Accounting*	Wendy	Crocker		X	X		
9	*Accounting*	Loretta	Johnson		X	X		X
10	*Sales*	Walter	Rivera		X			X
11	*Claims*	Misty	Whitfield		X			

To delete (clear) the cell content:

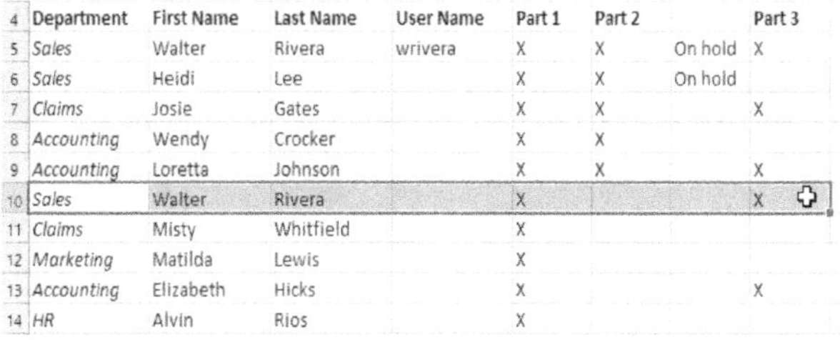

- If you wish to remove anything from a cell, you must first select it.
- Cells A10 through H10 will be used in this example.

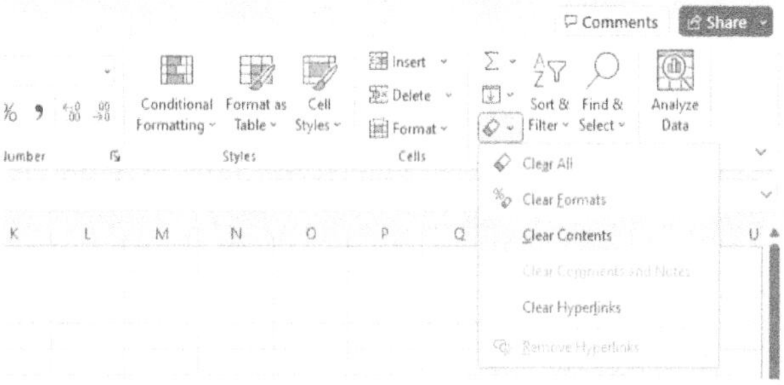

- Click Clear Contents after selecting the Clear command from the home menu.

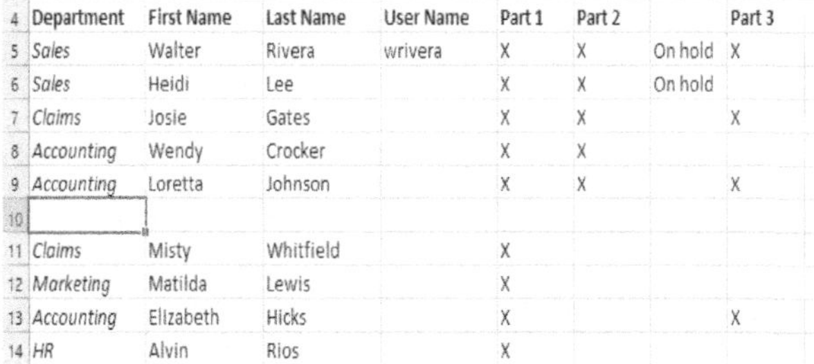

- The cell's contents will be wiped clean of all information.

Alternatively, you may erase many items from a cell at once by using the Delete button on the keyboard. Only one cell may be deleted at a time using the Backspace key.

To delete the cells:

A cell's content can be deleted; however, removing the cell itself is quite different. Delete the whole cell, and the cells below will relocate to fill within gaps & replace those cells that have been omitted.

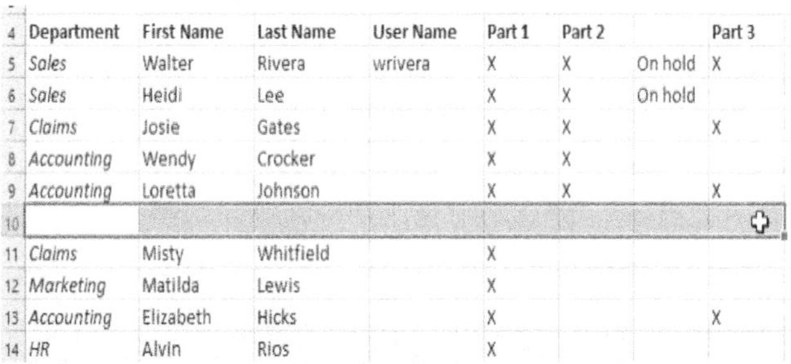

- To delete a cell, click on the cell you wish to remove. For illustration, let's use A 10: H 10.

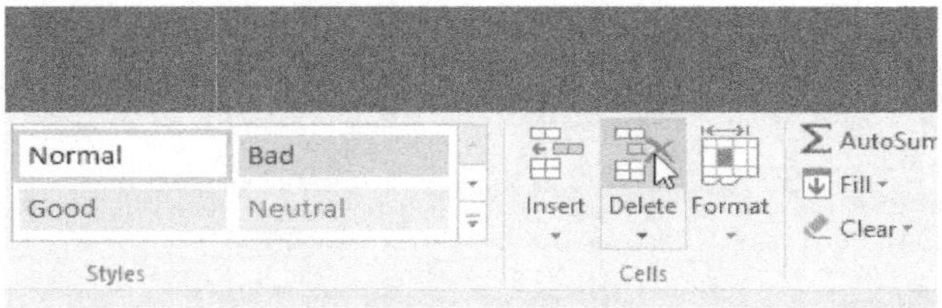

- You may access the delete option from your Ribbon home tab by pressing Ctrl-Delete.

- Those cells below should move up & fill up the voids left.

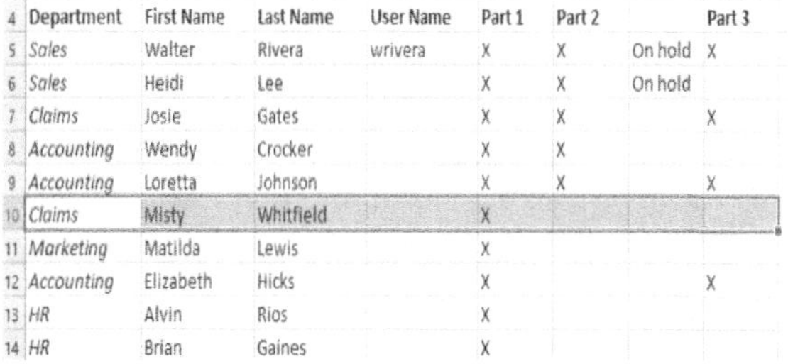

	Department	First Name	Last Name	User Name	Part 1	Part 2		Part 3
5	Sales	Walter	Rivera	wrivera	X	X	On hold	X
6	Sales	Heidi	Lee		X	X	On hold	
7	Claims	Josie	Gates		X	X		X
8	Accounting	Wendy	Crocker		X	X		
9	Accounting	Loretta	Johnson		X	X		X
10	Claims	Misty	Whitfield		X			
11	Marketing	Matilda	Lewis		X			
12	Accounting	Elizabeth	Hicks		X			X
13	HR	Alvin	Rios		X			
14	HR	Brian	Gaines		X			

To copy & paste the cell content:

To save effort and time, Excel provides the ability to cut / paste material that has already been put into your spreadsheet.

- Select the cell(s) you would like to copy. You'll use F9 as an example.

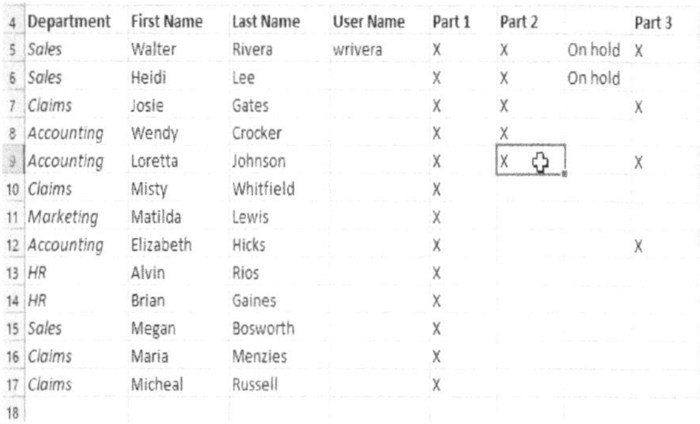

	Department	First Name	Last Name	User Name	Part 1	Part 2		Part 3
5	Sales	Walter	Rivera	wrivera	X	X	On hold	X
6	Sales	Heidi	Lee		X	X	On hold	
7	Claims	Josie	Gates		X	X		X
8	Accounting	Wendy	Crocker		X	X		
9	Accounting	Loretta	Johnson		X	X		X
10	Claims	Misty	Whitfield		X			
11	Marketing	Matilda	Lewis		X			
12	Accounting	Elizabeth	Hicks		X			X
13	HR	Alvin	Rios		X			
14	HR	Brian	Gaines		X			
15	Sales	Megan	Bosworth		X			
16	Claims	Maria	Menzies		X			
17	Claims	Micheal	Russell		X			
18								

- Press Ctrl + C on the keyboard or use the Copy option on your home tab.

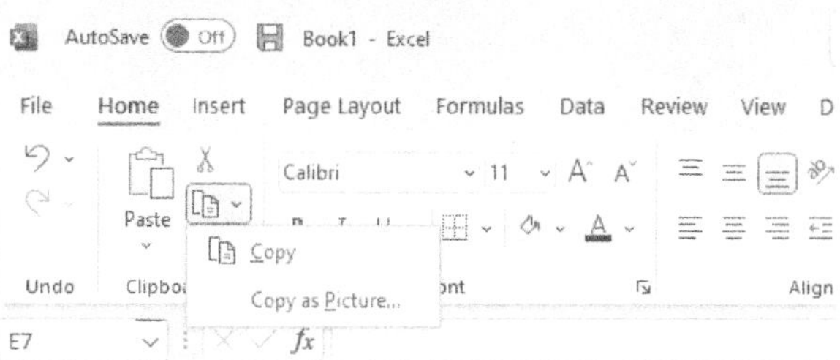

Identify whatever cell or cells you wish to put your data into by clicking on them. F 12: F 17 will be our selection in this scenario. A dashed box will appear around the duplicated cells.

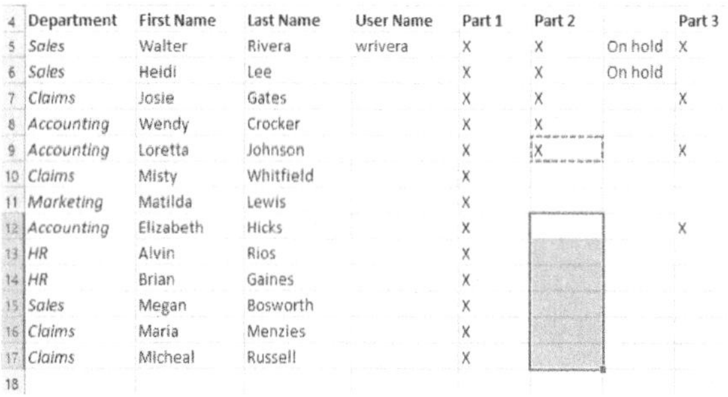

	Department	First Name	Last Name	User Name	Part 1	Part 2		Part 3
5	Sales	Walter	Rivera	wrivera	X	X	On hold	X
6	Sales	Heidi	Lee		X	X	On hold	
7	Claims	Josie	Gates		X	X		X
8	Accounting	Wendy	Crocker		X	X		
9	Accounting	Loretta	Johnson		X	X		X
10	Claims	Misty	Whitfield		X			
11	Marketing	Matilda	Lewis		X			
12	Accounting	Elizabeth	Hicks		X			X
13	HR	Alvin	Rios		X			
14	HR	Brian	Gaines		X			
15	Sales	Megan	Bosworth		X			
16	Claims	Maria	Menzies		X			
17	Claims	Micheal	Russell		X			
18								

- If you use a keyboard shortcut, press Ctrl+V after choosing Paste from your Home tab.

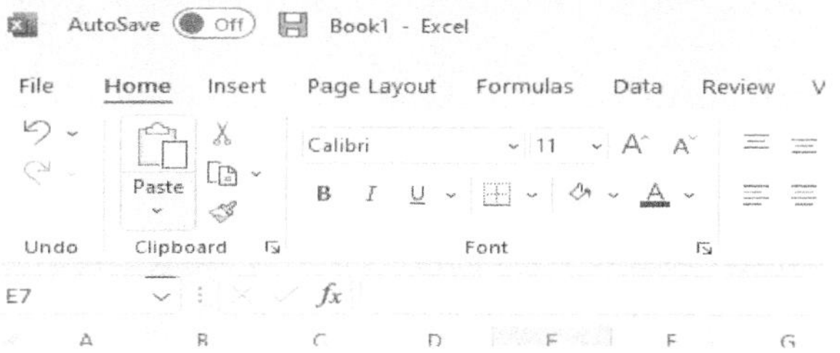

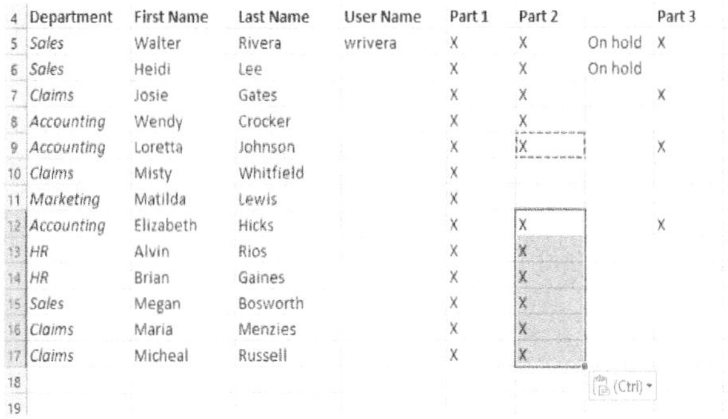

	Department	First Name	Last Name	User Name	Part 1	Part 2		Part 3
5	Sales	Walter	Rivera	wrivera	X	X	On hold	X
6	Sales	Heidi	Lee		X	X	On hold	
7	Claims	Josie	Gates		X	X		X
8	Accounting	Wendy	Crocker		X	X		
9	Accounting	Loretta	Johnson		X	X		X
10	Claims	Misty	Whitfield		X			
11	Marketing	Matilda	Lewis		X			
12	Accounting	Elizabeth	Hicks		X	X		X
13	HR	Alvin	Rios		X	X		
14	HR	Brian	Gaines		X	X		
15	Sales	Megan	Bosworth		X	X		
16	Claims	Maria	Menzies		X	X		
17	Claims	Micheal	Russell		X	X		
18								
19								

- The chosen cells will be filled with the content.

To access the additional paste option:

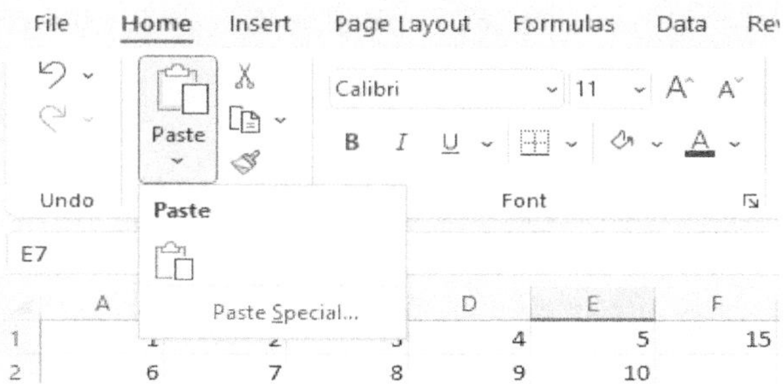

You may also access extra paste choices when dealing with cells that include formulae or formatting. This is all you need to do is choose to Paste & click your drop-down arrow to view all these alternatives.

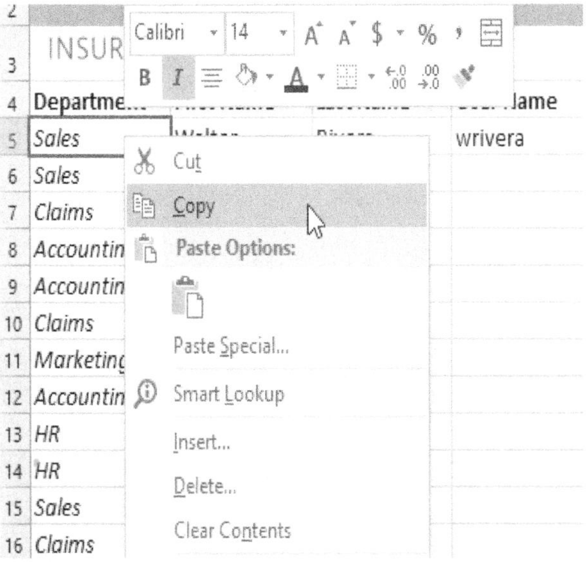

Right-clicking instead of using the Ribbon allows you to fast access commands. Just right-click on a cell and choose "format" to format a cell. Some commands also found on the Ribbon would appear within the drop-down menu.

To cut & paste the cell content:

It is possible to transfer material across cells instead of copy-pasting it.

- To cut a cell, choose the cell(s). You'll use G 5: G 6 as an example.
- Using the mouse's right-click menu, choose Cut. You may also hit Ctrl+X on your keyboard or the command just on the home tab.

Paste the material into the cells you've chosen. As a starting point, you'll choose F10:F11. A dashed box will now surround the cut cells.

Make a copy of the selected text and then paste it. You may also hit Ctrl+V on your keyboard or the command over your home tab.

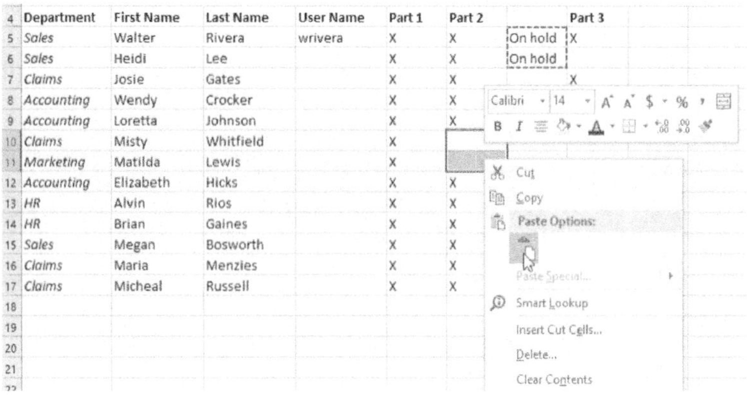

- The copied text will be deleted from the original cells & placed into the newly chosen cells instead.

	Department	First Name	Last Name	User Name	Part 1	Part 2		Part 3
4	Department	First Name	Last Name	User Name	Part 1	Part 2		Part 3
5	Sales	Walter	Rivera	wrivera	X	X		X
6	Sales	Heidi	Lee		X	X		
7	Claims	Josie	Gates		X	X		X
8	Accounting	Wendy	Crocker		X	X		
9	Accounting	Loretta	Johnson		X	X		X
10	Claims	Misty	Whitfield		X	On hold		
11	Marketing	Matilda	Lewis		X	On hold		
12	Accounting	Elizabeth	Hicks		X	X		X
13	HR	Alvin	Rios		X	X		
14	HR	Brian	Gaines		X	X		
15	Sales	Megan	Bosworth		X	X		
16	Claims	Maria	Menzies		X	X		
17	Claims	Micheal	Russell		X	X		
18								

To drag & drop cells:

Rather than copying, pasting, or cutting cells, you may just drag and drop them.

4	Department	First Name	Last Name	User Name	Part 1	Part 2		Part 3
5	Sales	Walter	Rivera	wrivera	X	X		X
6	Sales	Heidi	Lee		X	X		
7	Claims	Josie	Gates		X	X		X
8	Accounting	Wendy	Crocker		X	X		
9	Accounting	Loretta	Johnson		X	X		X
10	Claims	Misty	Whitfield		X	On hold		
11	Marketing	Matilda	Lewis		X	On hold		
12	Accounting	Elizabeth	Hicks		X	X		X
13	HR	Alvin	Rios		X	X		
14	HR	Brian	Gaines		X	X		
15	Sales	Megan	Bosworth		X	X		
16	Claims	Maria	Menzies		X	X		
17	Claims	Micheal	Russell		X	X		
18								

- To move a cell, you must first select it. You'll use H 4: H 12 as an example.
- A four arrows pointer appears when the mouse hovers over the chosen cells' borders.

4	Department	First Name	Last Name	User Name	Part 1	Part 2		Part 3
5	Sales	Walter	Rivera	wrivera	X	X		X
6	Sales	Heidi	Lee		X	X		
7	Claims	Josie	Gates		X	X		X G4:G12
8	Accounting	Wendy	Crocker		X	X		
9	Accounting	Loretta	Johnson		X	X		X
10	Claims	Misty	Whitfield		X	On hold		
11	Marketing	Matilda	Lewis		X	On hold		
12	Accounting	Elizabeth	Hicks		X	X		X
13	HR	Alvin	Rios		X	X		
14	HR	Brian	Gaines		X	X		
15	Sales	Megan	Bosworth		X	X		
16	Claims	Maria	Menzies		X	X		
17	Claims	Micheal	Russell		X	X		
18								

- The cells may be moved by clicking and dragging them to the appropriate position. These will be moved to G4:G12 in this case.

4	Department	First Name	Last Name	User Name	Part 1	Part 2	Part 3
5	Sales	Walter	Rivera	wrivera	X	X	X
6	Sales	Heidi	Lee		X	X	
7	Claims	Josie	Gates		X	X	X
8	Accounting	Wendy	Crocker		X	X	
9	Accounting	Loretta	Johnson		X	X	X
10	Claims	Misty	Whitfield		X	On hold	
11	Marketing	Matilda	Lewis		X	On hold	
12	Accounting	Elizabeth	Hicks		X	X	X
13	HR	Alvin	Rios		X	X	
14	HR	Brian	Gaines		X	X	
15	Sales	Megan	Bosworth		X	X	
16	Claims	Maria	Menzies		X	X	
17	Claims	Micheal	Russell		X	X	
18							

- Let go of the mouse. To place the cells where you want them, pick the desired spot.

To use your fill handle:

A fill handle is a handy alternative to copy / paste commands if you copy the cell content to consecutive cells within the same column or row.

- Hover your cursor over the lower-right corner of your cell to bring up the fill handle, then choose the cell(s) holding the desired content.

4	Department	First Name	Last Name	User Name	Part 1	Part 2	Part 3
5	Sales	Walter	Rivera	wrivera	X	X	X
6	Sales	Heidi	Lee		X	X	
7	Claims	Josie	Gates		X	X	X
8	Accounting	Wendy	Crocker		X	X	
9	Accounting	Loretta	Johnson		X	X	X
10	Claims	Misty	Whitfield		X	On hold	
11	Marketing	Matilda	Lewis		X	On hold	
12	Accounting	Elizabeth	Hicks		X	X	X
13	HR	Alvin	Rios		X	X	
14	HR	Brian	Gaines		X	X	
15	Sales	Megan	Bosworth		X	X	
16	Claims	Maria	Menzies		X	X	
17	Claims	Micheal	Russell		X	X	
18							

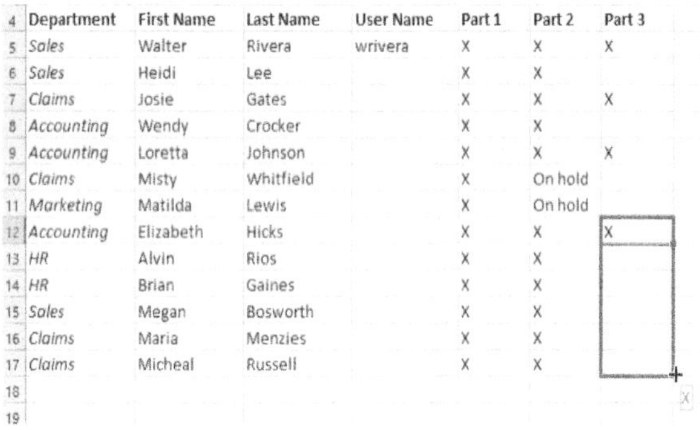

	Department	First Name	Last Name	User Name	Part 1	Part 2	Part 3
4	Department	First Name	Last Name	User Name	Part 1	Part 2	Part 3
5	Sales	Walter	Rivera	wrivera	X	X	X
6	Sales	Heidi	Lee		X	X	
7	Claims	Josie	Gates		X	X	X
8	Accounting	Wendy	Crocker		X	X	
9	Accounting	Loretta	Johnson		X	X	X
10	Claims	Misty	Whitfield		X	On hold	
11	Marketing	Matilda	Lewis		X	On hold	
12	Accounting	Elizabeth	Hicks		X	X	X
13	HR	Alvin	Rios		X	X	
14	HR	Brian	Gaines		X	X	
15	Sales	Megan	Bosworth		X	X	
16	Claims	Maria	Menzies		X	X	
17	Claims	Micheal	Russell		X	X	
18							
19							

- Fill all the cells you desire by clicking and dragging the fill handle. You'll use G 13: G 17 as an example.

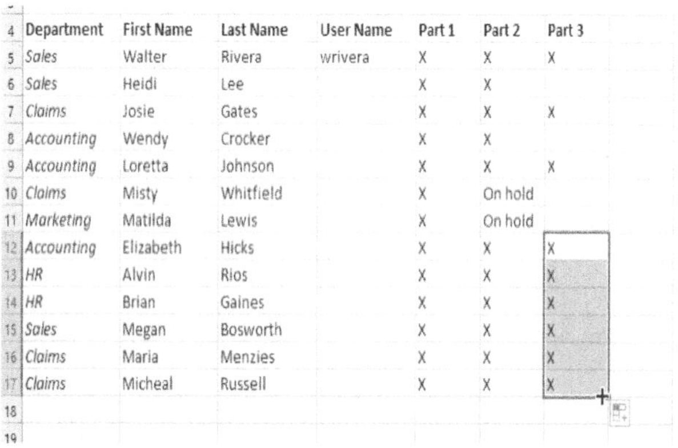

	Department	First Name	Last Name	User Name	Part 1	Part 2	Part 3
4	Department	First Name	Last Name	User Name	Part 1	Part 2	Part 3
5	Sales	Walter	Rivera	wrivera	X	X	X
6	Sales	Heidi	Lee		X	X	
7	Claims	Josie	Gates		X	X	X
8	Accounting	Wendy	Crocker		X	X	
9	Accounting	Loretta	Johnson		X	X	X
10	Claims	Misty	Whitfield		X	On hold	
11	Marketing	Matilda	Lewis		X	On hold	
12	Accounting	Elizabeth	Hicks		X	X	X
13	HR	Alvin	Rios		X	X	X
14	HR	Brian	Gaines		X	X	X
15	Sales	Megan	Bosworth		X	X	X
16	Claims	Maria	Menzies		X	X	X
17	Claims	Micheal	Russell		X	X	X
18							
19							

- To fill the chosen cells, just let go of the mouse button.

To continue the series with a fill handle:

It's possible to execute a series using the fill handle. The fill handle can predict the next row or column in a sequence, such as integers (1, 2, 3) or the days of the week (Monday, Tuesday, and Wednesday). Before filling in a series, you'll often need to pick several cells. In the meanwhile, here's a case study:

- Make sure the series you wish to continue is in the cell range you choose. You'll use E 4: G 4 as an example.
- Continue the sequence by clicking and dragging the fill handle.

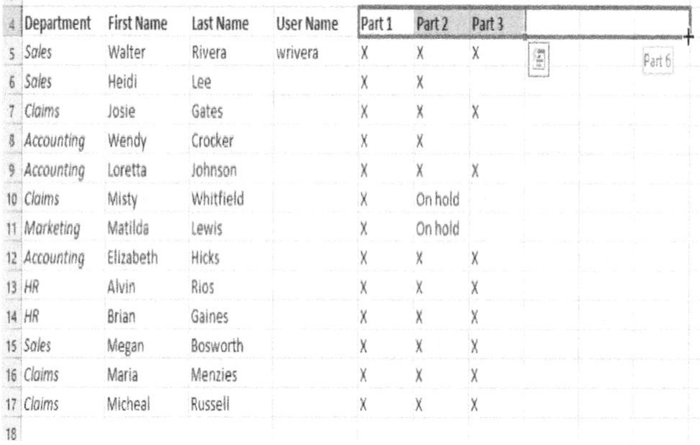

	Department	First Name	Last Name	User Name	Part 1	Part 2	Part 3
4	Department	First Name	Last Name	User Name	Part 1	Part 2	Part 3
5	Sales	Walter	Rivera	wrivera	X	X	X
6	Sales	Heidi	Lee		X	X	
7	Claims	Josie	Gates		X	X	X
8	Accounting	Wendy	Crocker		X	X	
9	Accounting	Loretta	Johnson		X	X	X
10	Claims	Misty	Whitfield		X	On hold	
11	Marketing	Matilda	Lewis		X	On hold	
12	Accounting	Elizabeth	Hicks		X	X	X
13	HR	Alvin	Rios		X	X	X
14	HR	Brian	Gaines		X	X	X
15	Sales	Megan	Bosworth		X	X	X
16	Claims	Maria	Menzies		X	X	X
17	Claims	Micheal	Russell		X	X	X
18							

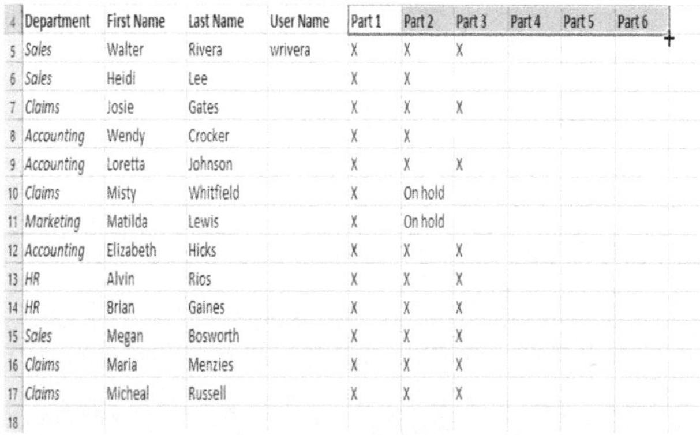

	Department	First Name	Last Name	User Name	Part 1	Part 2	Part 3	Part 4	Part 5	Part 6
4	Department	First Name	Last Name	User Name	Part 1	Part 2	Part 3	Part 4	Part 5	Part 6
5	Sales	Walter	Rivera	wrivera	X	X	X			
6	Sales	Heidi	Lee		X	X				
7	Claims	Josie	Gates		X	X	X			
8	Accounting	Wendy	Crocker		X	X				
9	Accounting	Loretta	Johnson		X	X	X			
10	Claims	Misty	Whitfield		X	On hold				
11	Marketing	Matilda	Lewis		X	On hold				
12	Accounting	Elizabeth	Hicks		X	X	X			
13	HR	Alvin	Rios		X	X	X			
14	HR	Brian	Gaines		X	X	X			
15	Sales	Megan	Bosworth		X	X	X			
16	Claims	Maria	Menzies		X	X	X			
17	Claims	Micheal	Russell		X	X	X			
18										

- Let go of the mouse. Selecting a cell will continue a series if Excel understands it. Parts 4, 5, & 6 were added to H 4: J 4 by Excel in this case.

In addition to clicking and dragging the fill handle, you may double-click it instead. With huge spreadsheets, when clicking & dragging might be cumbersome, this can be a handy tool.

2.6 HEADERS & FOOTERS IN THE WORKSHEET

In Excel, you can add headers and footers to printed worksheets. Create a footer, for instance, with the date, page numbers, and filename. You may design your headers and footers or choose from various pre-made options.

Only the Print Preview, Page Layout view, & printed pages show headers and footers. Adding headers and footers to many worksheets is also possible using the Page Setup dialogue box. Only the Page Setup dialogue box may be used to add headers and footers to other sheet kinds, including chart sheets and charts.

Change or Add footers or headers in the Page Layout view

- To add or edit headers or footers, choose the worksheet you'd want to work on.
- Click Header and Footer in the Text group on the Insert tab.

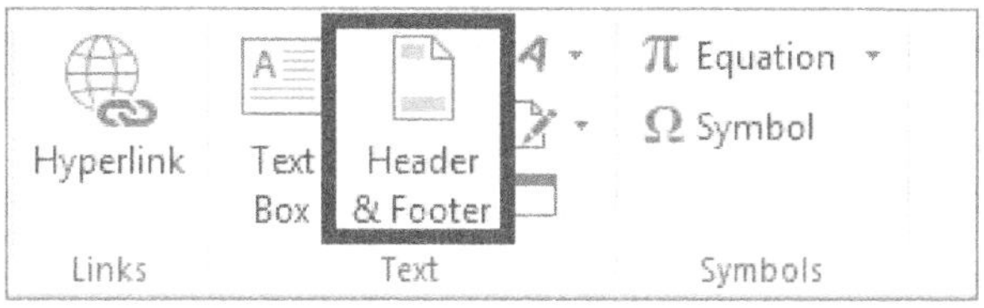

In-Page Layout mode, Excel shows the worksheet.

- Click the left, middle, or right footer or header text box over the bottom or top of a worksheet page to add or alter one (under the Header or the above Footer).
- Specify a new footer or header for the new page.

2.7 FORMATTING TABLES

An Excel table's formatting may be easily changed or removed without affecting the table's content, thanks to this guide. What do you want to do with the table you've just generated in Excel? Give it the appearance you want!

Excel has a range of preset table styles that can be applied or altered with a single click. Create your table style if none of your built-in styles match your requirements. Table components may also be shown or hidden, including header row, total row, banded rows, etc.

Excel table styles

Special features like integrated filter & structural references, calculated columns, sort options, total rows, etc., make examining and handling data in Excel tables much simpler. You'll get a good start formatting your data if you first convert it to the Microsoft Excel table. To make formatting easier, tables are pre-formatted when they are first added to a document.

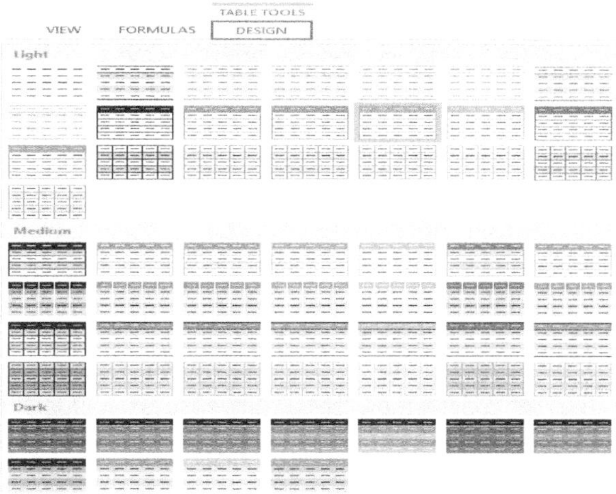

Changing the table format is as simple as picking one of the built-in table styles over the Design page of the application. Excel table styles may be accessed via the Design tab when you click on a cell in a table, the Table Tool contextual tab displays.

Your Table Designs gallery has a variety of 50+ built-in styles categorized into Medium, Light, & Dark.

To put it another way, an Excel table style is like a formatting template that automatically applies layouts to table columns and rows and headers and totals rows.

In addition to formatting tables, you may format the following table components using the Table Style Options:

- Table headers may be shown or hidden by using the header row option.
- The list includes functions for every cell in each cumulative row cell.
- Banded rows and columns, respectively, show alternate column or row shading.
- For the beginning and end columns of the table, you may apply specific formatting.
- In the header row, a button allows you to show or hide the arrows for filtering.

Table Style choices are shown in the image below:

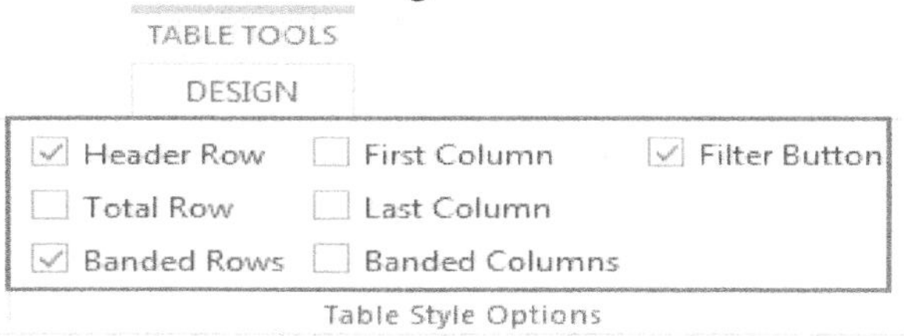

Making a table? Here's how to decide on a design style.

To format a table in a certain way, take these steps:

- Select the cells you wish to turn into a table and click the "Convert to Table" button.
- Format as the table may be found in the Styles section of the home tab.
- Make your selection from the Table Styles collection. Done!

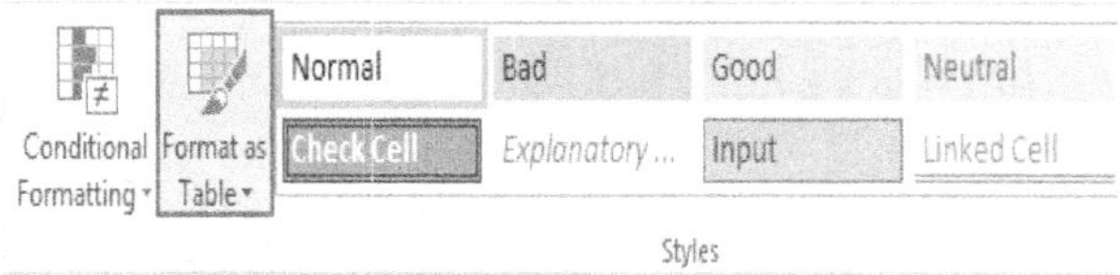

How can you change the table style to Excel

A new style may be applied by following these steps:

- To change the design of a cell, just click on it inside the table.
- You may see all the available table styles by clicking the More button in the Design tab's Table Styles group.
- Excel will offer you a live preview of the style you wish to apply by hovering your cursor over it.
- Just click on the new style to apply it.

Tip. A distinct Excel style will preserve whatever manual formatting you've made to the table.

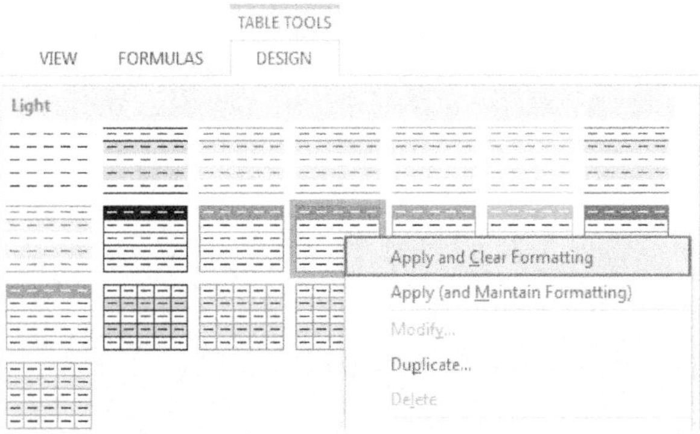

Examples of this would include making some cells bold or using a different font color.

Right-click on the style and choose "Apply and Clear Formatting" to apply the new style and erase any previous formatting.

Changing the table style using Excel is easy

For a specific workbook, right-click a table style within the Table design gallery and choose Set as Default:

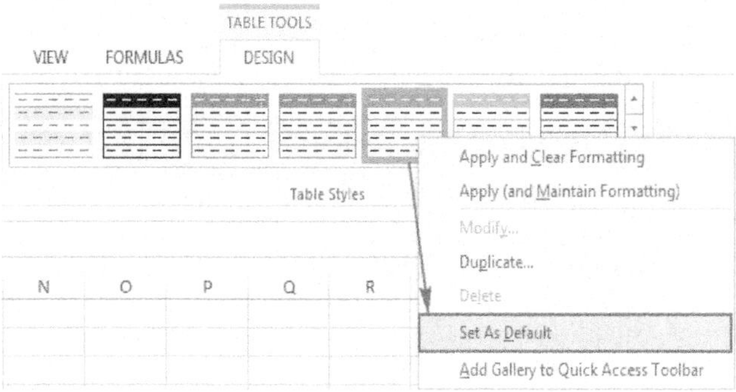

A table would now be produced every time you use Ctrl+T just on the Insert tab or click Table over your Insert tab.

How can you create the custom table styles

It is possible to develop a custom table style in Excel if one of the built-in styles doesn't exactly suit your needs:

- Format as the table may be found in the Styles section of the home tab. Or, if you already have a table open, select it and click on the More button to open the Design page.
- Select New Table Style from the drop-down menu below the preset options.
- You may name your customized table style within the Name field when you create a new table style.

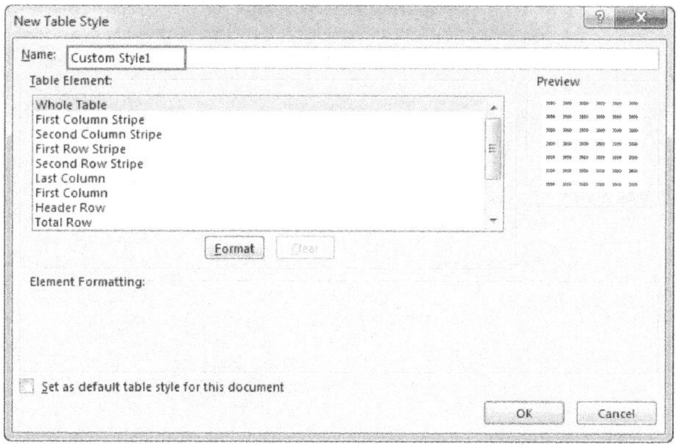

- To format an element, go to Table Elements, pick the desired element, and then click on the Format button. Open the Format Cells dialogue box and use the Border, Font, and Fill tabs to customize the appearance of the cells.
- Click the element & then the Clear button to erase any existing formatting.

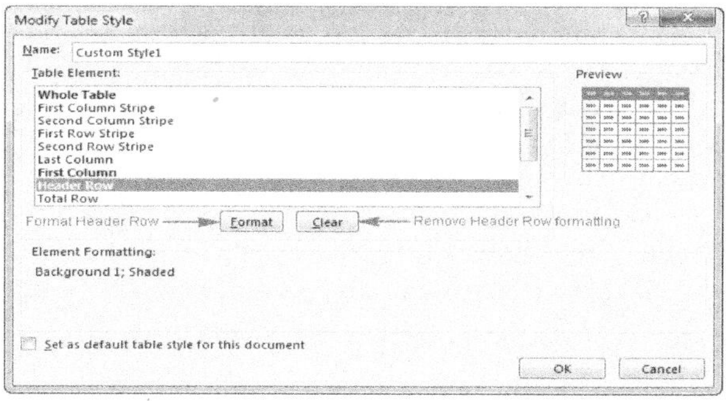

Tips:

Bold text appears in the Table Element field to denote formatted table elements.

The preview panel on the right reveals the formatting changes.

Select your Set as the quick default style for such a document box if you want to utilize the newly generated table style as the default style within a current worksheet.

- To save your customized table style, select OK.

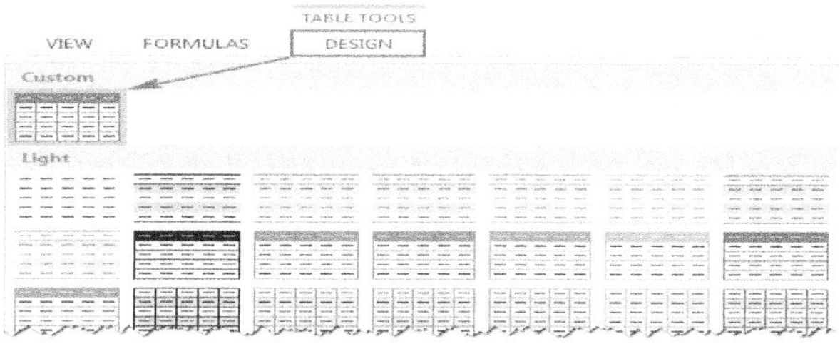

The Table Styles gallery is automatically updated each time a new custom style is created:

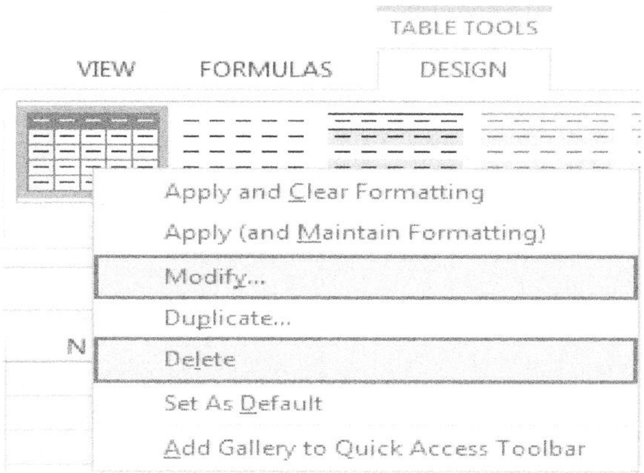

Select a table style from the Table Styles collection, right-click it, and select modify to make changes.

Right-click on a customized table style and choose to Delete to get rid of it.

You can't change or remove the built-in Microsoft Excel table styles.

Using a customized table style is only possible if you create one in the same worksheet. You may copy your table with custom style to another workbook if you wish to utilize it there. It's possible to remove the cloned table later & keep the custom style within the Table Styles gallery.

How to use a table design without having to create an actual table in Microsoft Excel

There is a simple workaround if you do not want to change a conventional Excel range to the Excel table and want to rapidly prepare the worksheet data using any of the native Excel table styles.

Apply the table style to a specific set of cells.

You may choose the required table style from the Styles category on the home page by clicking Format as Table.

Go to the Design tab ➔ Tools group & select Convert to Range on any cell in your freshly generated table.

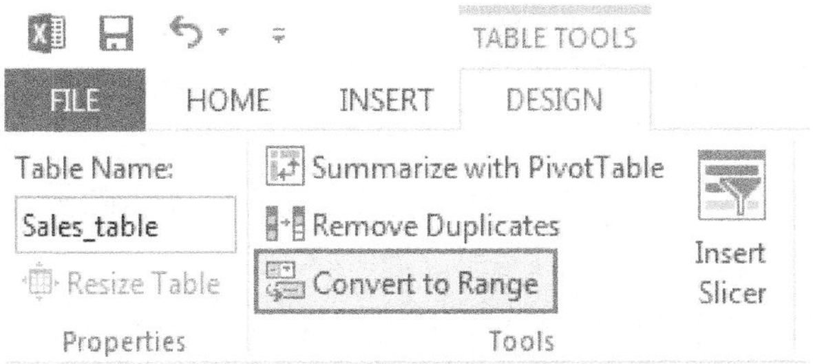

Use the right-click context menu, choose "Convert to Range," and select "Table."

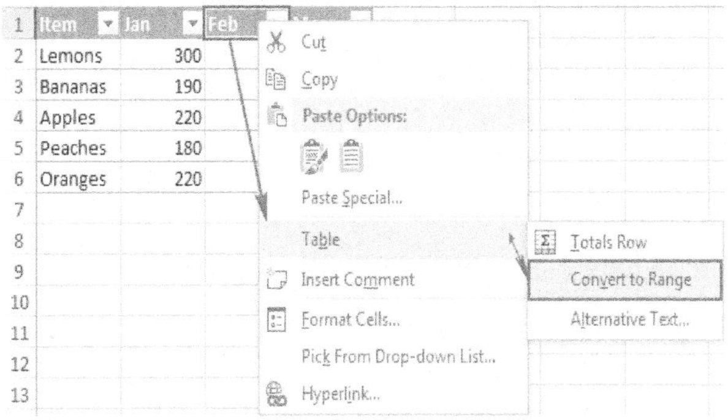

How to remove table formatting

Excel's built-in elements like banded rows, coloring, & borders may be removed, but the data in the table will remain intact.

Select a cell by clicking on it.

The More button can be found under the Table Styles category on the Design tab of the Ribbon.

Click Clear to remove the table-style templates.

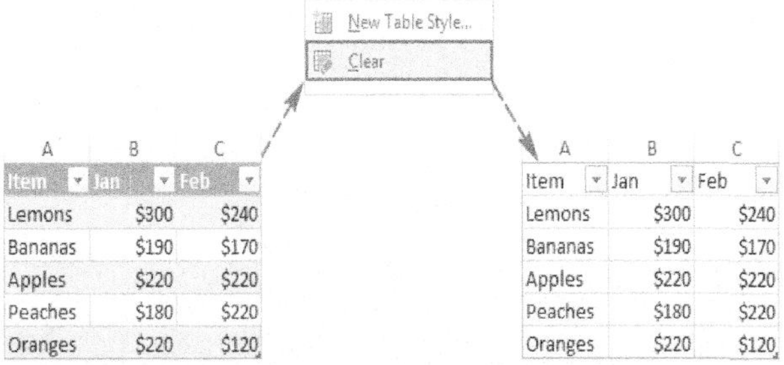

Using the Design menu Tools group, choose to Convert ➔ Range to eliminate a table while preserving data and layout. If you prefer, you may right-click anywhere in the table and pick Table ➔ Convert to Range from the menu.

Cell formats

Data may be formatted in a cell by following the instructions here. Only the appearance of the data in the spreadsheet cells may be altered using cell formats. It's vital to remember that this affects the presentation of the data, not the data itself.

More than only dates and times may be used in the formatting choices. To make it easier to distinguish between positive & negative numbers, several colors and formats might be used. Every time or date format may be found in one of a slew of date-and-time format variations. Select cells may also be formatted by changing the font, background, and border color.

You may further customize your spreadsheet by locking or limiting cell values and the range of data you can input in certain cells.

It's possible to utilize the Format Cells dialogue to update the formatting of a whole cell or selection or the Format Toolbar's buttons to access formatting components.

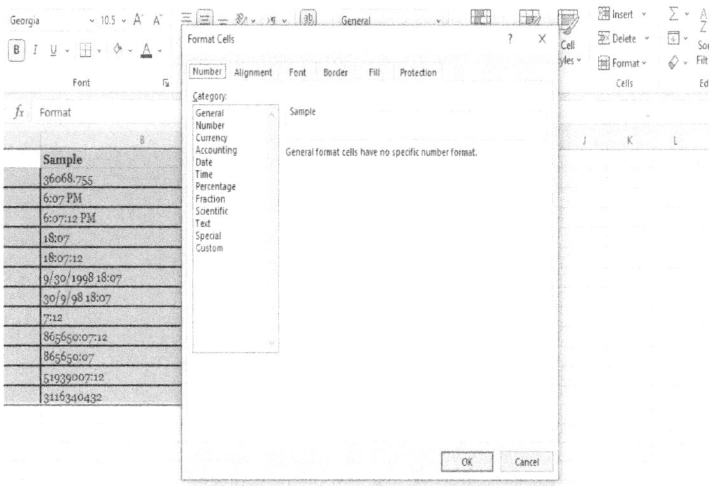

For this window, choose the range or cell of the cells you wish to format & then choose one from the following options:

- Use the Ctrl+1 keyboard shortcut (this is num one, not the letter l).
- From the menu bar, choose Format Cells.
- Right-click on cell grid areas & choose Format Cell. from the context menu to format the cells.

Number, Alignment, Background, Protection, Fonts, Border, and Validation are all tabs within Format Cells dialogue. In the next sections, you'll go through each of these tabs in further depth.

Make your selections & select OK to save changes to a specific formatting choice. The choices you specified in all tabs will be applied, and the Format Cells dialogue will be closed. You may also choose to implement the changes and keep the dialogue open or to dismiss the dialogue without making any changes by clicking on Apply or Close.

The buttons on the Format Toolbar may also be used to access some of the most often used formatting choices, including font, background, & alignment.

Number Formatting Tabs

Using this tab, you may change the cell's format. You may choose from various pre-formatted styles that should be sufficient in most circumstances. If neither option works for you, you may always make your own.

Select your format category (including Date or Number) by tapping the associated radio button on the dialog's left side to utilize one of its preset formats. The right-hand side of the dialogue will display how the chosen cell would appear in this format and provide other alternatives.

Below is a comprehensive list of the formats that are currently available:

General

In the style of the Swiss army knife. Values will be shown most efficiently feasible. Gnumeric's assumption of what sort of value is being shown influences the format of the cell (date, number, time).

Number

0-30 digits following the decimal point are shown in the numbers. It is possible to show negatives in several ways. Every third degree of magnitude may have a delimiter added as an alternative (thousand, million...). The comma and the hundreds separator have been approved for use in other languages.

Currency

A currency sign has been added to the Number. As of today, the most often used currency symbols are $, ¥, £, and ¤. Gnumeric's the default setting to display your locale's currency symbol and put it (either before or after the number).

Accounting

Positive and negative integers are aligned differently in this currency specialty. Positive integers are prepended with tiny spaces to correspond with negatives.

Date

In this section, you can find several ways to display dates. Gnumeric uses the date format native to your location by default (country & language setting).

The list on the right corner of the window lets you choose from various date formats. Examples of the codes used in various formats are shown below:

d: day of month (one or two digits). Example: 9
dd: day of month (two digits). Example: 09.
ddd: day of week. Example: Wed.
m: month (number, one or two digits). Example: 3.
mm: month (number, two digits). Example: 03.
mmm: month (abbreviated name). Example: Mar.
mmmm: month (full name). Example: March.
mmmmm: month (first letter). Example: M.
yyyy: year (four digits). Example: 1967.
yy: last two digits of year. Example: 67.

The codes listed below may be used to format dates containing the current time.

Time

There are various ways to display the current time in this category. You may choose from various time formats in the right-hand column of the window. Examples of the codes used in various formats are shown below:

- **h:** hour.
- **mm:** minute.
- **ss:** second.

Over 24 hours or 60 minutes/seconds may be required to show without increasing numbers by a bigger measure (e.g., twenty-five hours rather than a day + 1 hour). Codes '[h], [mm], & [ss] are used to do this.

Percentage

Value is multiplied by 100, with a percentage added. 0 to 30 digits following the decimal point may be utilized.

Fractions

Use a rational num with a certain denominator or a max number of digits within the denominator to approximate the value.

Scientific

5.334 E 6 = 5,334,000 is a scientific notation for the number. It supports decimal places up to Thirty digits long. Now, there is no way to adjust the exponent.

Text

Textual representation of quantitative data. This will display a number to the best of its ability, but it will have no idea whether it represents a date or an hour.

TIP

Select Text format for any items that include ID numbers, serial numbers, or other similar identifiers. 01124 will be displayed as 1124 whether you choose Number or General style in Gnumeric.

Custom

If you want a different format, this category is for you! Gnumeric's internal codes for specifying formats need an expert user's grasp of these codes.

So that you don't have to start from scratch, this category lists all existing formats' codes, so you may just edit one of them to develop your format.

Examples of the Date Formats

Format		Sample	
General		36068.755	
m/d/yy	d/m/yy	######	30/9/98
m/d/yyyy	d/m/yyyy	######	30/9/1998
d-mmm-yy	mmm-d-yy	######	Sep-30-98
d-mmm-yyyy	mmm-d-yyyy	######	Sep-30-1998
d-mmm	mmm-d	30-Sep	30-Sep
d-mm	mm-d	30-09	30-Sep
mmm/d	d/mmm	30-Sep	30-Sep
mm/d	d/mm	30-Sep	30/09
mm/dd/yy	dd/mm/yy	######	30/09/98
mm/dd/yyyy	dd/mm/yyyy	######	30/09/1998
mmm/dd/yy	dd/mmm/yy	Sep/30/98	######
mmm/dd/yyyy	dd/mmm/yyyy	Sep/30/1998	######
mmm/ddd/yy	ddd/mmm/yy	Sep/Wed/98	Wed/Sep/98
mmm/ddd/yyyy	ddd/mmm/yyyy	Sep/Wed/1998	Wed/Sep/1998
mm/ddd/yy	ddd/mm/yy	09/Wed/98	Wed/09/98
mm/ddd/yyyy	ddd/mm/yyyy	09/Wed/1998	Wed/09/1998
mmm-yy		Sep-98	
mmm-yyyy		Sep-98	
mmmm-yy		Sep-98	
mmmm-yyyy		Sep-98	
d/m/yy h:mm	m/d/yy h:mm	######	30/9/98 187:07
d/m/yyyy h:mm	m/d/yyyy h:mm	######	30/9/1998 187:07
yyyy/mm/d		9/30/1998	
yyyy/mmm/d		1998/Sep/30	
yyyy/mm/dd		9/30/1998	
yyyy/mmm/dd		1998/Sep/30	
yyyy-mm-d		9/30/1998	
yyyy-mmm-d		1998-Sep-3	
yyyy-mm-dd		9/30/1998	
yyyy-mmm-d		1998-Sep-30	
yy		98	
yyyy		1998	

Examples of The Time Formats

Format	Sample
General	36068.755
h:mm AM/PM	6:07 PM
h:mm:ss AM/PM	6:07:12 PM
h:mm	18:07
h:mm:ss	18:07:12
m/d/yy h:mm	9/30/1998 18:07
d/m/yy h:mm	30/9/98 18:07
mm:ss	7:12
[h]:mm:ss	865650:07:12
[h]:mm	865650:07
[mm]:ss	51939007:12
[ss]	3116340432

2.8 ALIGNMENT, FONT, BORDER, AND BACKGROUND TABS

Alignment Tab

This tab provides settings for vertical and horizontal alignment & justification.

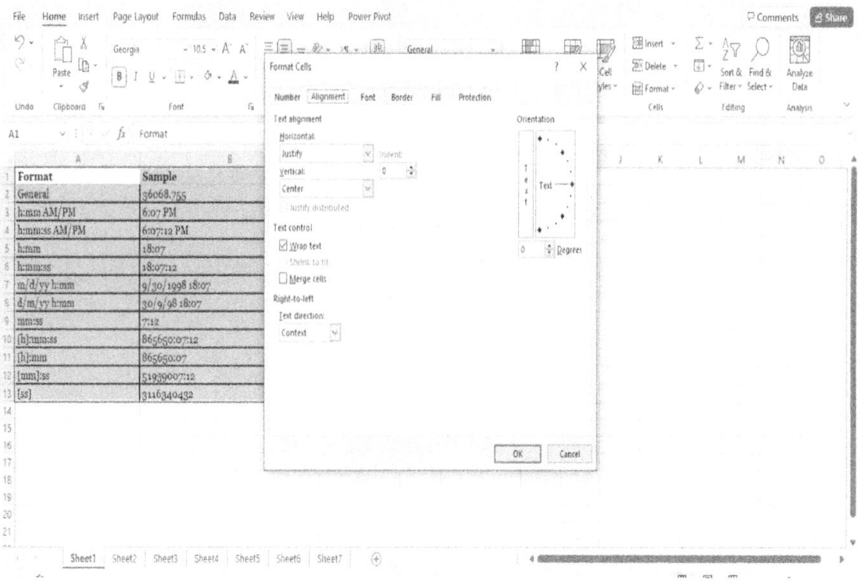

Horizontal justification options

General

This is the argument that most people use by default. For numbers and formulae, use right justification, whereas, for text strings, use left justification.

Left

All the contents of a cell should be aligned to the left.

Center

The contents of each cell should be centered.

Right

All cell contents should be right justified.

Fill

The contents of the cell should be added. Cell contents will be repeated as required to fill the cell's width.

Justify

Wrap large lines of text & left justify them. Same as Left for other formats.

Center across selection

The cell's contents are centered on ensuring that the middle of every line aligns with the middle of the other lines. Multiple cells are required to use this.

You may also define indent from the left (or right) side of the cell using the Left & Right justification options.

If the existing font size is 10, indent 4 indicates 40 pts; if the present font size is 12, indent 4 means 60 pts.

Vertical Justification Options

Top

Align the cell's contents at their highest point with its apex (or apex).

Center

Vertically align the cell contents with the same amount of room on each side.

Bottom

The elements of the cell should be aligned with the cell's bottom.

Justify

To fill the cell with text, wrap lengthy lines and distribute the content in each line uniformly.

Bottom justification may be used for formats (or whether the text does not include lengthy lines).

Font Tab

Change the typeface used for cell content by clicking this tab.

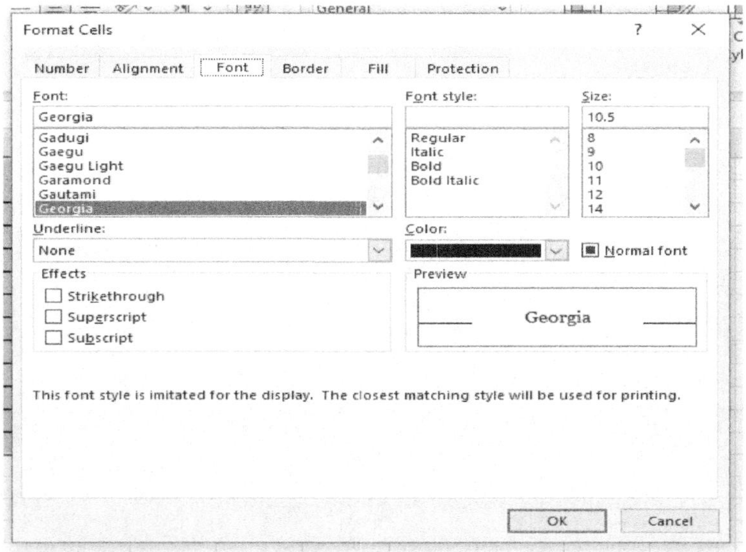

The font family, style, & point size (including Times New Roman, Helvetica, etc.) may all be changed to suit your preferences. Font effects like underlining and strikethrough are available, as are various font colors.

The gnome-print printing system's typefaces may be used with Gnumeric. A printed document will seem exactly like the one you're seeing on your computer screen since the same typefaces are used for both. The gnome-print package offers documentation for advanced users who want to learn more about the font control capabilities of GNOME.

TIP

Using the Format Toolbar is the quickest approach to alter the font of the chosen cells.

Border Tab

This tab enables you to pick the border for your chosen cells. To customize your borders, you may choose from various border designs and color options. Various borders may be used on various sides of a cell as well.

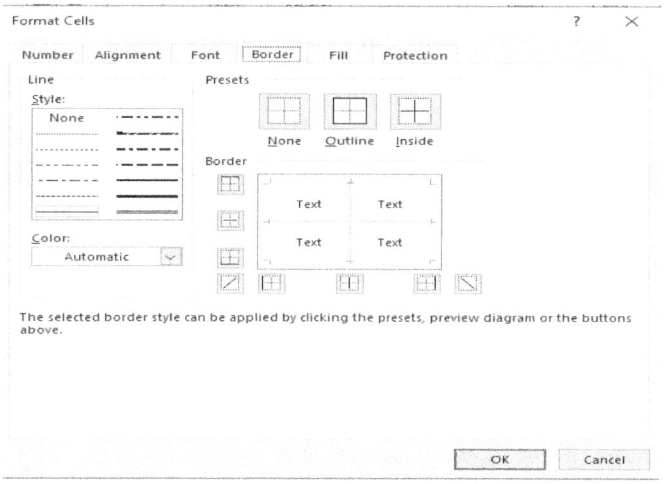

Cell or selection borders are selected by selecting border style and color on the right-side tab and then clicking on the buttons matching cell edges on the left-side tab, as seen in the screenshot below. The buttons for drawing the top, left, right, & those join the bottom sides of the cell for drawing the cell's diagonal and reverse diagonal. In a technical sense, they aren't boundaries, but they belong in this tab anyway.) There are two buttons on the bottom row: "None" and "Outline." None and Outline are two options for adding or removing boundaries from a cell or selection. When you use the buttons to border a range of cells, remember that they will only border one side of the selection. By illustration, selecting the Bottom button places the border at the bottom of the selected area, affecting just the cells within the bottom row. There are three buttons within the bottom row: Inside horizontal and inside vertical, which may be used to make choices. Inside vertical adds borders to all the selection's internal vertical borders; Inside horizontal adds borders to the selection's internal horizontal boundaries; and inside adds borders to the selection's internal vertical and horizontal borders. You may remove a current border from an edge of one cell or choice by re-clicking the button.

Background/Fill Tab

You may alter the background color of selected cells using this tab. The backdrop might be plain color or pattern. The right-hand side of the tab will provide a view of the chosen backdrop.

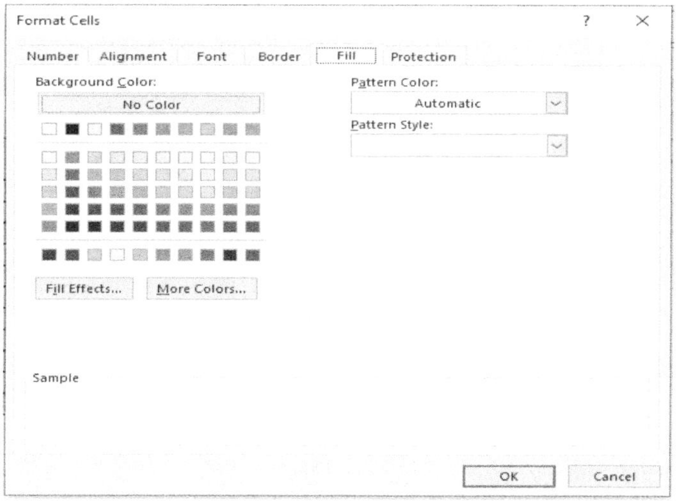

Select a color from the Backdrop Color drop-down box if you want a solid color background. If you want a custom color, just click the Custom Color option. Choosing the backdrop color in the Background Color area will allow you to pick a patterned background. After that, choose the pattern's color and style under the Pattern section. It's significant to consider that no matter what colors you choose for the pattern buttons, they'll always utilize a black pattern on a white backdrop.

Select the Solid pattern type if you want to get rid of the pattern (top left button, looking like the white square).

Protection and Validation Tabs

These tabs are being used to limit the kind of data that may be entered into a cell and to regulate which users have access to certain cells. Unlike other formatting choices, these two tabs have no impact on the look of a cell. Templates and forms meant to be filled out by others often take advantage of these features.

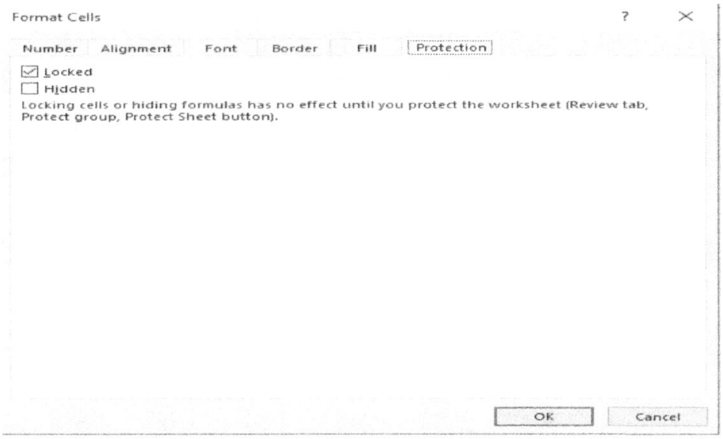

Imported Excel workbooks may have their cell protection settings managed using this tab. Gnumeric doesn't care whether a cell is tagged as protected or not; you may change it anyway. On the other hand, Gnumeric preserves the security settings of imported Excel files. Gnumeric will keep the protection information if you save the workbook in Excel format.

CHAPTER 3

BASIC FORMULAS

Beginners who want to become skilled in financial analysis should focus on learning the fundamentals of Excel formulae.

Microsoft Excel is the de facto industry standard for data analysis workstations. Investment bankers & financial analysts choose Microsoft's Excel spreadsheet tool for data processing, financial modeling, and presentation. Basic Excel functions are covered in detail in this chapter.

In Excel, there are two primary methods for calculating: Formulas & functions are the building blocks of mathematics.

1. Formulas

A formula in Excel is a phrase that affects the values in various cells and a single cell in the workbook.

For example, consider the formula =A1+A2+A3, which calculates the total values in cells A1 through A3.

2. Functions

In Excel, functions are preset formulae that may be used to do calculations.

Formulas no longer need time-consuming manual input since they have human-friendly names instead.

For example, =SUM (A 1: A 3). The function sums up all values from A1 through A3.

3.1 FIVE TIME-SAVING WAYS TO INSERT DATA INTO EXCEL

There are five standard methods for entering simple formulae when evaluating your data in Excel.

The pros and disadvantages of each technique are unique. So, before we go into the key formulae, we'll go through those approaches so that you may design your process.

1. Simple insertions: Typing your formula inside your cell

Basic Excel formulae may be entered by simply typing them into a cell or even the formula bar. This normally begins with an equal sign and an Excel function name.

When you enter the name of a function in Excel, a function suggestion appears in a pop-up window. You'll be able to choose your favorite option from this list.

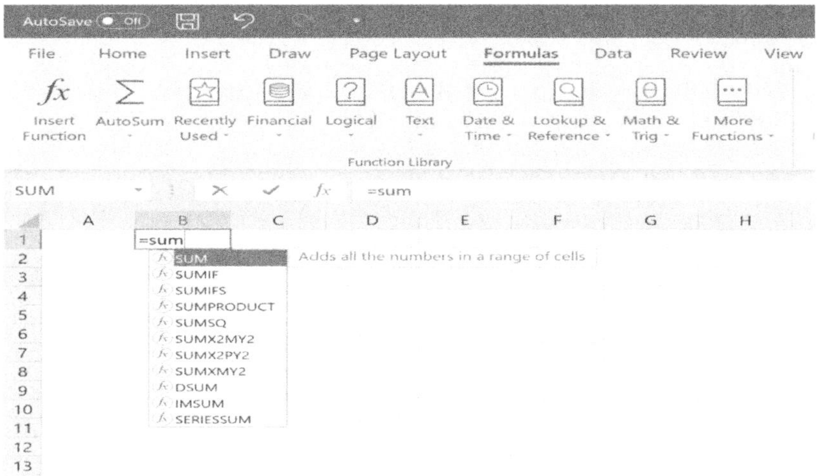

The Enter key is not required. As an alternative, hit the Tab key to continue adding choices.

Otherwise, you may get an incorrect name problem, which will appear as '#NAME?' in your browser.

Re-select the cell in question, and then type in your function within the formula bar to get it working properly.

2. Using the Insert Function from your Formulas Tab

Inserting functions in Excel is as simple as utilizing the Insert Function dialogue box. You may accomplish this by clicking on the Formulas tab & selecting the Insert Function option. You may use the dialogue box's functionalities to finish your financial analysis.

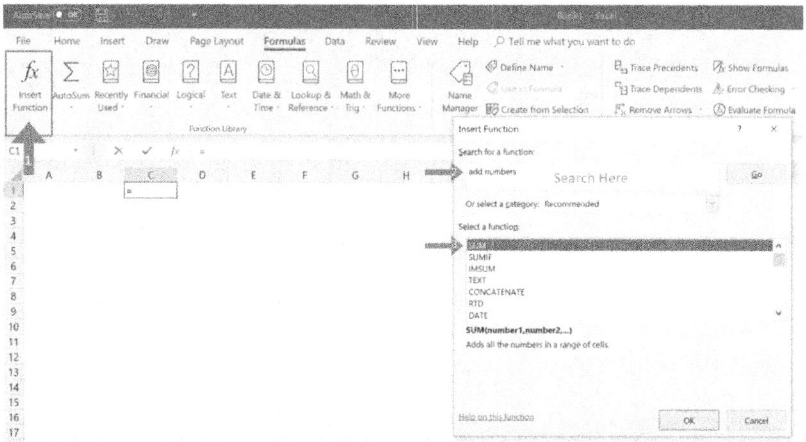

3. Selecting a Formula from One of the Groups in the Formula Tab

This is a good choice to get right into your favorite features. Choose your favorite group from the Formulas tab to access this menu. To open a sub-menu containing a list of functions, just click.

Once you've made your choice, you'll be able to proceed. Click over the More Functions option if your selected group isn't listed there; it may be buried there.

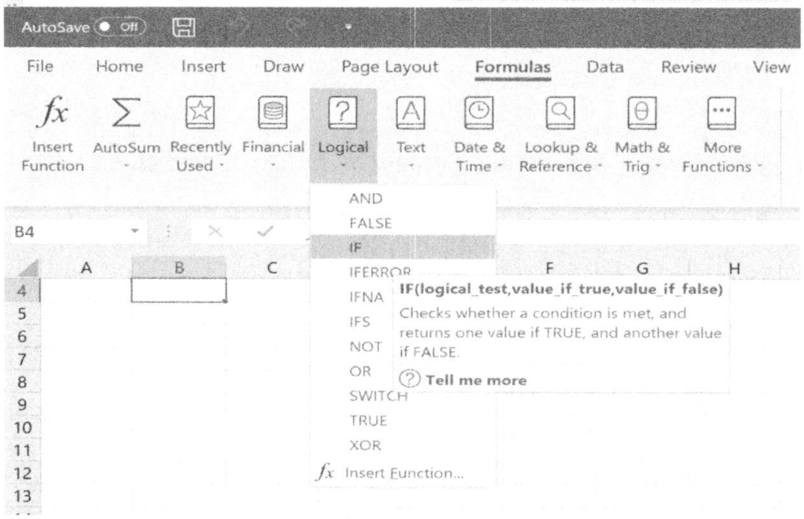

4. Using AutoSum Option

The AutoSum tool is your best bet for routine jobs. So, go to the home tab within the right corner and choose AutoSum.

Clicking the caret will reveal other formulae that are concealed. The formulas tab, following the Insert Function option, also has this option.

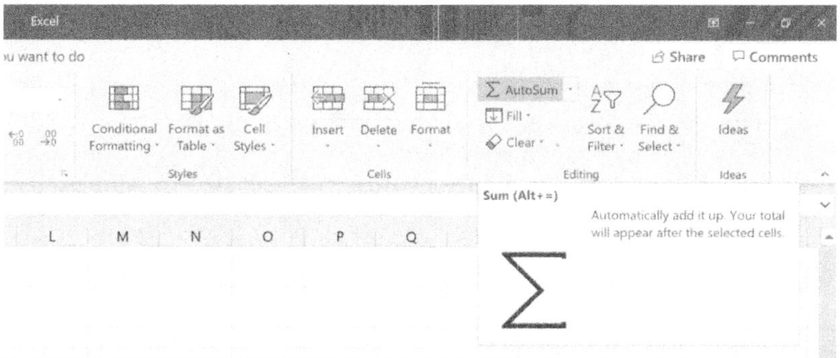

5. Quick Insert: Use Recently Used Tabs

Using the Recently Used option will save you from having to repeatedly type in your most recent formula. The third menu item next to AutoSum is "Formulas" on the Formulas tab."

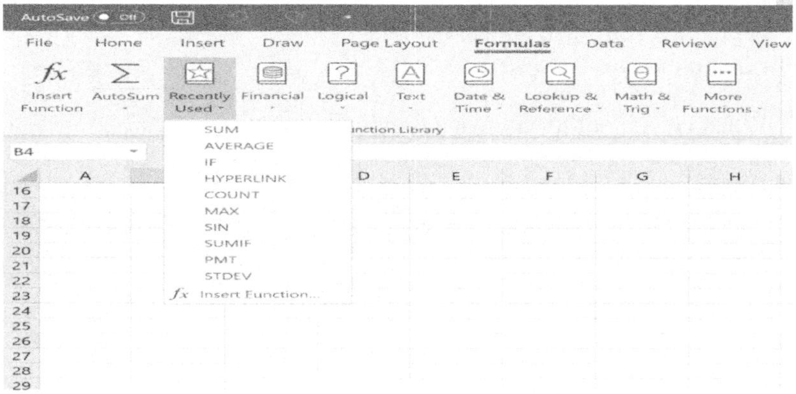

3.2 SUM FUNCTION

The SUM function may add or sum the values of several rows or columns.

=SUM (num 1, [num 2])

=SUM (number1, [number2], [number3]......)

- **Number1(Required Argument)**: This is the first value to sum
- **Number2 (Optional Argument):** This is the second value to sum
- **Number3 (Optional Argument):** This is the third value to sum

To utilize the SUM function, follow these steps.

In the cell, create the SUM feature.

- Go to the Function argument to choose cells for the cell range box.
- After that, hit the Enter key.

The SUM function takes the following inputs.

Let's utilize the table and the Aggregate function to calculate the total income from Monday through Friday.

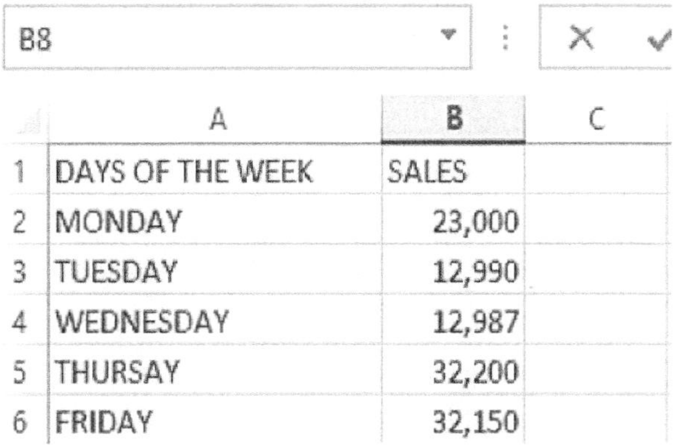

Use Total to track income from Monday through Friday by following the steps below.

To summarize, fill in the feature with the cell set in an empty cell; =SUM (A2:B6)

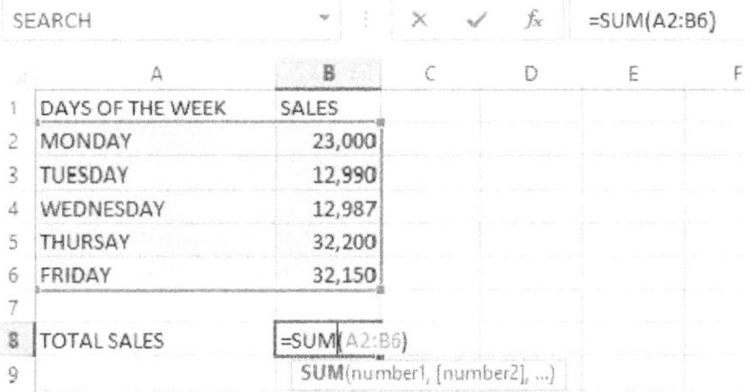

If you completed the parameters above, your net revenue from Monday through Friday would be 113327.

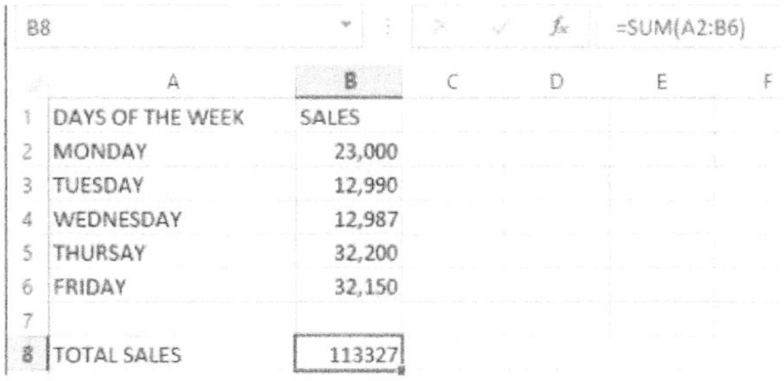

Take this into account when using the SUM function.

- A value error occurs if the criteria supplied are greater than 255 characters.
- Empty cell types with text values are immediately disqualified by the SUM method.
- You may utilize constants, sets, ranges, and cell references as parameters.
- For each statement that contains problems, the SUM function produces an error.

3.3 COUNT.VALUES FUNCTION

SUM =COUNT(B2:B13)

	A	B	C
1	Country	Population	
2	China	1,389,618,778	
3	India	1,311,559,204	
4	USA	331,883,986	
5	Indonesia	264,935,824	
6	Pakistan	210,797,836	
7		Empty	Skips non-numerical values
8	Brazil	210,301,591	
9	Nigeria	208,679,114	
10			Skips empty cells
11	Bangladesh	161,062,905	
12	Russia	141,944,641	
13	Mexico	127,318,112	
14	COUNT	=COUNT(B2:B13)	Output = 10
15			
16			

3.4 AVERAGE FUNCTION

Thanks to the AVERAGE function, data such as the typical number of owners in a certain shareholding pool will be familiar.

=AVERAGE (number 1, [number 2], ...)

Example:

=AVERAGE (B 2: B 11) – Shows the simple average, like (SUM (B 2: B 11)/10)

SUM =AVERAGE(B2:B11)

	A	B	C
1	Country	Population	
2	China	1,389,618,778	
3	India	1,311,559,204	
4	USA	331,883,986	
5	Indonesia	264,935,824	
6	Pakistan	210,797,836	
7	Brazil	210,301,591	
8	Nigeria	208,679,114	
9	Bangladesh	161,062,905	
10	Russia	141,944,641	
11	Mexico	127,318,112	
12	Average	=AVERAGE(B2:B11)	Output = 435,810,199
13			
14			

3.5 LENGTH FUNCTION

When you need to estimate the words in a cell, utilize the LEN function- which counts letters, digits, characters, & all spaces. For example, "It's 98 degrees today; therefore, you'll go swimming" (except for the quotations) has a total of 42 characters - 2 figures, 31 letters, a comma, 8 spaces, & 2 apostrophes.

Click on your keyboard to activate the function by typing within formula bar =LEN (cell).

With many cells, you may drag your fill handles down (or across) a range of cells to apply a formula over numerous cells at once.

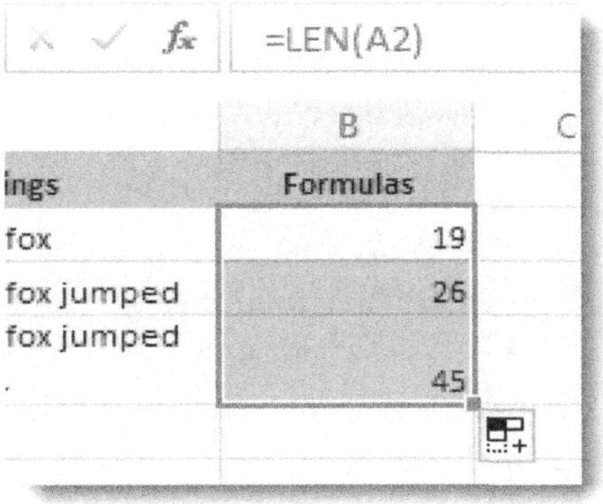

The SUM and LEN functions may retrieve the number of characters in many cells. Each cell is counted with the LEN function, and the SUM function combines the numbers:

=SUM ((LEN (cell1), LEN (cell2), (LEN (cell3)))).

Try to apply the LEN formula

The LEN function may be seen in action in the following instances.

Cell A 1 in the Excel worksheet should contain the copied table. For a quick look at how much text is in each cell in column A, drag your formula from B 2 to B 4.

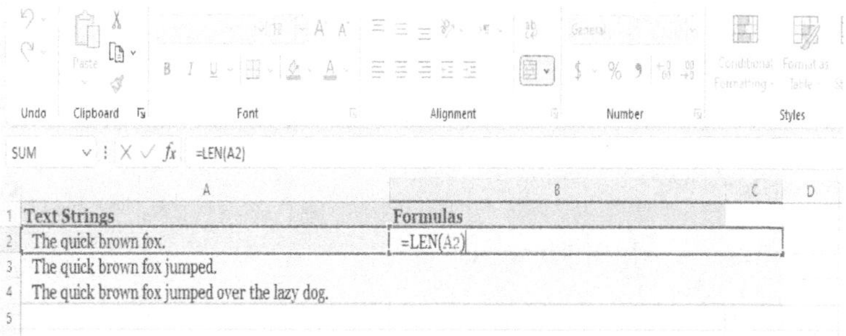

Count characters into one cell

1. Click on cell B 2.
2. Enter =LEN (A2).

If you include up all spaces and punctuation, A2's characters total 27, including both punctuation and spaces.

LEN includes any whitespace that follows the final character.

Count characters into multiple cells

- Click on cell B 2.
- Cell B2 may be copied by Ctrl+C, followed by Ctrl+ V to insert this formula in cells B 3: B 4.

This function tallies the words in every cell after copying the equation to cells B3 & B 4 (20, 27, & 45).

Count the total number of characters

- In your sample workbook, select cell B 6.
- In your cell, type =SUM (LEN (A 2), LEN (A 3), LEN (A 4)) & press Enter.

The characters for all the 3 cells are counted, and the sum is computed (92).

3.6 TRIM FUNCTION

The TRIM function eliminates unnecessary spaces from a letter, leaving just one space between words and no room for characters at the start or conclusion. The TRIM function uses the following statements to conduct its activities.

To remove the blank space from the text of the table.

- In an empty cell, write the purpose and the argument. =TEXTJOIN (",", TRUE, A2, A3, A4, A5, A6).

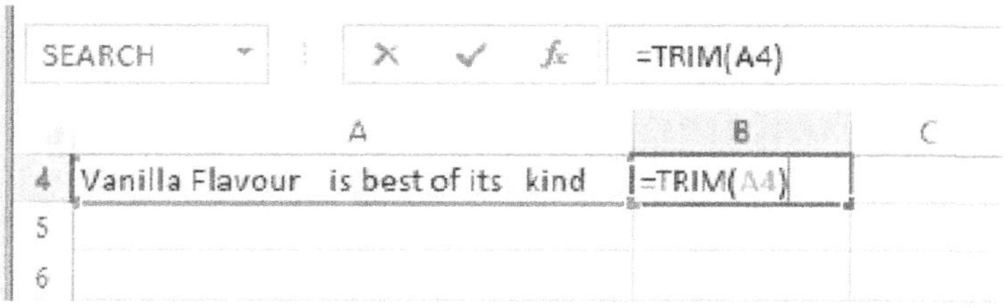

- The texts will be concatenated into a single text string when you hit enter, as shown below.

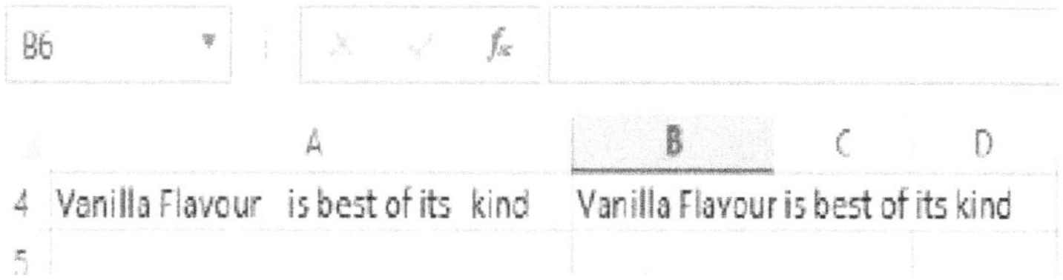

3.7 MIN AND MAX FUNCTION

Using the MAX function in Excel, you may find out which cell or range of cells has the highest numeric value. The MIN function is the inverse of the MAX function; it returns the cell in a variety of cells with the lowest numeric value.

Creating the MAX Formula

- To insert the formula, choose the cell you wish to work in.
- Select the Sum button from the drop-down menu.
- Max must be selected.

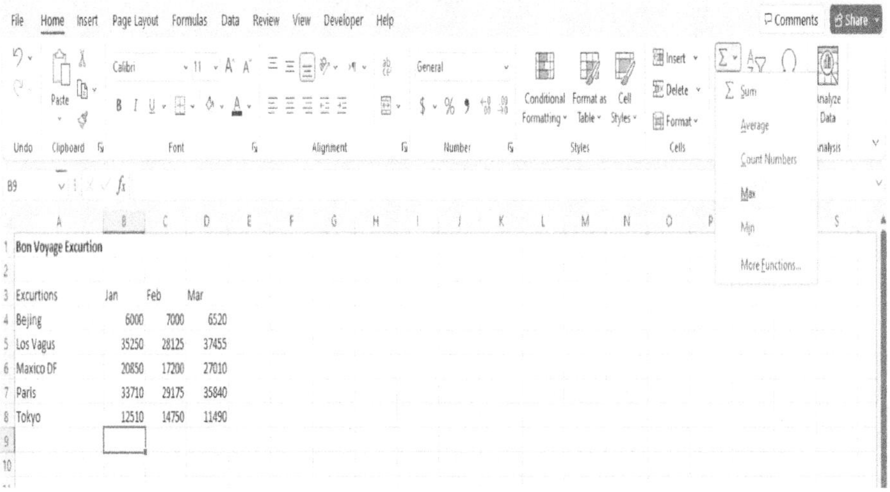

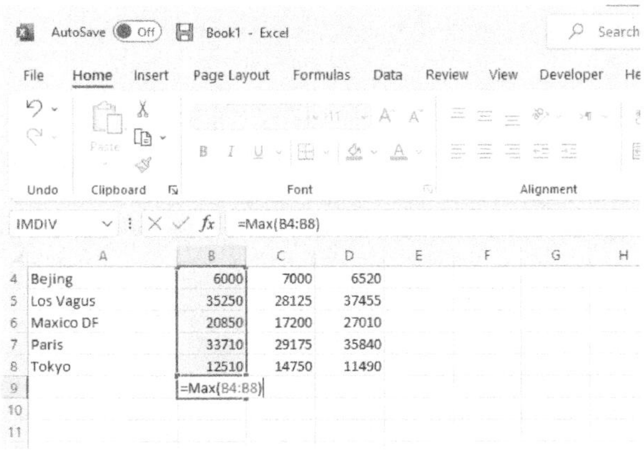

- If that's the case, just choose the range of cells you need.
- Just press Enter button or click your mouse.

Inserting the MAX formula into Excel will show you the highest value in your range.

Creating the MIN Formula

To insert the formula, choose the cell you wish to work in.

Move the list arrow to the AutoSum button.

To choose the Minimum, click here.

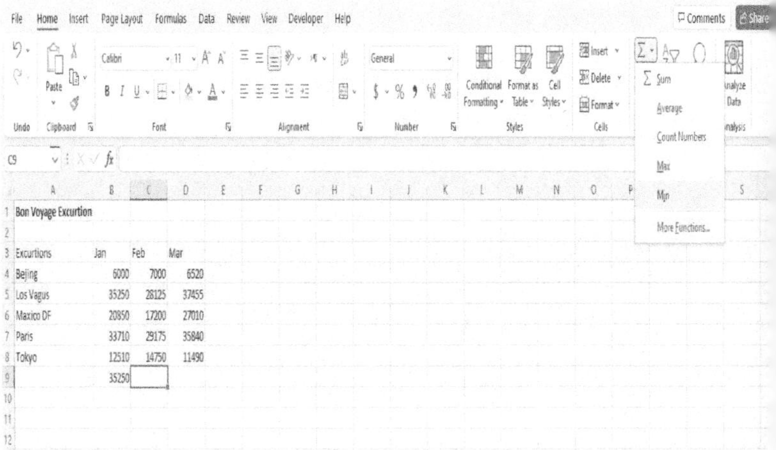

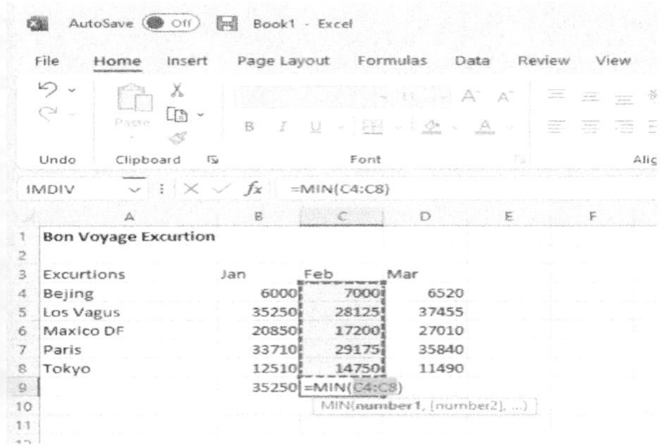

- If that's the case, just choose the range of cells you need.
- Just press Enter button or click your mouse.

A MIN formula is added to Excel, & the range's lowest value is shown.

CHAPTER 4

INTERMEDIATE EXCEL

In this chapter, you will go through sorting, advanced filters, slicers, and adding comments and images in an excel spreadsheet.

4.1 SORTING & ADVANCED FILTERS

Excel's built-in sorting and filtering functions are some of the most useful in managing data. You may use the filter tool to narrow down a table's data to only show the relevant elements. Sort by number, date, alphabetical order, & more with this handy feature. Sorting and filtering are used within the following example to demonstrate some sophisticated sorting methods.

You'll use the following spreadsheet as an example:

Order Number	Product	Salesperson	Price	Date	Customer
333222	ABC	John Smith	$100.00	2/3/2016	Eastern Company
333221	DEF	Rachel Adams	$200.00	2/2/2016	Western Company
333223	ABC	John Smith	$100.00	2/4/2016	Eastern Company
333220	XYZ	Cheryl Myers	$800.00	2/1/2016	Southern Company
333119	GHI	Rachel Adams	$300.00	1/31/2016	Northern Company
333224	JKL	Michael Brent	$400.00	2/5/2016	Northern Company
333118	DEF	Cheryl Myers	$200.00	1/30/2016	Western Company
333225	MNO	Dylan Rogers	$500.00	2/6/2016	Eastern Company
333117	PQR	Michael Brent	$600.00	1/29/2016	Southern Company
333226	STU	Cheryl Myers	$700.00	2/7/2016	Northern Company
333116	ABC	Rachel Adams	$100.00	1/28/2016	Western Company
333227	MNO	John Smith	$500.00	2/3/2016	Eastern Company
333228	PQR	Rachel Adams	$600.00	2/2/2016	Western Company
333229	ABC	John Smith	$100.00	2/4/2016	Eastern Company
333230	XYZ	Cheryl Myers	$800.00	2/1/2016	Southern Company
333231	DEF	Rachel Adams	$200.00	1/31/2016	Northern Company
333232	STU	Michael Brent	$700.00	2/5/2016	Northern Company
333233	GHI	Cheryl Myers	$300.00	1/30/2016	Western Company
333234	DEF	Dylan Rogers	$200.00	2/6/2016	Eastern Company
333235	ABC	Michael Brent	$100.00	2/3/2016	Southern Company

It's easy to notice that everything from the order dates to the order numbers to the pricing is out of sync. So, let's go to work sorting & filtering our data.

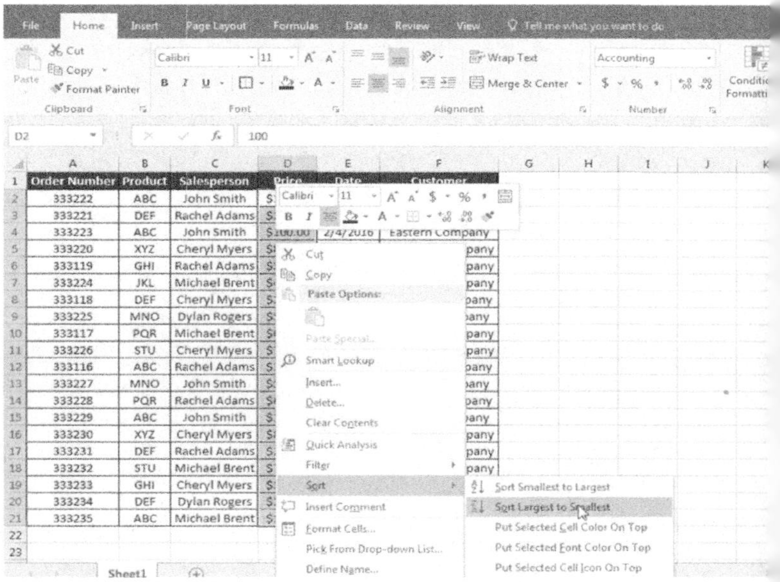

Sorting Data

Assume you already have the spreadsheet and wish to sort it according to pricing. This is a straightforward procedure. To begin, you may choose the entire column or just click on the first cell of the column. After that, you'll:

- Open the context menu by doing a right-click.
- When you hover your mouse over Sort, a sub-menu will emerge. Select Largest to Smallest from the drop-down menu. Expand the options available to you.
- Select "OK"

The sorted column has now been included in the whole table. Note: Expand the selection should be selected when data in a column is connected to data in other columns of the table. This ensures that the data within this row is transferred to the sorted column data.

Filtering Data

To narrow a table, you may use the filter tool, which displays a drop-down option for each column heading. Let's imagine you wish to filter the table by Salesperson and Company, like in the previous example. The quantity of transactions Dylan Rogers produced to Eastern Company is what you're looking for.

You can accomplish this using the filter:

- Open the Excel ribbon and choose the Data tab.
- Look at the Filter option
- Drop down the options and choose Eastern Company.
- Choose Dylan Rogers in the dropdown menu for "Salesperson."

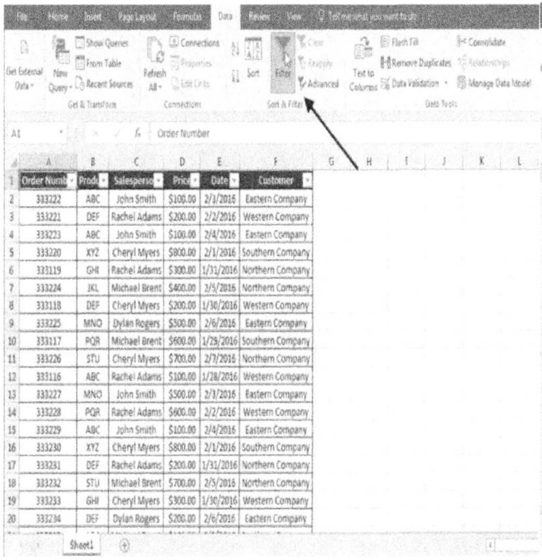

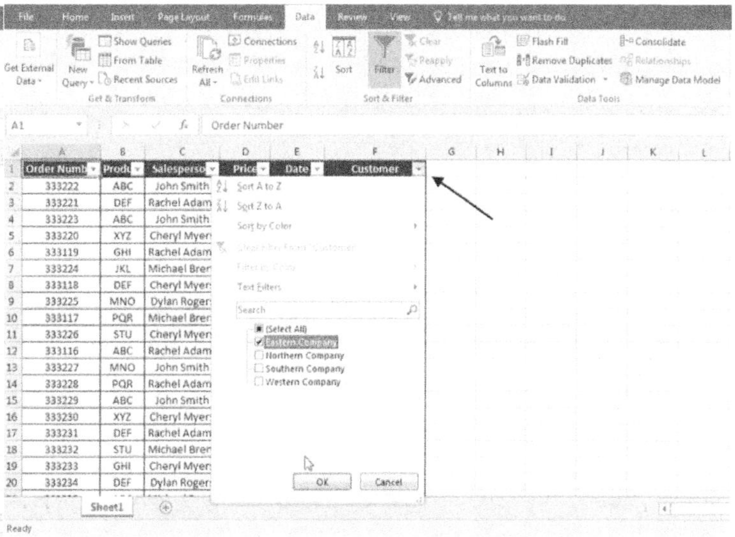

You now know exactly how many Eastern Company sales Dylan Rogers made.

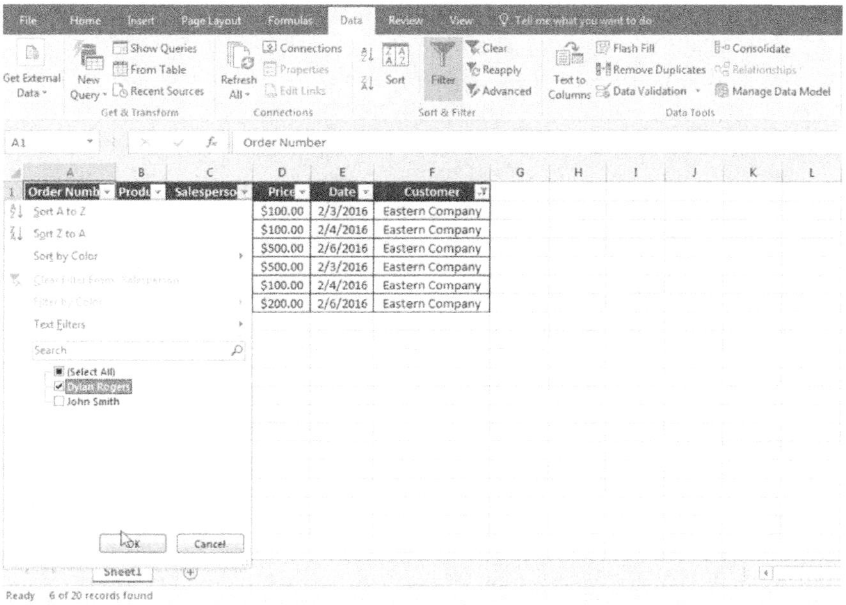

The Filter & Sort Tool

Custom sorting in Excel is possible using the Filter & Sort tool and the right-click sorting menu and Filter tool over the Data ribbon. The Custom Sorting tool may be used to sort price or date ranges, as seen in the accompanying images.

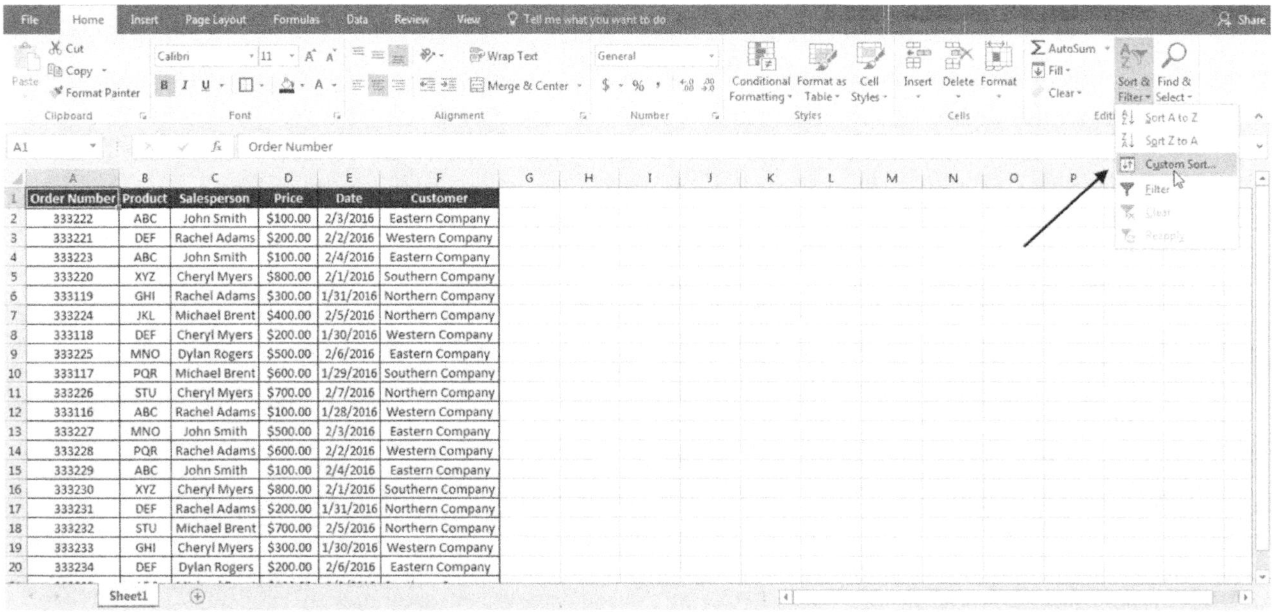

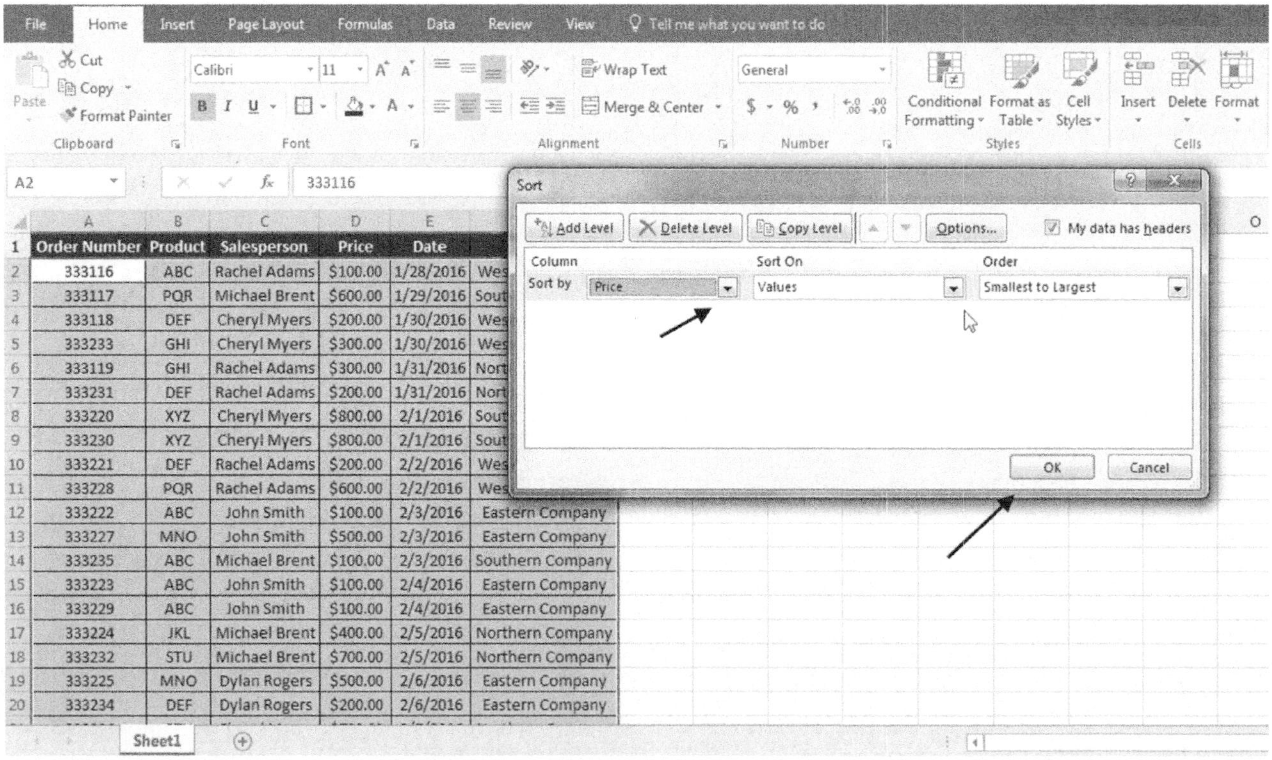

However, observe how this case is either/or in nature. So, what if price and data were combined in a search? In this case, the Custom Sorting option is a lifesaver. You may increase the precision of your event data by choosing an additional level after choosing your initial set of sorting criteria:

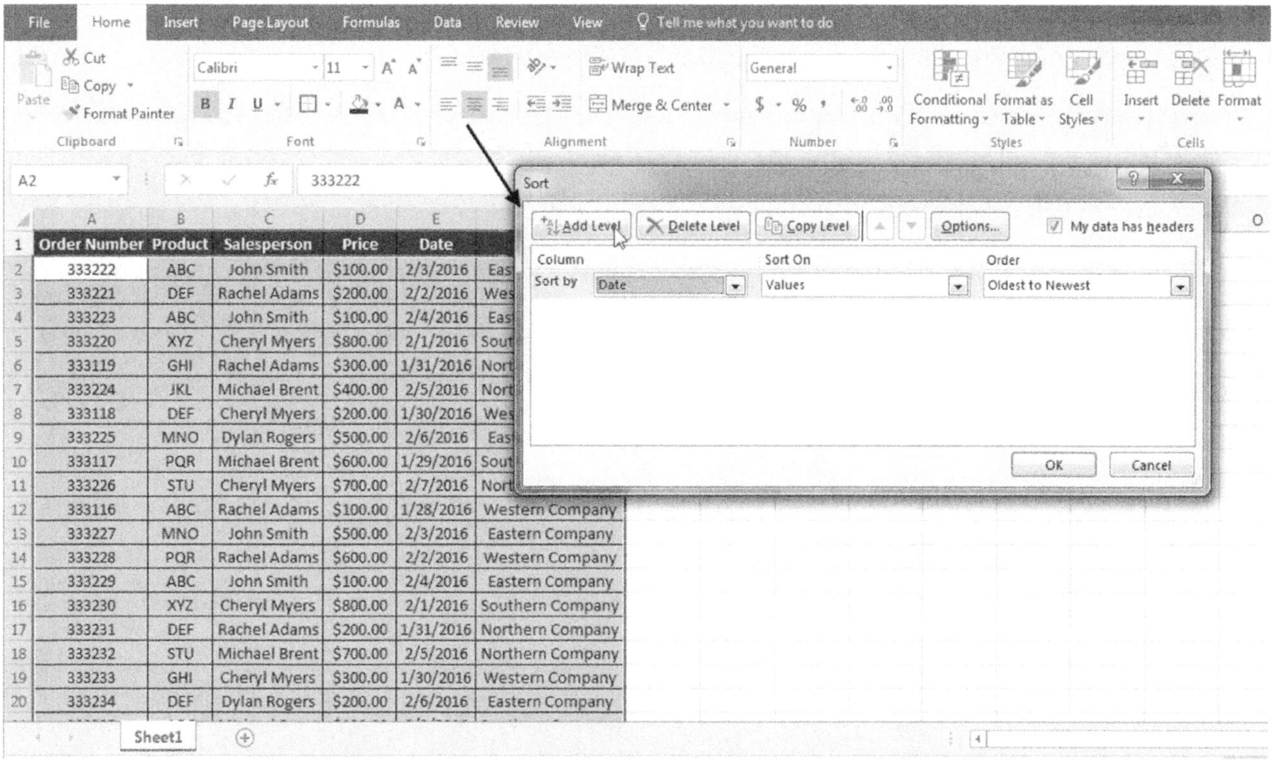

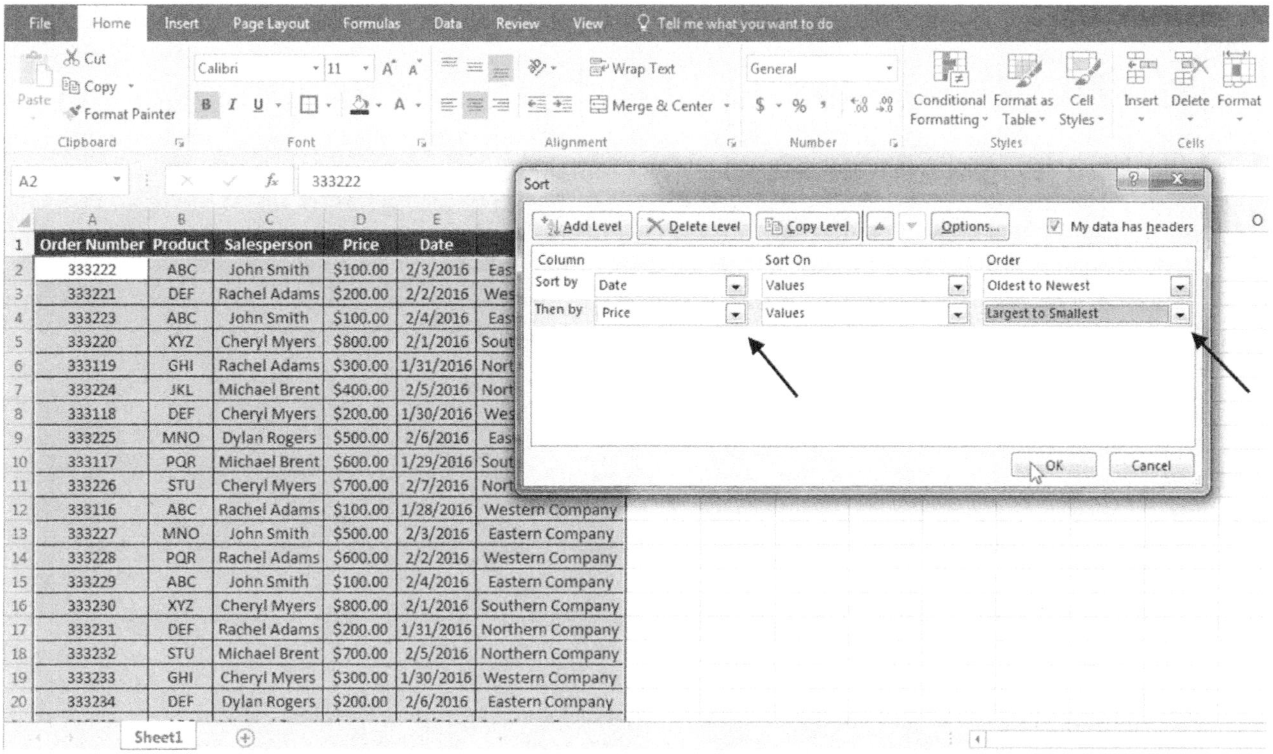

Excel has a wide range of sorting & filtering options that may help you organize your data and make it simpler to find what you're searching for.

Thank you for reading, and we wish you the best of luck in the future. It's up to you to manage your information.

4.2 SLICERS IN EXCEL

One-click software filters may be applied to a vast amount of data in a fraction of a second by using slicers in Excel, which are implemented alongside Excel tables & pivot tables.

You will be able to make a few slicers after completing this chapter since you will have a strong knowledge of Excel Slicers and can construct them.

What Are the Slicers into Excel?

In Excel, slicers are software filtering for massive amounts of data in pivot tables or Excel tables. S

licers do more than remove irrelevant data; they also make it easier to grasp what has been retrieved and put on the screen.

For both Windows & Macintosh operating systems, Microsoft Excel Slicers is available.

You'll be able to construct realistic Excel slicers as you go along.

How to Use Slicers in Excel?

Just follow these two steps to add slicers to Excel or pivot tables.

- Step 1: Prepare the data by converting it to a table or pivot table.
- Step 2: Insert slicers by selecting a cell in an Excel pivot table or simple table.

In this section, you'll go into further depth about each stage.

<u>Step 1</u>

Tables or pivot tables may be used to present the data more efficiently. Excel manages your data as a database by default; thus, adding slicers is not always feasible. For the argument, let me point out that you might have started by transforming the data into an Excel table or a pivot table.

- The pivot table may be built from any Excel column.

Q17 fx

	A	B	C	D	E	F	G	H
1	Employee _ID	Employee_Name	Designation	Department	Salary	Employee_DOB	Employee_DOJ	
2	10012	Jack	Trainee	HR	10000	10-03-1995	19-02-2020	
3	10013	Jennifer	Associate	Development	20000	12-06-1996	15-08-2019	
4	10014	Brock	Senior	Testing	50000	08-08-1998	06-06-2018	
5	10015	Emily	Manager	Knowledge Transfer	35000	09-04-1994	06-05-2018	
6	10016	Martha	Contract	Analytics	30000	01-01-1995	09-08-2019	
7	10017	Clark	Intern	Admin	10000	12-12-1996	06-05-2020	
8	10018	Tony	Senior	IT Support	80000	11-12-1995	03-05-2020	
9	10019	Ben	Trainee	Analytics	12000	30-12-1995	05-02-2019	
10	10020	Alfred	Associate	Admin	25000	05-06-1992	25-02-2019	
11	10021	Steve	Senior	IT Support	60000	06-07-1995	06-05-2018	
12	10022	Barnes	Manager	HR	40000	13-11-1995	09-08-2019	
13	10023	Banner	Contract	Development	35000	30-09-1993	06-05-2020	
14	10024	Fred	Intern	Testing	10000	23-02-1995	03-05-2020	
15	10025	Peter	Senior	Knowledge Transfer	45000	23-05-1995	19-02-2020	
16	10026	Stephanie	Manager	IT Support	40000	06-05-1995	15-08-2019	
17	10027	John	Contract	HR	25000	03-03-1996	06-06-2018	
18	10028	Mack	Intern	Knowledge Transfer	12000	03-04-1994	06-05-2018	
19	10029	Rob	Manager	Analytics	30000	03-05-1995	09-08-2019	
20	10030	Bobby	Contract	Admin	30000	12-12-1995	25-02-2019	
21	10031	Sam	Intern	IT Support	5000	11-12-1995	06-05-2018	
22	10032	Pepper	Senior	Analytics	80000	12-11-1996	09-08-2019	
23	10033	Morgan	Trainee	Admin	10000	13-12-1994	06-05-2020	
24	10034	Chris	Associate	IT Support	20000	19-05-1995	03-05-2020	
25	10035	Idris Elba	Senior	HR	35000	12-09-1996	19-02-2020	
26	10036	Paul	Manager	Development	60000	11-08-1996	15-08-2019	
27	10037	Dominic	Contract	IT Support	50000	12-08-1996	06-06-2018	
28	10038	Letty	Intern	HR	10000	23-09-1994	03-05-2020	
29	10039	Brian	Manager	Knowledge Transfer	50000	30-08-1996	19-02-2020	
30	10040	Luke Hobbs	Contract	Analytics	65000	26-05-1999	19-02-2021	
31	10041	Jayson	Contract	Admin	65000	12-01-1999	18-03-2021	

- Select the pivot table from the insert option over the toolbar.

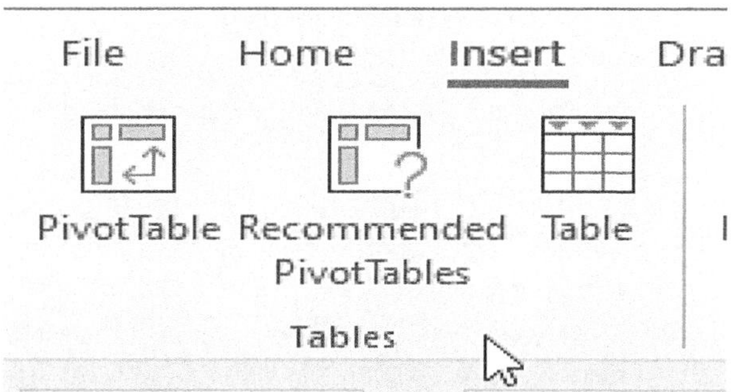

- Select your option to put slicers within pivot table sheets by going to the insert option.

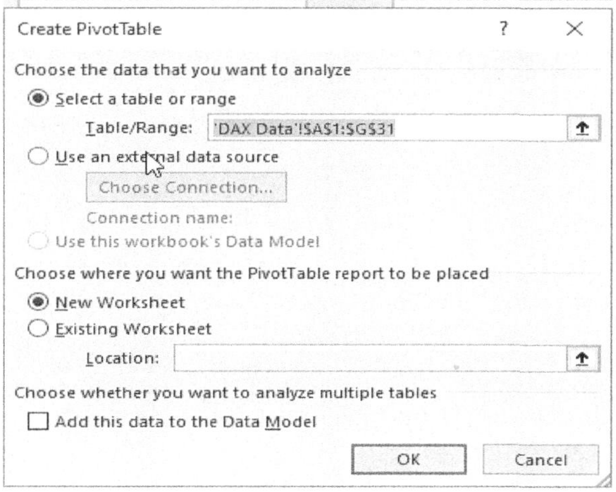

Try Excel's standard table now.

- Any cell on the Excel sheet may be selected.

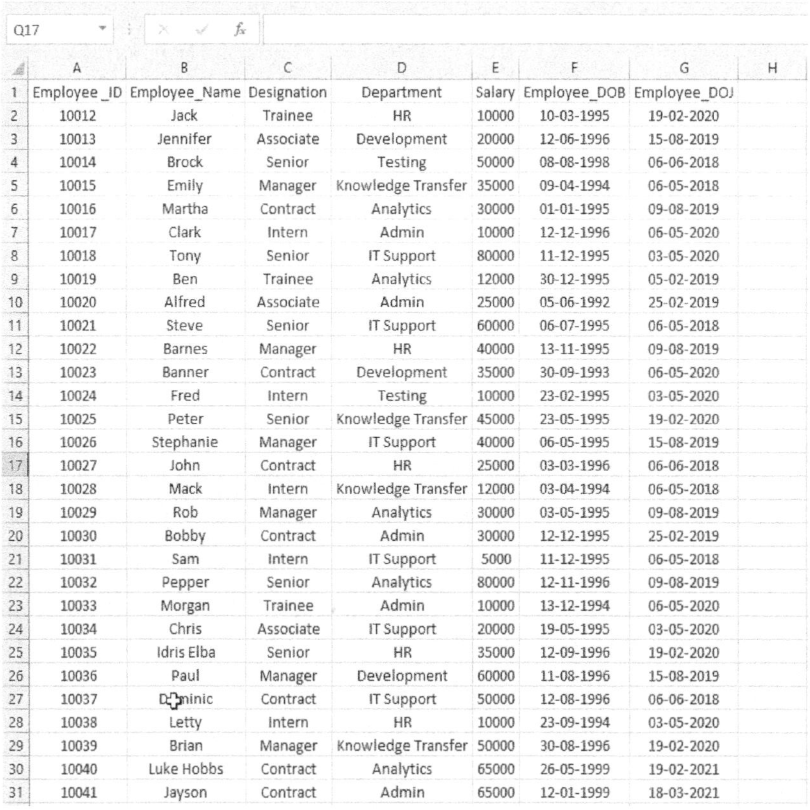

	A	B	C	D	E	F	G
1	Employee_ID	Employee_Name	Designation	Department	Salary	Employee_DOB	Employee_DOJ
2	10012	Jack	Trainee	HR	10000	10-03-1995	19-02-2020
3	10013	Jennifer	Associate	Development	20000	12-06-1996	15-08-2019
4	10014	Brock	Senior	Testing	50000	08-08-1998	06-06-2018
5	10015	Emily	Manager	Knowledge Transfer	35000	09-04-1994	06-05-2018
6	10016	Martha	Contract	Analytics	30000	01-01-1995	09-08-2019
7	10017	Clark	Intern	Admin	10000	12-12-1996	06-05-2020
8	10018	Tony	Senior	IT Support	80000	11-12-1995	03-05-2020
9	10019	Ben	Trainee	Analytics	12000	30-12-1995	05-02-2019
10	10020	Alfred	Associate	Admin	25000	05-06-1992	25-02-2019
11	10021	Steve	Senior	IT Support	60000	06-07-1995	06-05-2018
12	10022	Barnes	Manager	HR	40000	13-11-1995	09-08-2019
13	10023	Banner	Contract	Development	35000	30-09-1993	06-05-2020
14	10024	Fred	Intern	Testing	10000	23-02-1995	03-05-2020
15	10025	Peter	Senior	Knowledge Transfer	45000	23-05-1995	19-02-2020
16	10026	Stephanie	Manager	IT Support	40000	06-05-1995	15-08-2019
17	10027	John	Contract	HR	25000	03-03-1996	06-06-2018
18	10028	Mack	Intern	Knowledge Transfer	12000	03-04-1994	06-05-2018
19	10029	Rob	Manager	Analytics	30000	03-05-1995	09-08-2019
20	10030	Bobby	Contract	Admin	30000	12-12-1995	25-02-2019
21	10031	Sam	Intern	IT Support	5000	11-12-1995	06-05-2018
22	10032	Pepper	Senior	Analytics	80000	12-11-1996	09-08-2019
23	10033	Morgan	Trainee	Admin	10000	13-12-1994	06-05-2020
24	10034	Chris	Associate	IT Support	20000	19-05-1995	03-05-2020
25	10035	Idris Elba	Senior	HR	35000	12-09-1996	19-02-2020
26	10036	Paul	Manager	Development	60000	11-08-1996	15-08-2019
27	10037	Dominic	Contract	IT Support	50000	12-08-1996	06-06-2018
28	10038	Letty	Intern	HR	10000	23-09-1994	03-05-2020
29	10039	Brian	Manager	Knowledge Transfer	50000	30-08-1996	19-02-2020
30	10040	Luke Hobbs	Contract	Analytics	65000	26-05-1999	19-02-2021
31	10041	Jayson	Contract	Admin	65000	12-01-1999	18-03-2021

- To make a table of the data, click Ctrl + T at the same time.
- Click OK to accept your table range selection.

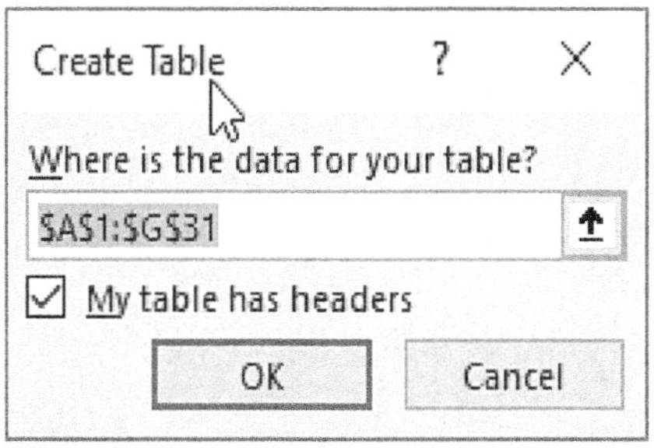

- This is how the final table will appear.

	A	B	C	D	E	F	G
1	Employee_I	Employee_Nam	Designatio	Department	Salar	Employee_DO	Employee_DO
2	10012	Jack	Trainee	HR	10000	10-03-1995	19-02-2020
3	10013	Jennifer	Associate	Development	20000	12-06-1996	15-08-2019
4	10014	Brock	Senior	Testing	50000	08-08-1998	06-06-2018
5	10015	Emily	Manager	Knowledge Transfer	35000	09-04-1994	06-05-2018
6	10016	Martha	Contract	Analytics	30000	01-01-1995	09-08-2019
7	10017	Clark	Intern	Admin	10000	12-12-1996	06-05-2020
8	10018	Tony	Senior	IT Support	80000	11-12-1995	03-05-2020
9	10019	Ben	Trainee	Analytics	12000	30-12-1995	05-02-2019
10	10020	Alfred	Associate	Admin	25000	05-06-1992	25-02-2019
11	10021	Steve	Senior	IT Support	60000	06-07-1995	06-05-2018
12	10022	Barnes	Manager	HR	40000	13-11-1995	09-08-2019
13	10023	Banner	Contract	Development	35000	30-09-1993	06-05-2020
14	10024	Fred	Intern	Testing	10000	23-02-1995	03-05-2020
15	10025	Peter	Senior	Knowledge Transfer	45000	23-05-1995	19-02-2020
16	10026	Stephanie	Manager	IT Support	40000	06-05-1995	15-08-2019
17	10027	John	Contract	HR	25000	03-03-1996	06-06-2018
18	10028	Mack	Intern	Knowledge Transfer	12000	03-04-1994	06-05-2018
19	10029	Rob	Manager	Analytics	30000	03-05-1995	09-08-2019
20	10030	Bobby	Contract	Admin	30000	12-12-1995	25-02-2019
21	10031	Sam	Intern	IT Support	5000	11-12-1995	06-05-2018
22	10032	Pepper	Senior	Analytics	80000	12-11-1996	09-08-2019
23	10033	Morgan	Trainee	Admin	10000	13-12-1994	06-05-2020
24	10034	Chris	Associate	IT Support	20000	19-05-1995	03-05-2020
25	10035	Idris Elba	Senior	HR	35000	12-09-1996	19-02-2020
26	10036	Paul	Manager	Development	60000	11-08-1996	15-08-2019
27	10037	Dominic	Contract	IT Support	50000	12-08-1996	06-06-2018
28	10038	Letty	Intern	HR	10000	23-09-1994	03-05-2020
29	10039	Brian	Manager	Knowledge Transfer	50000	30-08-1996	19-02-2020
30	10040	Luke Hobbs	Contract	Analytics	65000	26-05-1999	19-02-2021
31	10041	Jayson	Contract	Admin	65000	12-01-1999	18-03-2021

Step 2

Slicers may be added to any cell in an Excel pivot table or standard table.

The slicers are now in place. If you want to insert slicers, you may do so just as you would in the pivot table.

- Any cell within a table may be selected.
- On your toolbar, choose the insert option.

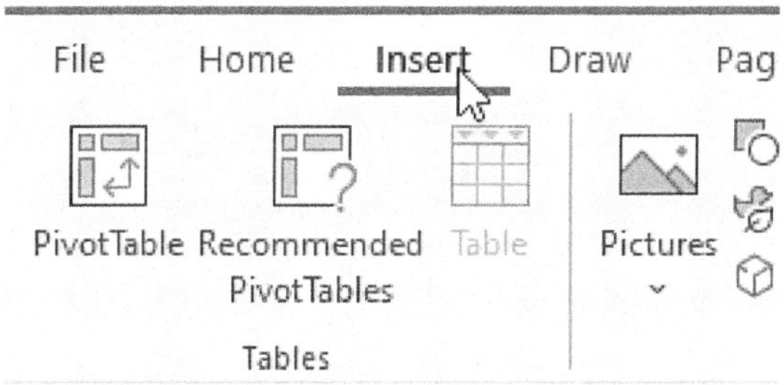

- Choosy insert a slicer

- A new page will appear up and ask for the necessary information. Click ok to finalize your selections

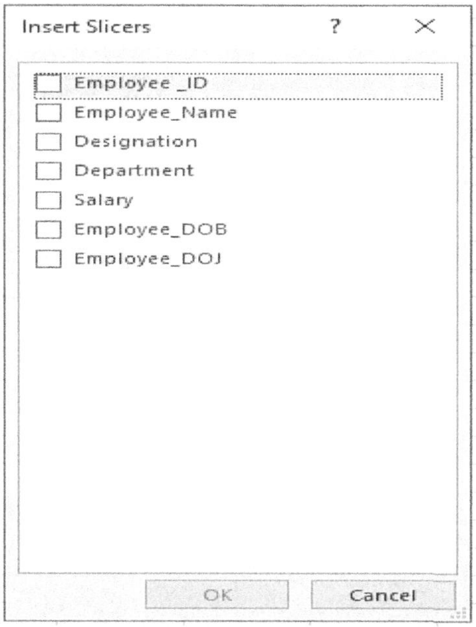

- To use the slicers, they will be shown on the screen.

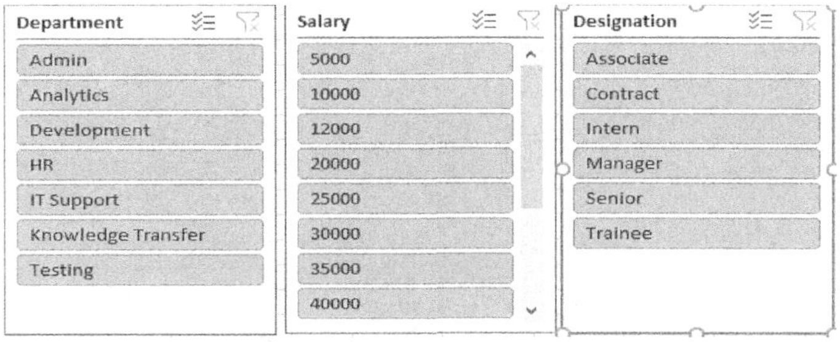

- Slicers may be used to filter data and produce results like the one seen below.

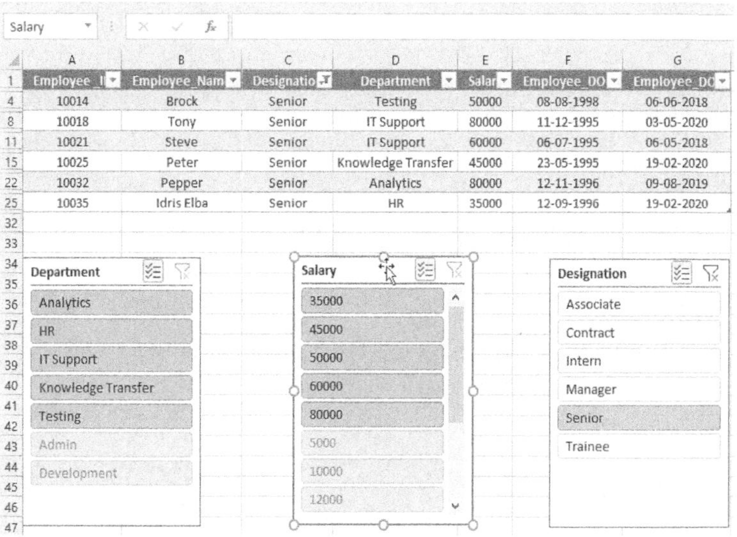

Using slicers within Excel has several advantages, and you will learn about some of those advantages now.

Benefits of Utilizing Slicers in Excel

Using Excel slicers has several benefits and makes real-time data processing simpler and more efficient. It's worth noting that there are a few notable advantages.

- Copying and moving the Slicer formulae to another table is easy. When you use Slicers, getting the information you need in a quarter of the time eliminates the time-consuming process of manually sifting through the data.
- If the user is solely interested in filtering out the relevant data, Slicers in Excel serve to keep data safe and secure.

4.3 INSERT A COMMENT

Use Excel 2019's comment feature to start a discussion or provide input on a cell's content. Notes, the new name for the old kind of comments is still accessible.

Insert Comment

Follow these instructions to add a comment.

- A cell may be selected by clicking on it.
- Then click on New Comment from the context menu that appears after you've performed a right-click.

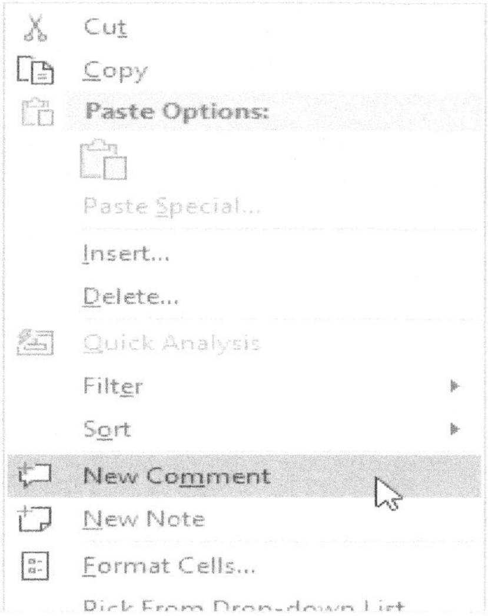

To add an old-style remark, just click New Note and type your message.

- The third step is to submit your remark.

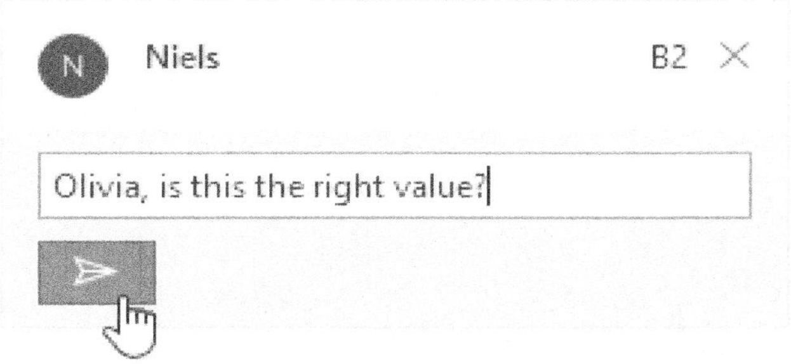

In Excel, the cell's upper-right corner shows a purple signal.

- To read the remark, just place your cursor over the cell.

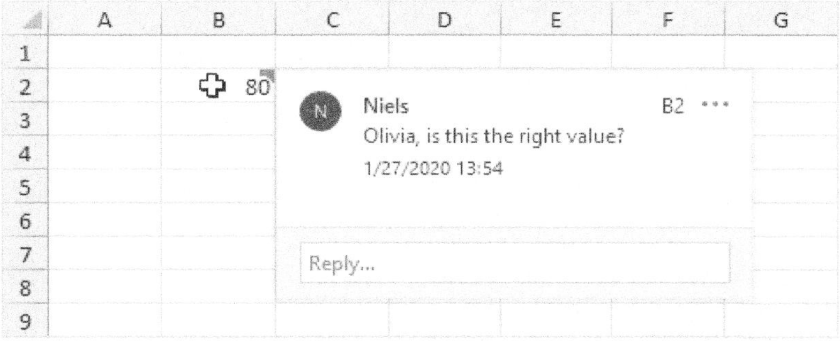

- Edit a remark by hovering your mouse over a comment and selecting Edit.

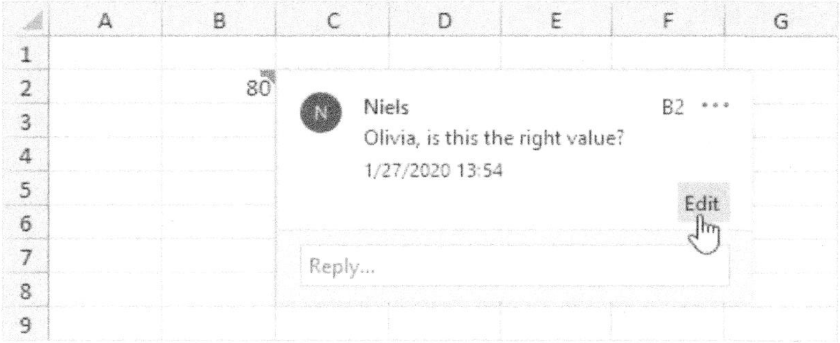

- Your comment will now be open to further discussion.

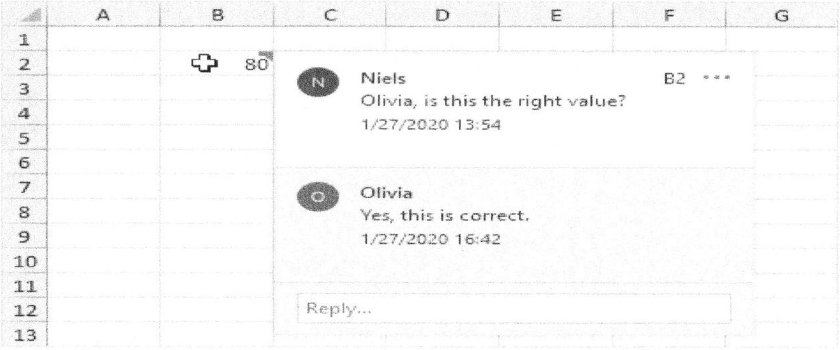

4.4 DELETE COMMENT

Follow these methods to get rid of a remark.

1. Click on the cell that contains the remark.

2. Click your right mouse button, then choose Delete Comment.

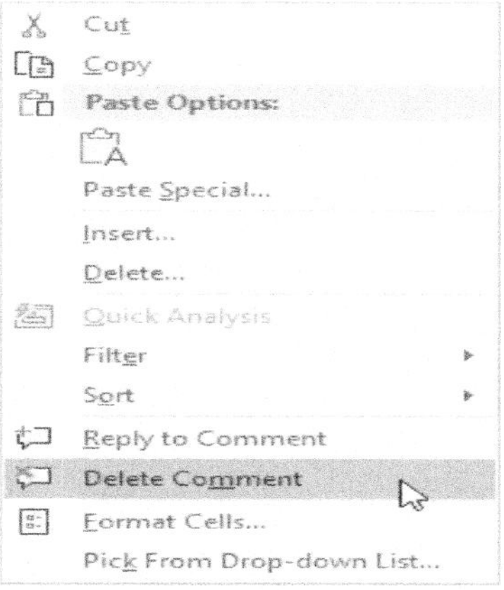

Show Comments

Execute the following procedures to see all comments inside an Excel file.

1. Click Show Comments within the Comments group on the Review tab.

Tip: Rather than selecting Review, select Comments, located in the ribbon's top right corner.

In the Comments pane, Excel displays all the comments in this Excel document.

You can also edit, respond, and remove comments from this window.

4.5 INSERTING IMAGES, BACKGROUNDS OR 3D

It's simple to place an image in an Excel spreadsheet so that as you move, resize, or filter it, the image also changes.

In the sample below, the logos of a few well-known firms have been placed in the adjacent column, & as the cells are sorted, so are the logos.

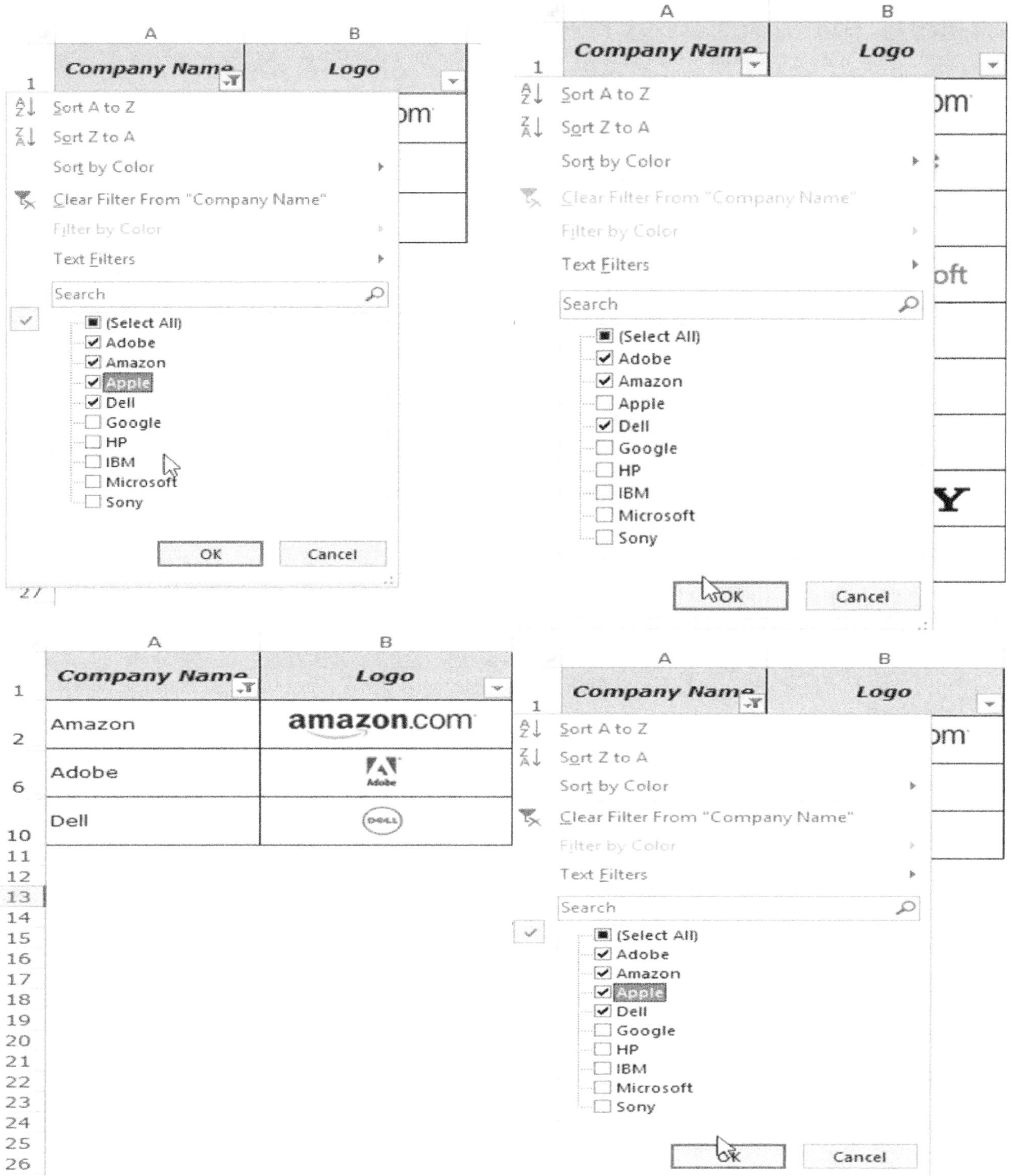

This may be helpful if you're working with product images or SKUs.

Images in Excel are not connected to cells; therefore, you can't filter, hide, or resize them in conjunction with the cells.

You will understand how to do the following things in this demo:

- You may add a picture to any cell in Excel by dragging and dropping.
- As a result, the Picture will be able to move, resize and filter together with the cells in the cell.

4.6 INSERT PICTURE INTO A CELL IN EXCEL

To add a photo to an Excel cell, follow these steps:

- Navigate to the Insert menu.
- Select "Pictures" from the Illustrations drop-down menu.

- To put photographs into an Excel column, go to the 'Insert Picture' dialogue box and choose the images you wish to use.

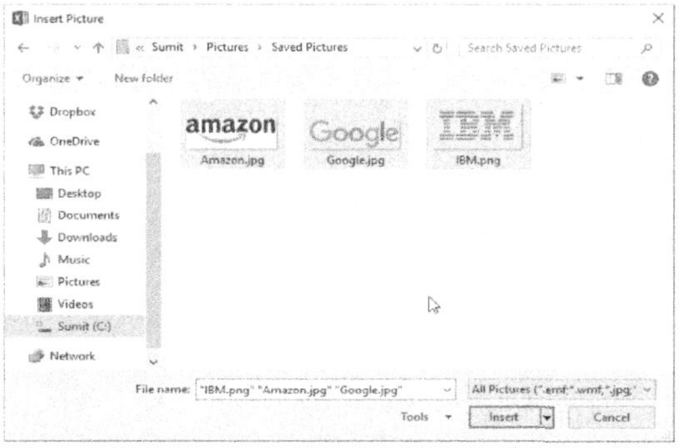

- The Insert button should be clicked.

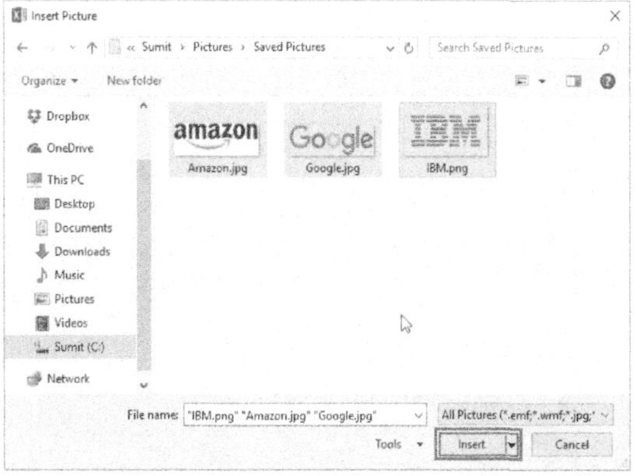

Adjust the image's size so that it precisely fills the cell.

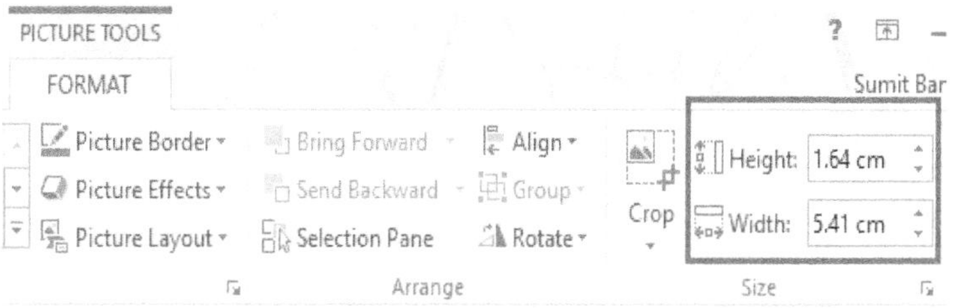

Put the image within the cell.

The ALT key is a great shortcut to utilize before dragging the image with the mouse. As soon as it approaches the cell's boundary, it will snap into place and align itself with it.

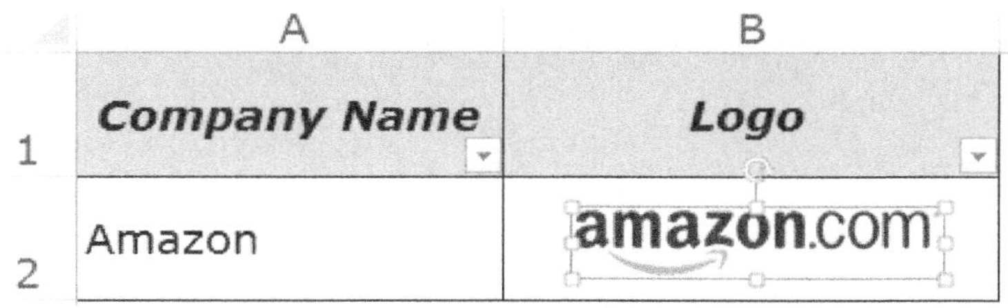

If you have many photographs, you may choose them and put them at once (as displayed in step 4).

Images may also be resized by choosing them and dragging their edges. You may wish to maintain the image's aspect ratio when using logos or product graphics. Just use the corners of the picture to resize it while maintaining the aspect ratio.

If you use the following instructions to insert an image into a cell, all pictures will not stay there even if you filter, resize, or hide all cells. Locking the picture to the cell where it is inserted must adhere to it.

To accomplish this, you must do the extra actions detailed in the section below.

Lock the Picture with the specified Cell into Excel

The picture must be locked so that it moves, filters, & hides with the cell after being entered into the workbook, scaled to fit inside a cell, & placed in the cell.

The procedures to lock a photo in a cell are as follows:

- Select Format Image by doing a right-click on the image.

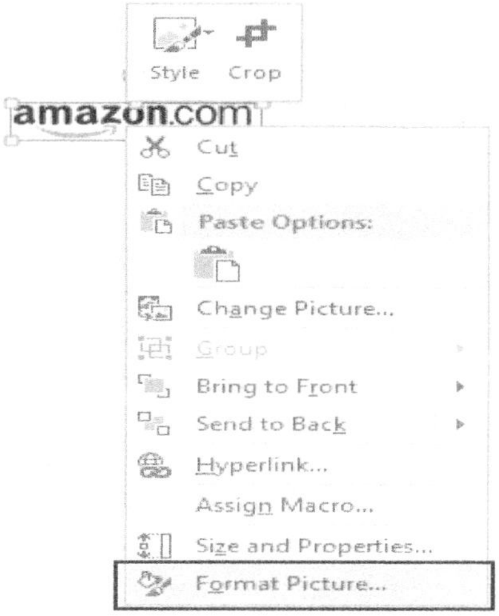

Choose "Move & size with cells" from the list of choices under "Properties" under "Size & Properties" within the Format Picture window.

It's done!

Now that the image has been moved, filtered, or hidden, the cells may be moved, too.

This might be a helpful tip if you have a list of items with their photographs and would like to filter out certain product categories with their images.

4.7 INSERTING BACKGROUND

If you have a sheet with certain data and want to add a vibrant backdrop behind the cells for a more eye-catching appearance, as seen in the picture below, do you know how to achieve it with Excel?

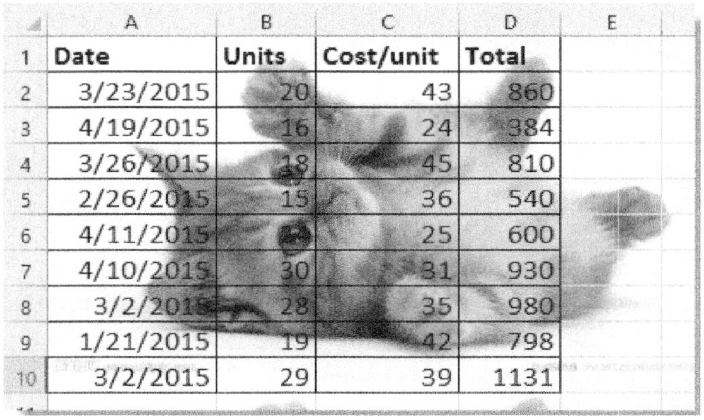

	A	B	C	D	E
1	Date	Units	Cost/unit	Total	
2	3/23/2015	20	43	860	
3	4/19/2015	16	24	384	
4	3/26/2015	18	45	810	
5	2/26/2015	15	36	540	
6	4/11/2015	24	25	600	
7	4/10/2015	30	31	930	
8	3/2/2015	28	35	980	
9	1/21/2015	19	42	798	
10	3/2/2015	29	39	1131	

Inserting Background Behind the Cells Using Background Function

The Background function lets you put a picture behind the current worksheet's cells.

Click on Page Layout ➔ Background. See the image below:

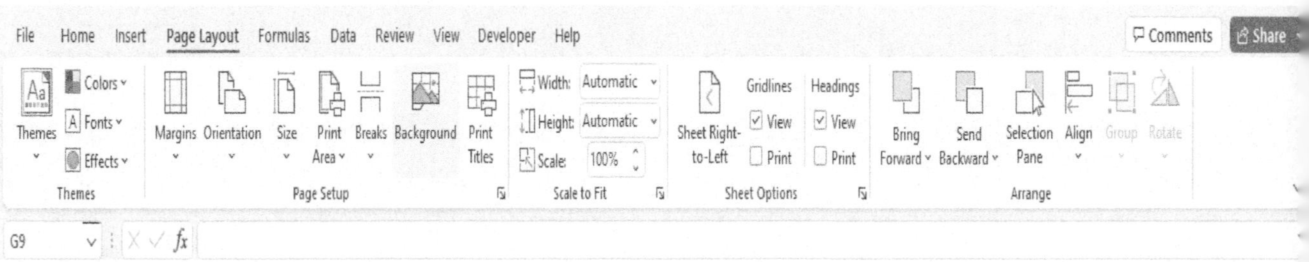

When the Insert Pictures dialogue appears, pick a photo you wish to use as the backdrop from a folder within the Sheet Background dialogue by clicking the Explore button next to the file option. See the example below:

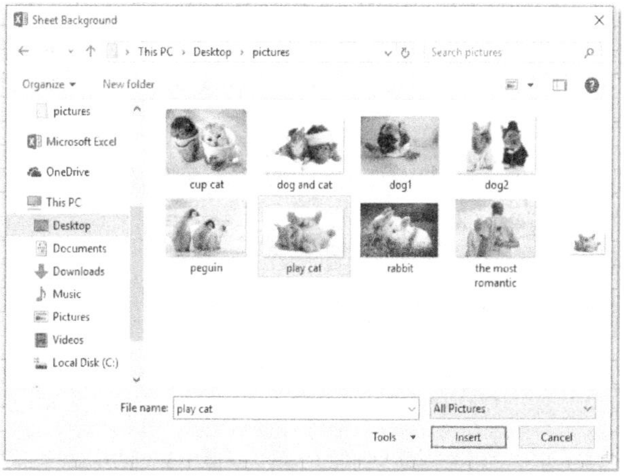

- Press Insert. Additionally, cells have been added to hide the backdrop picture.

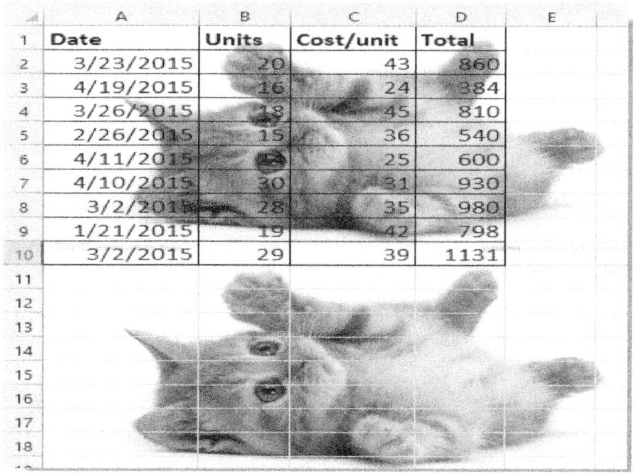

Tip: For deleting background, click on Page Layout ➔ Delete Background.

Inserting Background Behind the Cells With specified Kutools for the Excel

You may enter a photo as a watermark embedded behind data cells if you've Kutools for Excel.

After installation of Kutools for Excel, kindly do as under:

Click Kutools ➔ Insert ➔ Insert Watermark. See the example below:

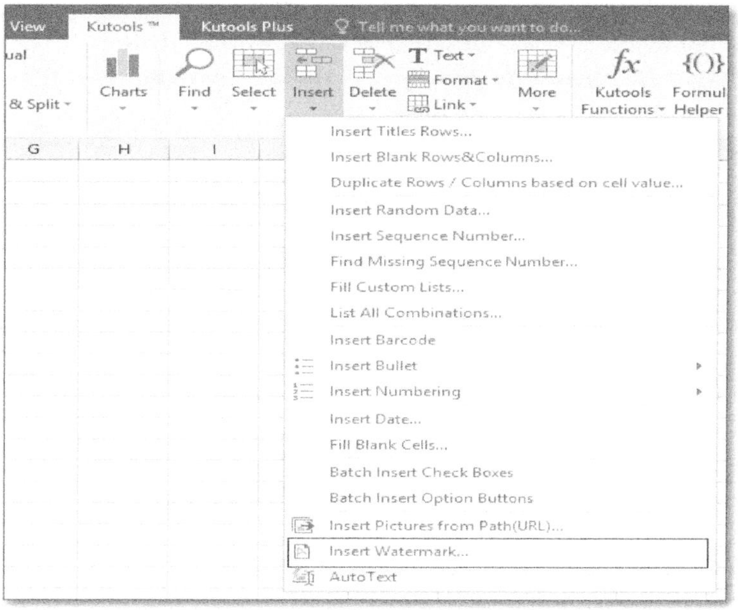

You have the option to enter a photo watermark from a folder or a text watermark using formatting within the Insert Watermark box, as seen in the screenshot:

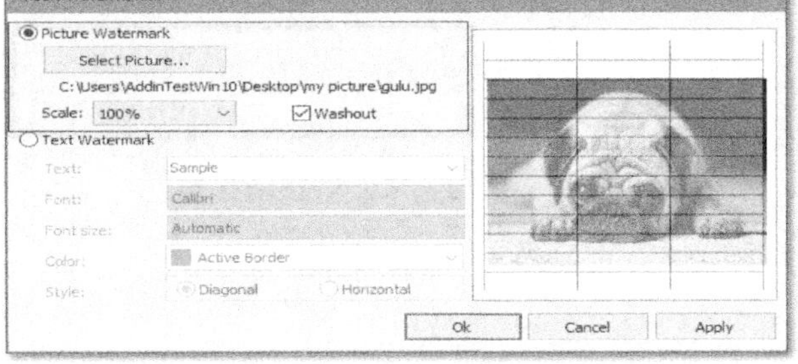

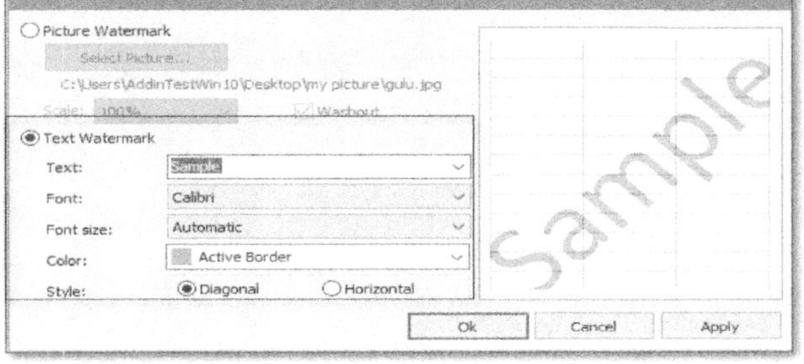

Once you select Apply and Ok, your background image will be placed.

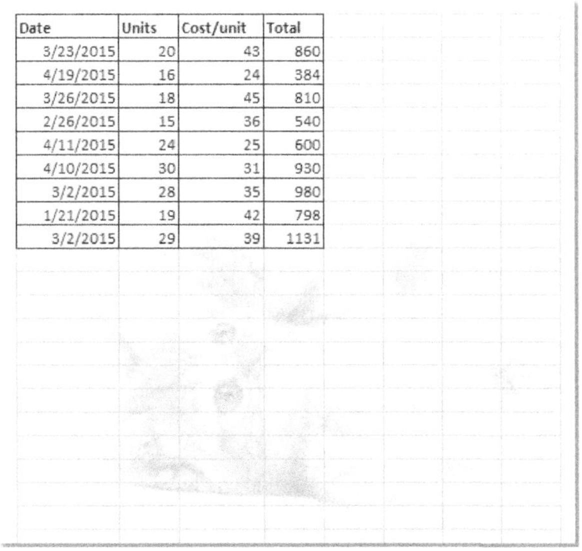

Date	Units	Cost/unit	Total
3/23/2015	20	43	860
4/19/2015	16	24	384
3/26/2015	18	45	810
2/26/2015	15	36	540
4/11/2015	24	25	600
4/10/2015	30	31	930
3/2/2015	28	35	980
1/21/2015	19	42	798
3/2/2015	29	39	1131

Tip: This Erosion option is default selected when you enter a photo watermark in the Insert Watermark window. If you don't check the Erosion option, your watermark will appear as follows:

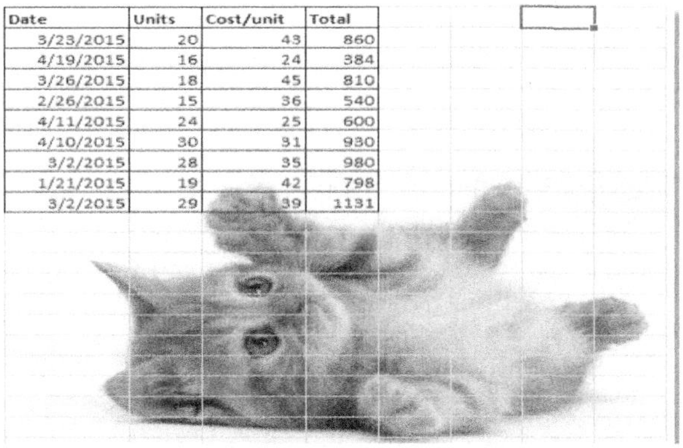

Date	Units	Cost/unit	Total
3/23/2015	20	43	860
4/19/2015	16	24	384
3/26/2015	18	45	810
2/26/2015	15	36	540
4/11/2015	24	25	600
4/10/2015	30	31	930
3/2/2015	28	35	980
1/21/2015	19	42	798
3/2/2015	29	39	1131

To remove your watermark, click on Kutools ➔ Delete ➔ Delete Watermark. Check the image below:

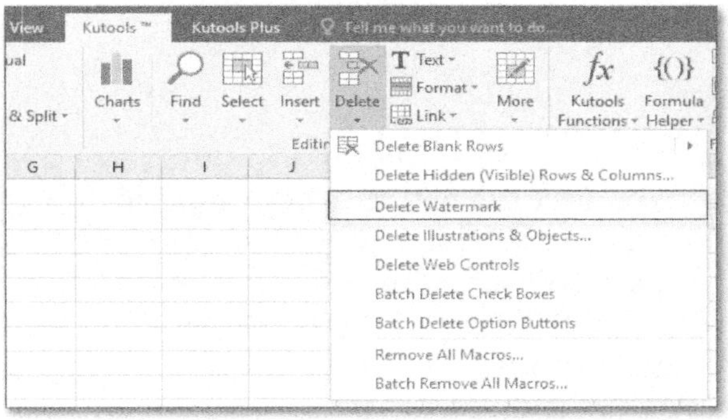

Inserting Background Behind the Cell Contents

Suppose you'd want to insert images in a certain sequence based on the provided names rather than entering them one at a time. In that case, you may use the Match Import Photographs tool in Kutools for Excel to quickly locate photographs from the folder based on the specified picture names & then input picture match names.

4.8 3D PLOT IN EXCEL

For data sets that may not provide much visibility, comparative viability with the other data sets, or charting the region when we have enormous numbers of data points, we employ Excel's 3D Plot feature. Excel's 3D Plot is a clever approach to converting a straightforward 2D graph into a 3D one.

How can you Plot a 3D Graph into Excel?

When we wish to transform data, pie charts, and graphs into the 3D format, displaying 3D graphs within Excel is quite simple and helpful. Let's look at some examples to better understand how you can plot a 3D Graph into Excel.

From the Insert menu, choose the Charts option and 3D Plot.

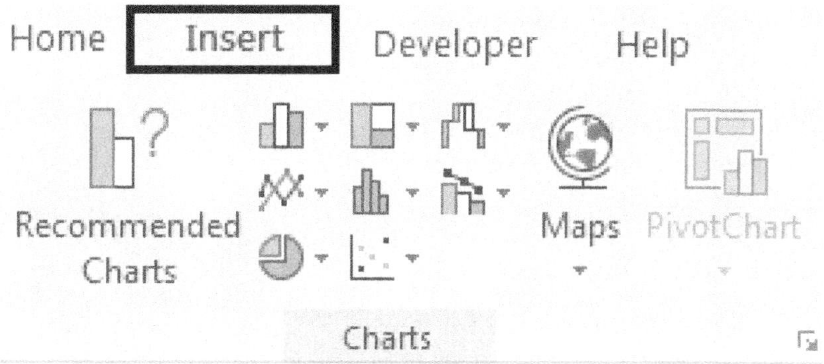

3D Plot into Excel – Example # 1

You have information on how far certain sportsmen could climb in meters. The distance was reached on an hourly basis in one instance. Every athlete has climbed a certain distance for five hours, and the one who has climbed the most distance at the end of the race wins. You may not be able to draw a conclusion from the data or make comparisons. It will be simple to verify the case scenario if you plot such data on 3D graphs.

	A	B	C	D	E	F	G
1	Athelete	1st hour	2nd hour	3rd hour	4th hour	5th hour	
2	Ben	54	56	24	52	54	
3	Chris	38	82	54	54	52	
4	John	38	64	30	50	52	
5	Mary	42	80	22	50	52	
6							

Select the data before making a 3-D Plot for the data above collection.

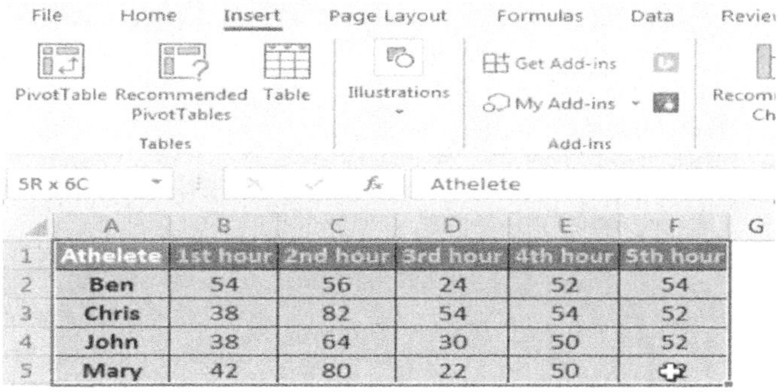

Then pick a column chart from the chart menu under the Insert menu tab. When you click over it, a drop-down list of options will appear. Select a 3-D Column from there, as shown below.

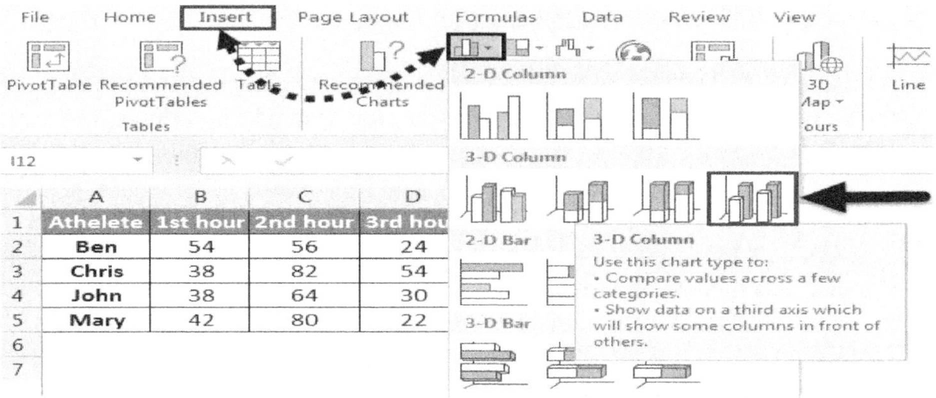

As seen in the example below, choosing the 3-D Column option results in a 3-D plot with a Column. Data labels, Heading, Axis Titles, and even 3-D column design may all be added in this section.

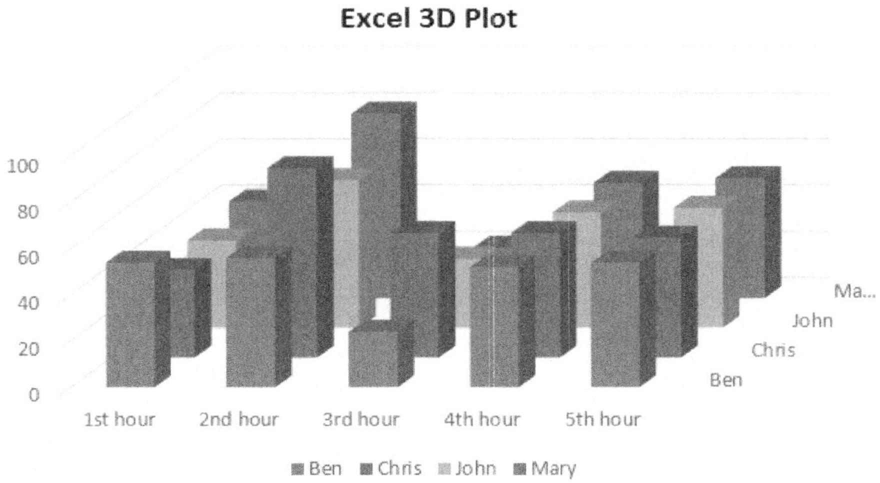

Columns of data are shown in the graph above, and such columns are framed with data in parallel. Column heights have been mapped, and the height parameters for each column are presented above. Let's re-plot this data in 3D this time. The next step is to create a three-dimensional graph. Here's how it works: First, choose the data; then go to your Insert menu and select Waterfall (stock), Surface (radar) and other charts from the drop-down menu. You may also choose Other Charts if you use a different Excel version.

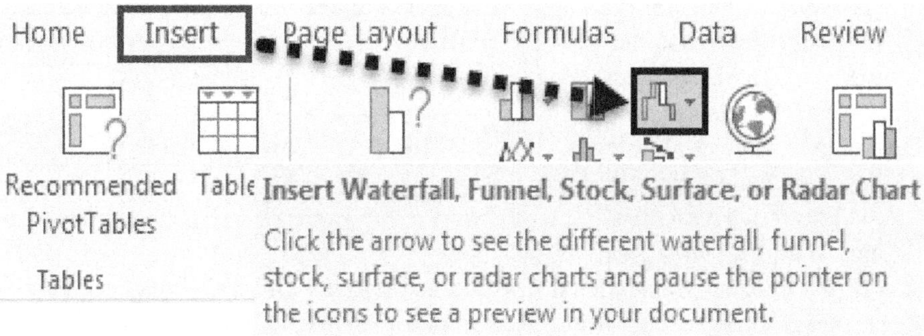

Once you do so, you will receive a drop-down option of Surface Stok & Radar chart, which can be seen below. From there, pick 3D Surface.

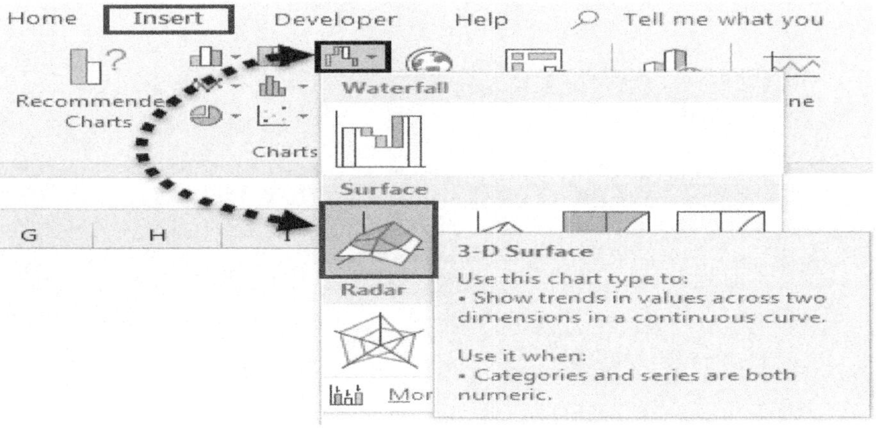

This is what the 3-D Surface Plot looks like after you're done.

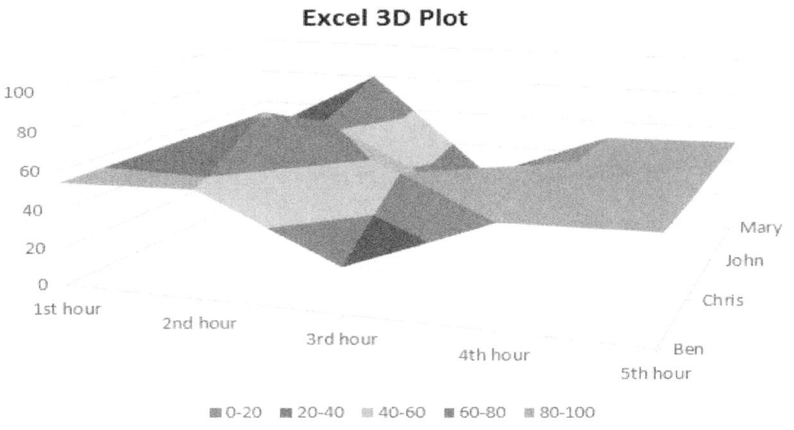

The peak and trough distance hiked by athletes is shown in the above data, with each hue indicating a distinct distance range. Therefore, you may play with various Excel 3D Plot possibilities.

3D Plot into Excel – Example # 2

Consider that height is determined every ten meters from a set of predetermined sites on the surface. The height of the land's surface varies dramatically from one place to the next. Below, you can see the data.

	A	B	C	D	E	F	G	H
1	Point	10M	20M	30M	40M	50M	60M	70M
2	Point 1	40	35	90	100	100	90	70
3	Point 2	40	9333333	90	1333333	100	90	70
4	Point 3	60	21	135	150	150	6333333	105
5	Point 4	56	112	126	140	140	126	98
6	Point 5	5333333	1166667	120	1333333	1333333	120	9333333
7	Point 6	5142857	120	1157143	1285714	128 5714	1157143	90
8	Point 7	60	122.5	135	150	150	135	105
9								

Now that you've selected all your data, you can begin plotting the 3D graph. Select a column chart from the Charts area of the Insert menu, as seen in the image below. When you choose it, a submenu will display. Select a 3-D Column from the drop-down menu given below.

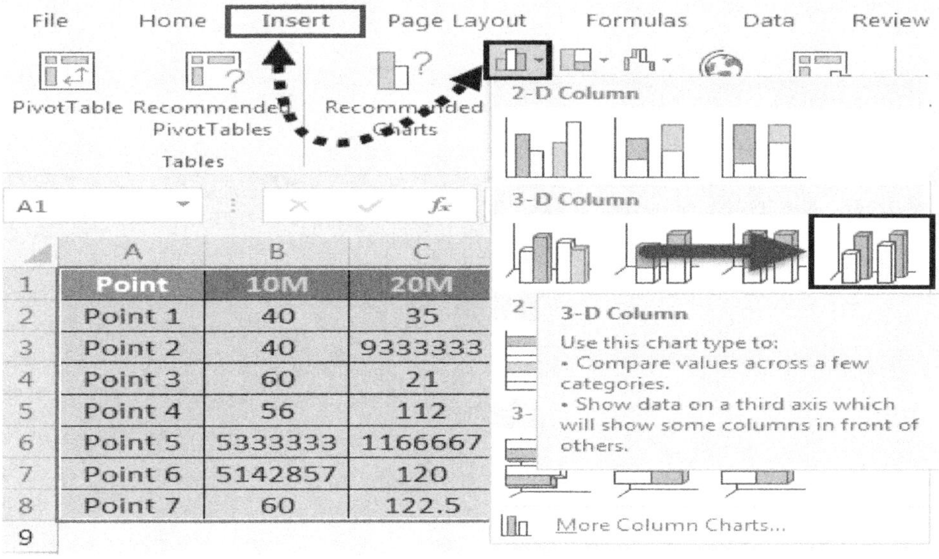

As seen in the example below, choosing the 3-D Column option results in a 3-D plot with a Column.

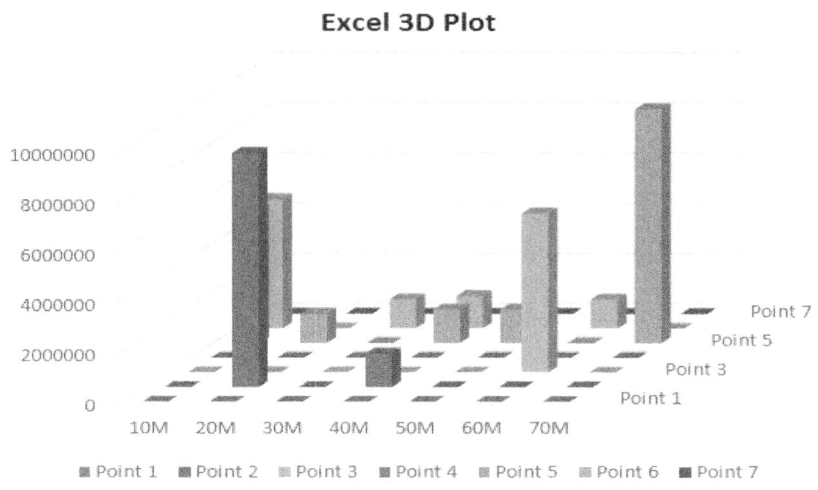

A few large skyscrapers and a few flat buildings can be seen. This data may be shown in 3D charts, which makes it clear where the process has highs and lows. Data labels may be added here. Try creating a 3D graph with the same data. To do so, choose the data and then go to the Insert menu; underneath the Charts section, choose either an Area or Line Chart.

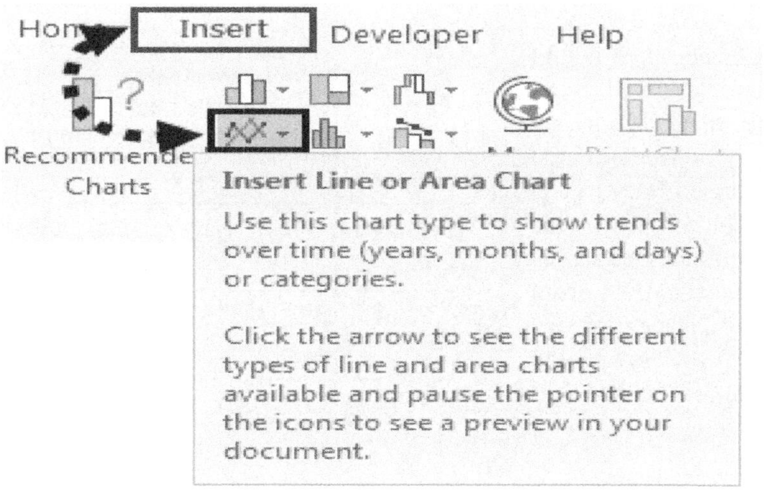

You'll then get a list of Graphs like the one below. 3-D Line charts may be selected from this menu.

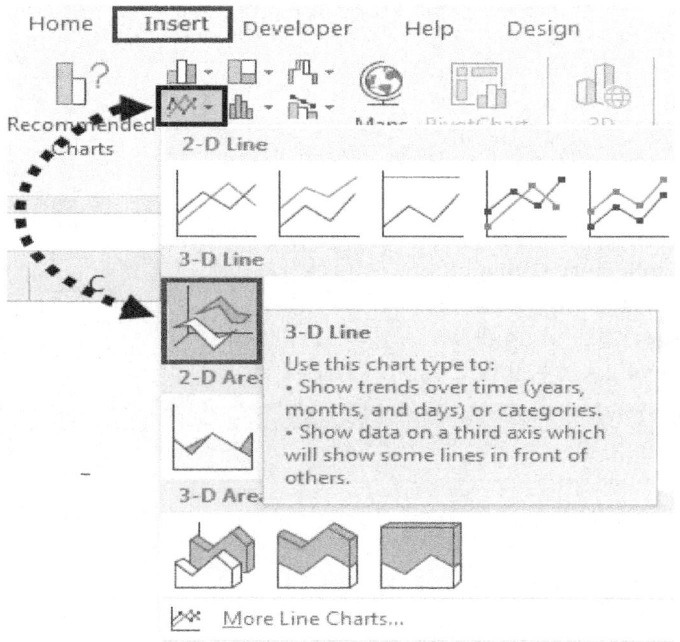

As can be seen by hovering over it and clicking, the 3D Plotted graph plot appears, as shown below.

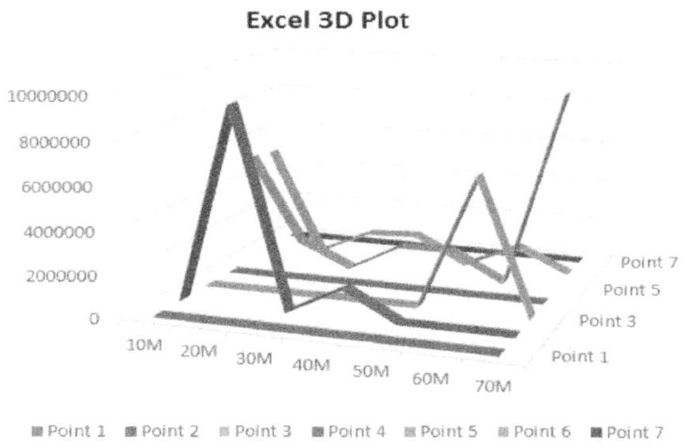

That's the most logical and straightforward three-dimensional plot we could develop. Because the data are divided, this graphic is simple to comprehend. It's easy to see the differences in the data, too. A 3-D Line plot is an excellent choice when the data is separated.

The 3D plots, like the one seen above, are an excellent illustration of this kind of display. If the data enables you to depict varied and needed viewpoints, you can make a 3-D plot for Bar Chart, Area Chart, Pie Chart, and Combo Charts.

A 3D plot may not be capable of providing us with the appropriate perspective if you use the Pie chart for data presented in the instances above. For this reason, it is finest to 1st comprehend what you want to view before mapping it onto the required 3D representation.

Pros of 3-D Plot in Excel

- When data includes dimensions, a 3D Plot allows for a broader view of the information.
- These 3-D or basic graphs make it easy to keep track of changes made in the backend. To plot contour graphs, you need to know the height of the surface.

Things you should Remember

- When you have a basic data structure, you don't necessarily need to draw a 3-D graph using Excel.
- To ensure that the final graph does not alter, always paste the graph with the picture attached.
- Data should be organized to make it easy to modify a graph if necessary. Data labels within 3D Graphs clog up the plot and should be avoided at all costs.
- When data labels can be seen, they should be used.

4.9 ALIGNING OR ARRANGING OBJECTS

It's easy to align items in Microsoft Office products (such as text box, SmartArt visual, and WordArt).

Aligning multiple objects

It's time to choose your alignment targets! After clicking the first item, you must hold down the Ctrl key while clicking the other items.

Make the following action:

- The Format tab in Photograph Tools may be used to align a picture.
- Under Drawing Tools, choose the Format option to align any text box shape or WordArt.

When you click Align within Arrange group, you may pick one of the following instructions from the menu:

Option	Description
Align Left	Aligns objects along their left edges
Align Center	Aligns objects vertically through their centers.
Align Right	Aligns objects along their right edges
Align Top	Aligns objects along their top edges
Align Middle	Aligns objects horizontally through their middles.
Align Bottom	Aligns objects along their bottom edges

You can only pick one item if the Align choices are unavailable. You must be able to proceed after selecting one or even more things.

Arranging objects at equal distances from one another

If you wish to place at least three things at identical distances from each other, choose at least three. Click one item, and then tap & hold the Ctrl key as you click the remaining objects in a selection.

Do the following to select concealed, stacked, or behind-the-text objects:

Draw one box over the items you want to choose and click Find & Select within the Editing group on the home page to get started.

Do any of the following:

- You may do this by going to the Format tab in Picture Tools.
- Using the Format option in the Drawing Tools, you may organize a set of text boxes, shapes, or WordArt equally.

You may perform one of the following within the Alignment group:

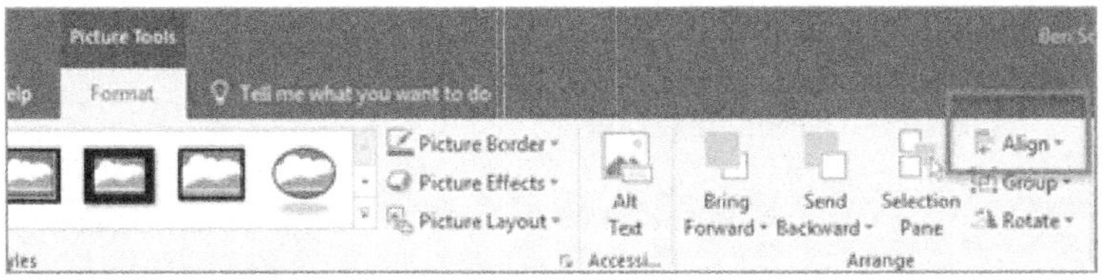

Click Distribute Horizontally to arrange the elements horizontally.

Click the Distribute Vertically button to vertically distribute the items.

4.10 CHARTS AND GRAPHS

Microsoft Excel's charts and graphs make it possible to view numerical data. Compared to graphs, charts are more complicated, diversified, dynamic, and vary in their presentation of data points. Several examples of charts and graphs are used to communicate progress or outcomes in presentations to management, clients, or team members. Using a graph or a chart to show your quantitative data can save you time and stress by allowing you to quickly identify patterns and correlations. Because you can keep your data straight in an Excel Spreadsheet rather than importing it from another tool, creating graphs and charts with Excel is a breeze. Excel provides a wide range of pre-made chart & graph kinds regarding charting and graphing.

Although Excel is well-known, it was never designed to be used as a management tool. Comparing work visibility, accessibility, management, collaboration, and connectors between Excel & Smartsheet is easy with this side-by-side comparison.

When to Use Excel's Different Chart & Graph Types.

Your data may be shown using one of the many charts & graph types available in Excel. Choosing the right chart type for your data collection is important, even when numerous options may be available.

There are five primary types of charts in Excel 2023:

Column Charts: Charts such as column charts are ideal for comparing data or if you have numerous categories of a single variable to examine (for instance, multiple genres or products).

It's possible to create various column charts in Excel: the clustered and stacked, the 100 percent stacked, and 3-D. Choose the data visualization that best reveals the narrative of your data.

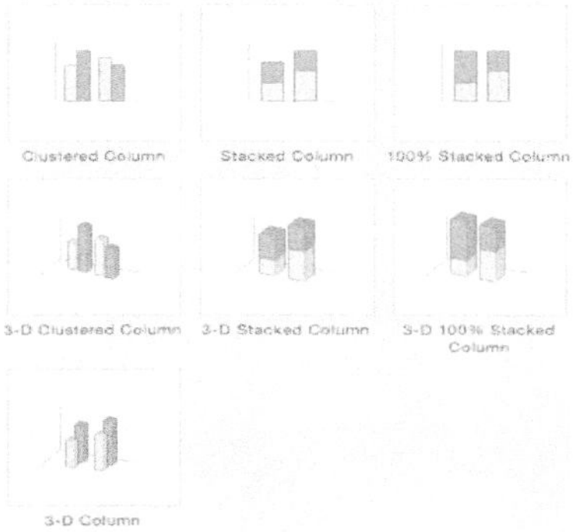

Bar Charts: Column and bar charts are quite similar, except that bar charts have horizontal bars rather than vertical. Bar charts and column charts are sometimes used interchangeably; however, some favor column charts since it is simpler to see negative values vertically on a y-axis using a column chart.

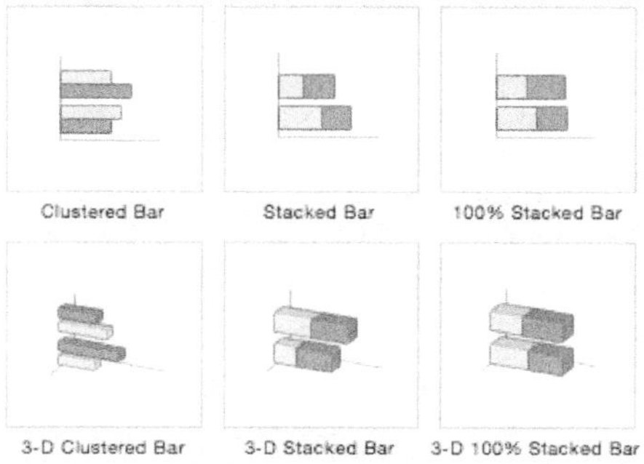

Pie Charts: When comparing percentages of the whole, use pie charts. All values are shown as one slice of the pie, allowing you to see the proportions. It's possible to create various Pie Charts: Pie, 3-D Pie, Bar of Pie, Pie of Pie, and Doughnut. There are five different forms.

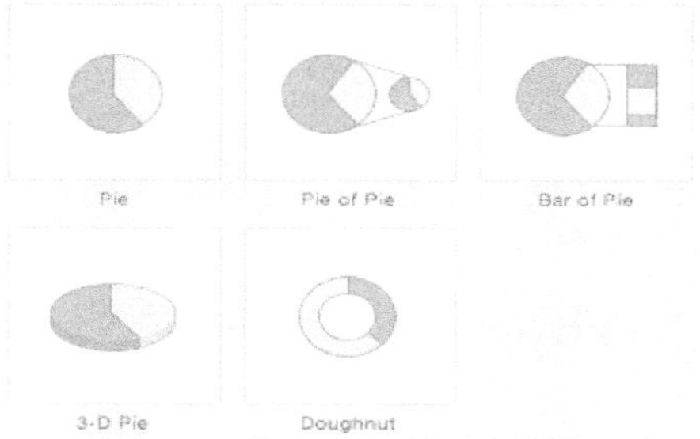

Line Charts: A line graph best illustrates patterns over time rather than individual data points. To observe how the values changed over time, each data point is connected by a series of lines. Line, stacked line, 100 percent stacked line, stacked line with the markers, line with the markers, 100 percent stacked line with markers, and 3-D line are the seven-line chart possibilities.

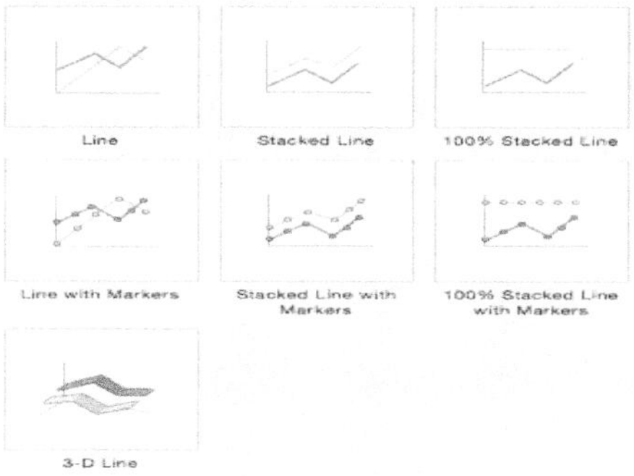

Scatter Charts: A scatter chart is a visual representation of the relationship between two variables that may be used to demonstrate how one changes the other over time, much like line graphs. It's known as correlation. There are several types of scatter charts, including bubble charts. There are seven types of scatter charts: scatter, bubble, scatter with some smooth lines & markers, scatter with straight lines, scatter with the straight lines & markers, scatter with smooth lines, and a 3-D version of the 3-D bubble scatter.

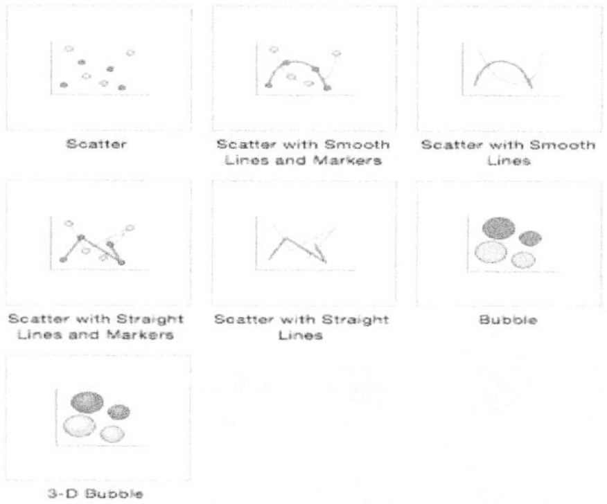

Additionally, there are four subcategories of lesser importance. Use-case-specific charts are shown in this section.

Area: Area graphs, like line graphs, depict the evolution of values through time.

On the other hand, area charts are valuable because the solid area under each line highlights the disparities in change across numerous variables.

There are six area charts available: 2-D area, 2-D stacked area, 3D area, & 3-D area with 100% stacking.

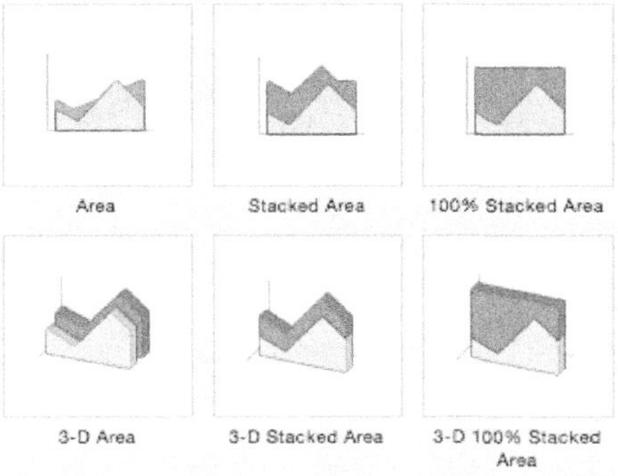

Stock: This chart style is utilized in financial research and by investors to show a stock's high, low, & closing price of a stock. If you wish to show both the possible values for a given number and the precise number, you may put them to effective use in any situation. Stock charts may be displayed in a variety of ways: high / low / close, volume / high / low / close, open / high / low / close, and volume / open / high / low / close.

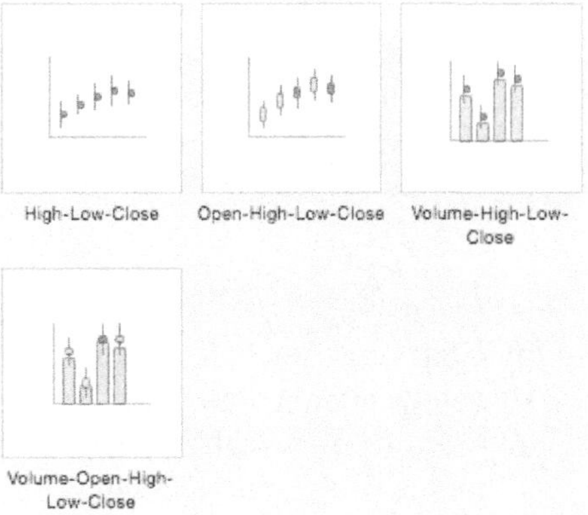

Surface: Using a surface chart to visualize data across three-dimensional space. It's good for huge data sets, or those multiple categories inside a single variable, because of the extra plane. As a result, ensure that the audience is acquainted with surface charts before presenting them. All these options are available to you on a 3-D surface, including wireframe 3-D surface & contour.

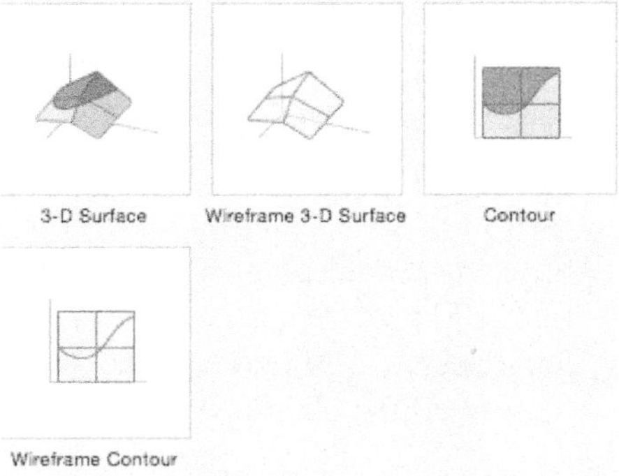

Radar: A radar chart is the best choice to show many factors' relationships. The crucial point is the starting point for all variables. These charts may assist you in assessing the strengths and shortcomings of various goods and personnel and are widely used for this purpose. In the world of radar charts, you may choose from three types: radar, filled radar, and radar with markers.

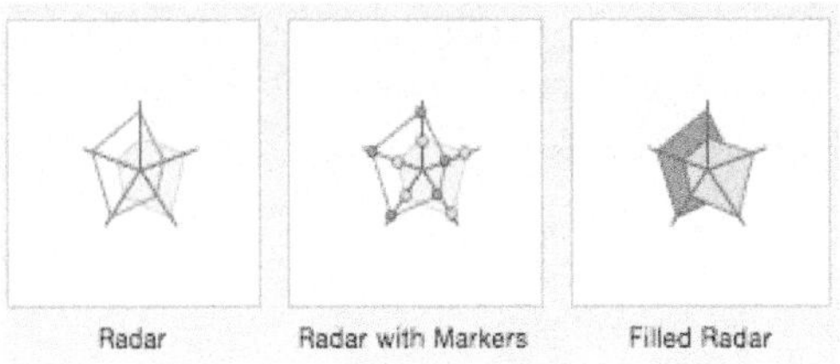

A waterfall chart, which is simply a succession of column graphs showing negative and positive changes over time, is another common chart type. Although a waterfall chart is not an Excel default, you may use a template to streamline the process.

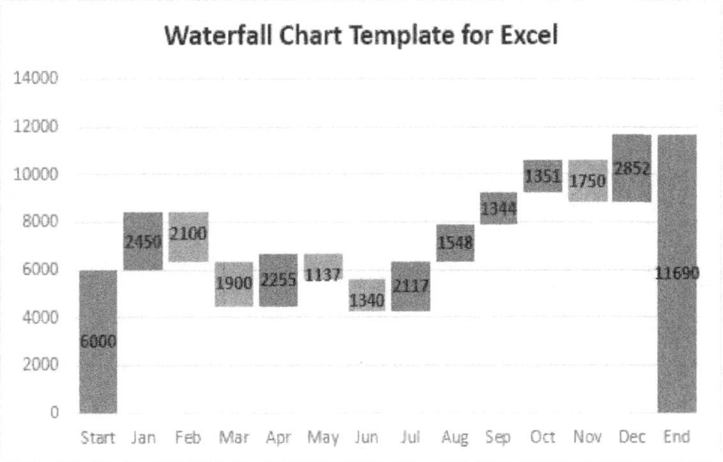

Top Five Excel Graph and Chart Best Practices

It's possible to get the most out of Excel's built-in style and formatting options for your charts by using alternative techniques. To maximize the use of your charts and graphs, follow these recommended practices:

- Clean Up Your Act: Intensely colored or text-heavy graphs may be distracting and difficult to understand. Get rid of extraneous details so your audience can concentrate on what you're trying to say.
- Selecting the Right Topics: A theme should be chosen that is appropriate for your audience, subject matter, and the primary goal of the chart. Try out various approaches but stick to one that is most appropriate for the task at hand.
- Make Good Use of Text: There is a good chance you will include some text in your charts and graphs (such as axis or title labels). It's important to keep your writing brief while using descriptive language, and you should also pay attention to the direction in which any content is written.
- Organize Elements Wisely: Always pay attention to the placement of graphics, such as the names of components in a diagram or the symbols they represent. They shouldn't distract from your graph but instead add something new.
- Before creating the chart, sort the data as follows: After sorting or removing duplicates, people frequently create unintuitive charts that may lead to mistakes.

How You can Chart Data in Excel

To create a graph or chart in Excel, you should first input the data you wish to show into the application. Chart data using Excel 2023 by following the instructions below.

Step 1: Enter the Data into your Worksheet

Select a New Workbook in Excel.

Make a list of the data you wish to utilize to make a graph or a chart. From 2013 to 2017, you'll compare five distinct goods' earnings. Ensure that the columns & rows of your table are labeled. The data may then be visualized as an easy-to-understand chart or graph. Here are some example data for you to play around with.

	A	B	C	D	E	F
1	Product	2013	2014	2015	2016	2017
2	Product A	$18,580	$49,225	$16,326	$10,017	$26,134
3	Product B	$78,970	$82,262	$48,640	$48,640	$48,640
4	Product C	$24,236	$131,390	$79,022	$71,009	$81,474
5	Product D	$16,730	$19,730	$12,109	$11,355	$17,686
6	Product E	$35,358	$42,685	$20,893	$16,065	$21,388
7						

Step 2: Select Range for Creating Graph or Chart from your Workbook Data

By clicking & dragging the mouse over the cells, you may choose the data you wish to include in your graph.

Once you've selected a chart type, the cells in your range will be highlighted in grey.

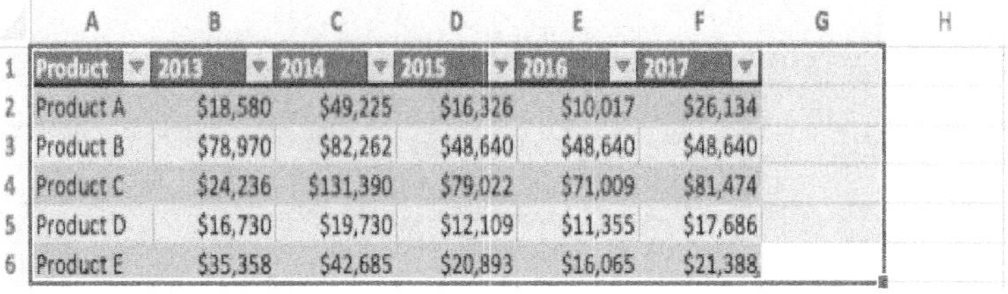

Product	2013	2014	2015	2016	2017
Product A	$18,580	$49,225	$16,326	$10,017	$26,134
Product B	$78,970	$82,262	$48,640	$48,640	$48,640
Product C	$24,236	$131,390	$79,022	$71,009	$81,474
Product D	$16,730	$19,730	$12,109	$11,355	$17,686
Product E	$35,358	$42,685	$20,893	$16,065	$21,388

Suppose you want to learn how to create a cluster column chart using Excel 2023. In the following section, you'll go step-by-step through the process of generating clustered columns chart in Excel, beginning with the basics.

How can you Make a Chart with your Excel

After entering your data and choosing the cell range, you can pick the chart you want to use. Using the data from the previous example as a starting point, you will construct clustered column charts in this section.

Step 1: Select a Chart Type

After highlighting your data in the Workbook, choose the Insert tab on the window's top banner. A section with many charting choices may be found halfway across the toolbar. Excel gives Suggested Charts depending on popularity, but you may choose a unique design by clicking any dropdown menus. Excel also provides Recommended Charts.

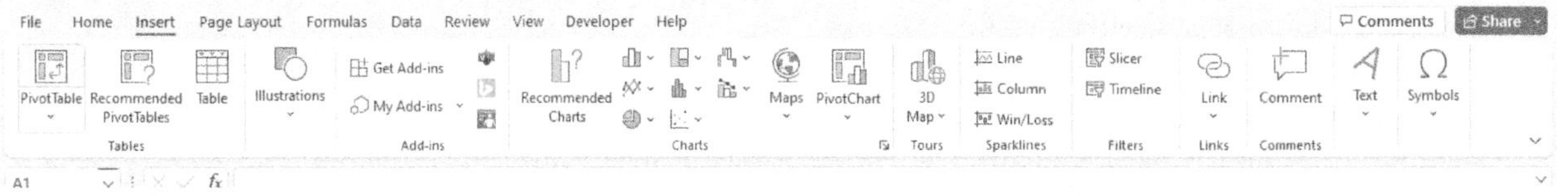

Step 2: Create the Chart

Click your column chart symbol under the Insert tab, and then pick the Clustered Column option.

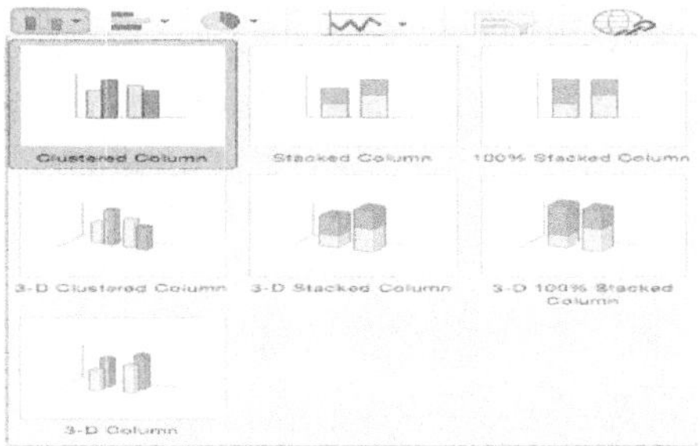

Excel will automatically generate a cluster chart column based on the data you specify in the worksheet. Your workbook's middle section will become the location of the chart. To give your chart a name, double-click the text "Chart Title" on the chart, and then write in a name. This chart will be known as "Product Profit 2013-2017."

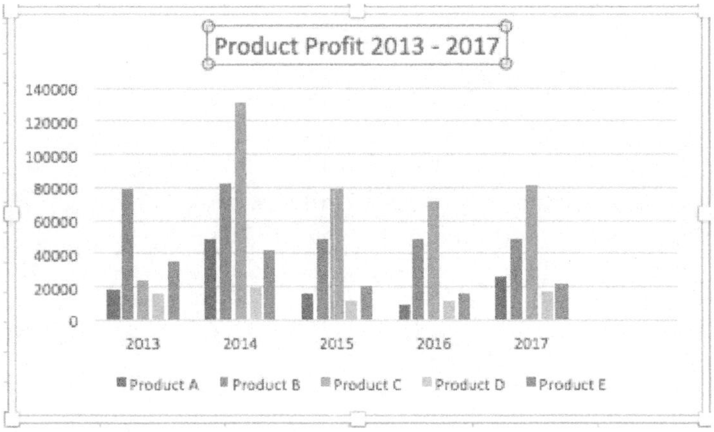

COLUMN CHART TEMPLATE

PRODUCT	2013	2014	2015	2016	2017
Product A	$18,580	$49,225	$16,326	$10,017	$26,134
Product B	$78,970	$82,262	$48,640	$48,640	$48,640
Product C	$24,236	$131,390	$79,022	$71,009	$81,474
Product D	$16,730	$19,730	$12,109	$11,355	$17,686
Product E	$35,358	$42,685	$20,893	$16,065	$21,388

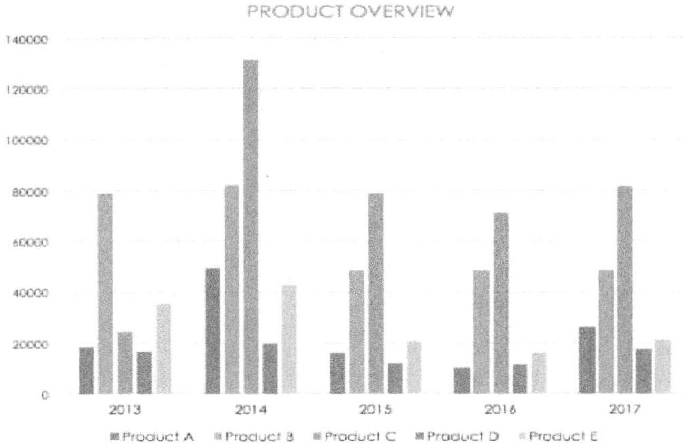

Chart Design & Format are the 2 tabs on the toolbar which you will utilize to make alterations to your chart. You may access both tabs by clicking the Chart Design button. Excel will apply design, style, and format settings to graphs and charts automatically; however, you have the option to add more customization by examining the tabs. Following that, you will step by step go through all the Chart Design modifications that are currently accessible.

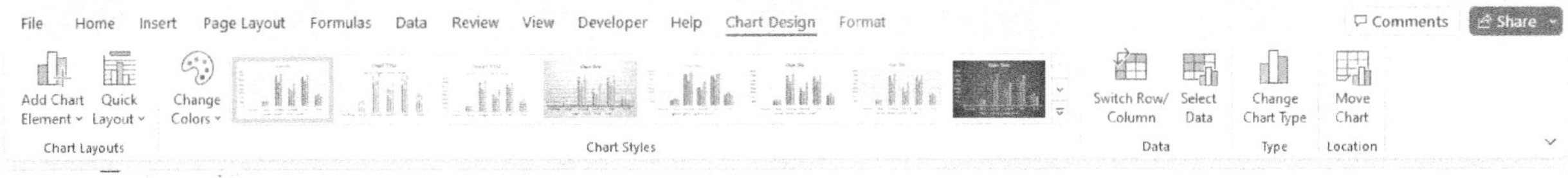

Step 3: Adding your Chart Elements

Your graph or chart will seem better if you add chart components since these items will clarify the data or provide more information. You may choose a chart element by going to the upper left corner of the screen and clicking on the dropdown menu labeled Add Chart Element (underneath your home tab).

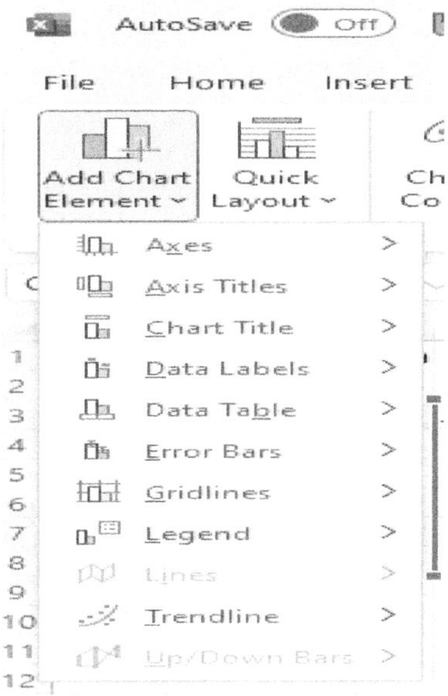

To Hide or Display Axes:

Select Axes. Excel would automatically populate your chart with horizontal & vertical axes based on the specified cell range's column and row headers

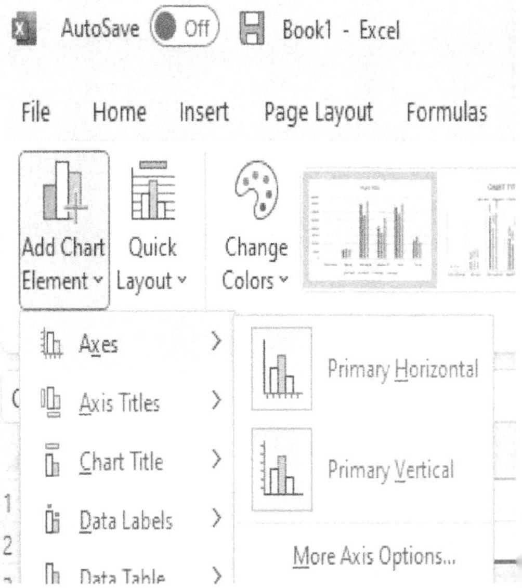

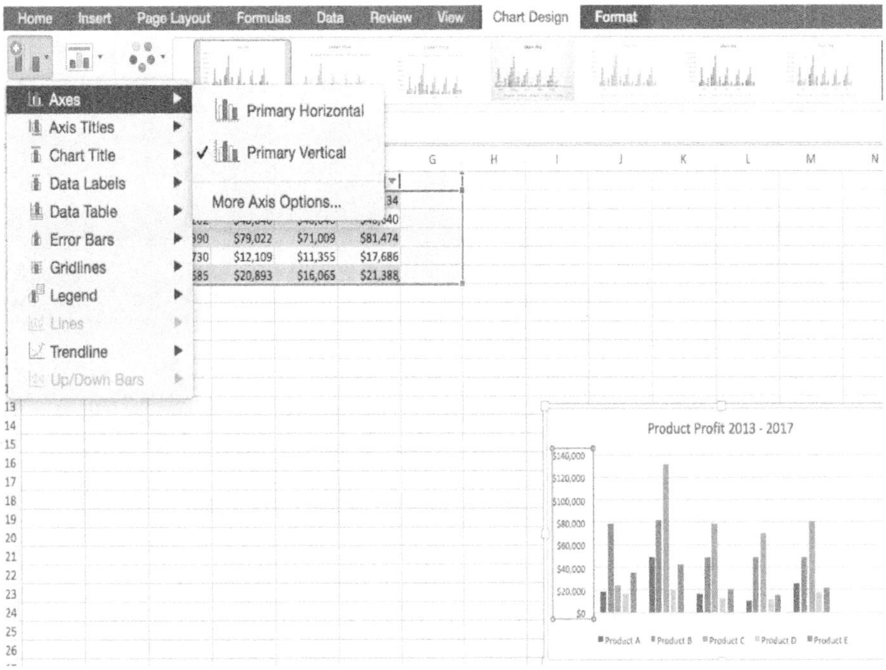

Remove the chart's display axis by unchecking these boxes. Primary Horizontal would eliminate the year labels from the x plane of the chart in this example.

To access more text and formatting choices, including inserting tick marks, numbers, labels, or altering text color and size, choose More Axis Options from the Axes dropdown menu.

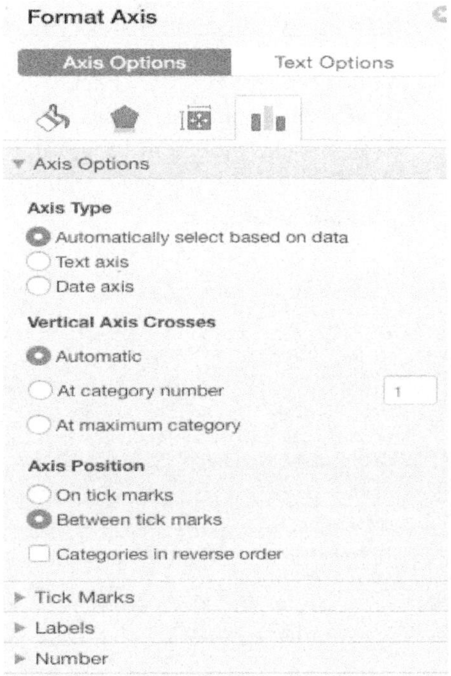

To Add the Axis Titles:

Select Axis Title from the Add Chart Element dropdown box after clicking Add Chart Element. The Primary Horizontal & Primary Vertical checkboxes will be unchecked since Excel does not immediately add axis names to your chart.

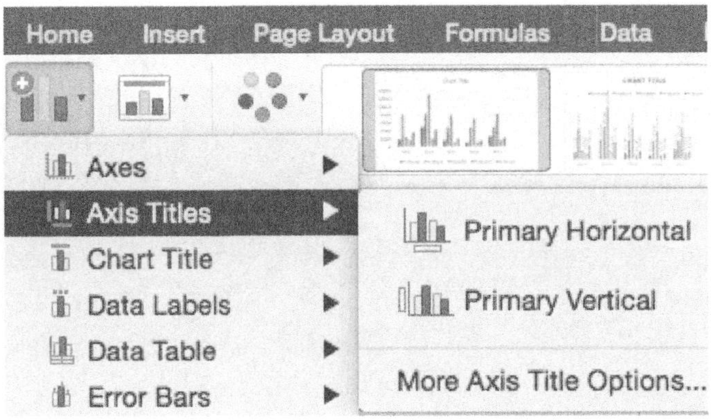

Primary Vertical or Horizontal axis titles may be created by clicking on the text box on your chart. In this example, you used both of our mouse buttons. Input the names of the axes. You added the names "Year" (horizontal) & "Profit" (vertical) to this example (vertical).

To Move or Remove Chart Title:

Add a Chart Element and choose Chart Title. There are four alternatives to choose from: none, above the chart, centering the overlay, and additional title options.

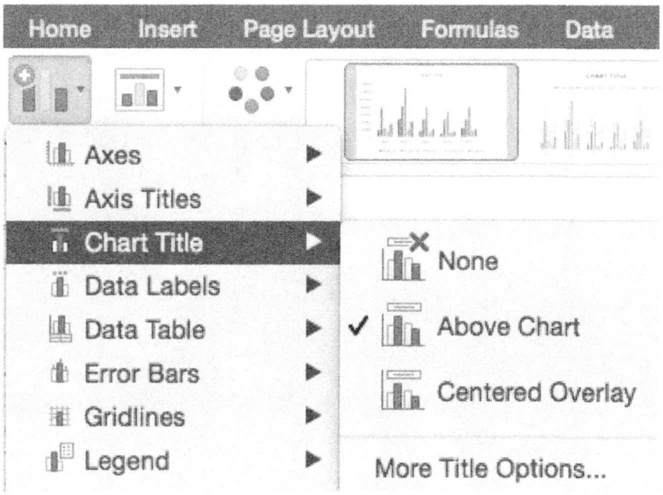

To delete the chart title, choose None.

The title will appear above the chart when you choose to Display Above Chart. Excel places the chart title automatically if one is created.

To center the title inside the chart's gridlines, choose Centered Overlay from the Format menu. Keep an eye out for this choice since you do not want the title to obscure any information in the graph and make it difficult to read (as shown in the example below).

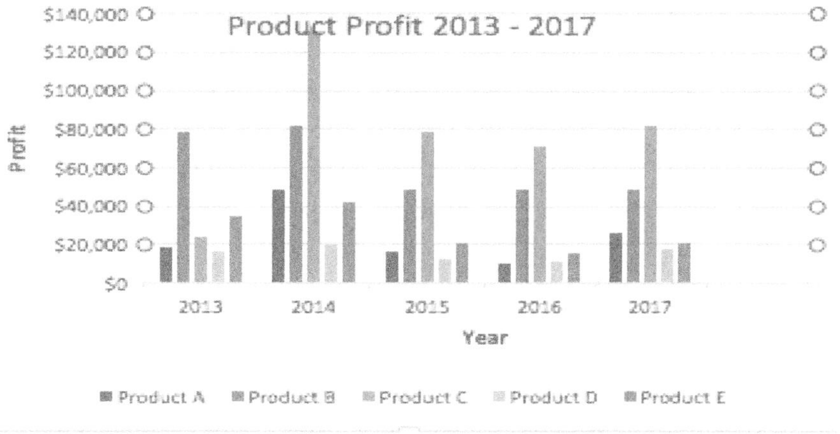

To Add the Data Labels:

Right-click and choose Data Labels. Among the six possibilities for labeling data: none (default), center, inside end, outside end, inside base, and other alternatives.

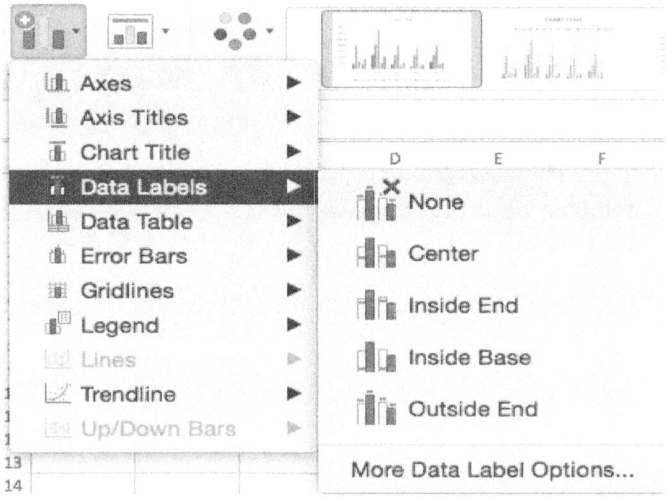

You may choose from one of four labeling choices for every data point measured. Please select the one you want by clicking on it. This tweak might be useful if you have a small quantity of exact data or a lot of additional space in your chart. On the other hand, adding data labels to a cluster column chart is likely to seem overly busy. Here's what it looks like to use Center data labels:

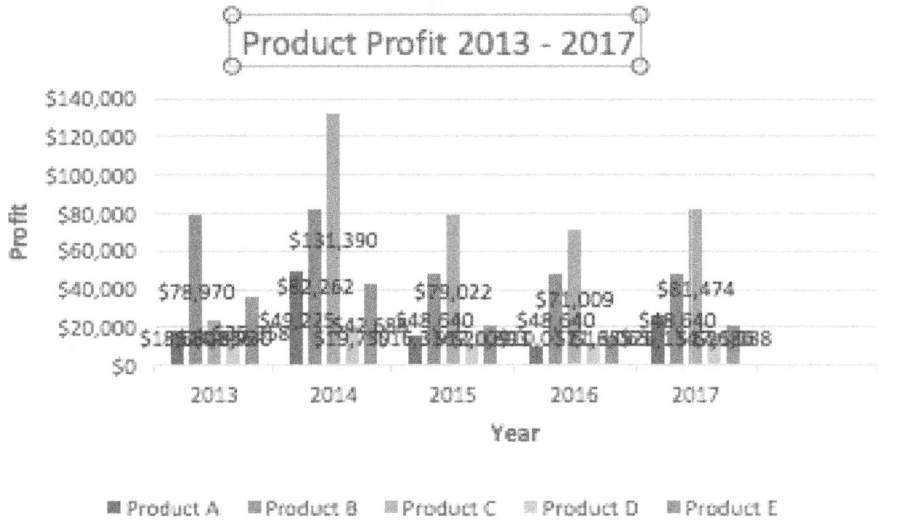

To Add the Data Table:

Using the Add Chart Element button, choose Data Table. There are 3 pre-formatted choices, as well as an expanded menu that may be accessed by choosing Additional Data Table Alternatives:

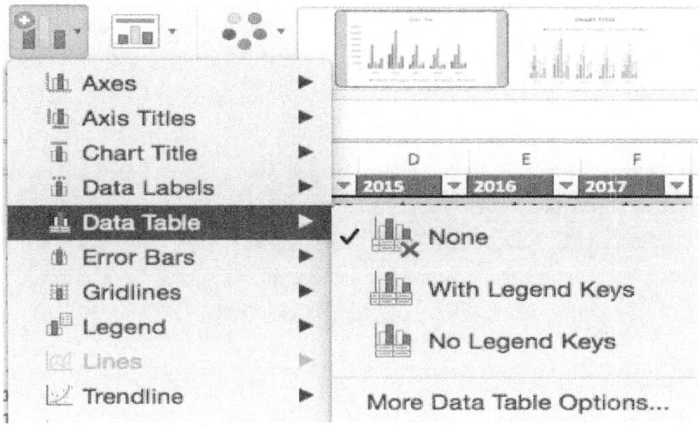

Non-duplicate: The data table isn't included in the graphic by default. The data range is shown in the data table below the graphic using Legend Keys. There will also be a legend with a color-coded system.

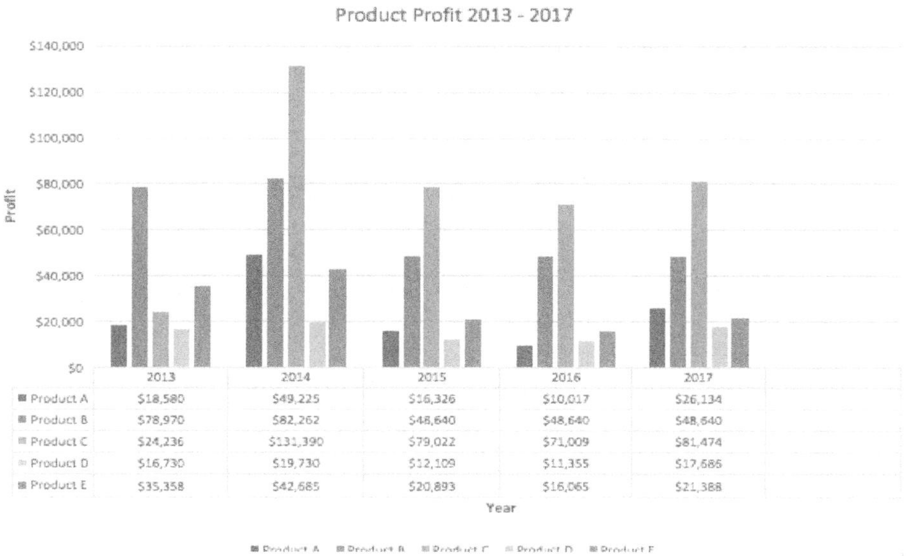

The data table behind the chart is likewise shown, but the legend is absent when using the No Legend Keys.

For this reason, if you add the data table, you should increase the size of your chart. To enlarge your chart, just click and drag one of its corners.

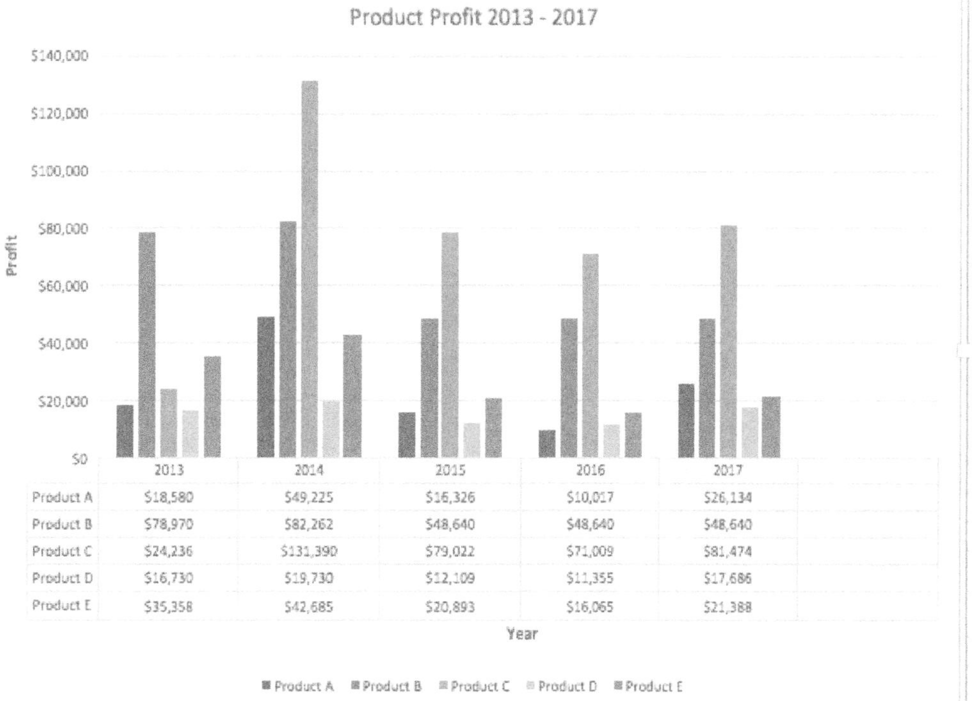

To Add the Error Bars:

Then choose Error Bars from the Add Chart Element menu. There are four other options: None (as default), Standard Error, 5 percent (Percentage), & Standard Deviation. Using conventional formulae for calculating error, error bars may be added to the data to illustrate the possibility of inaccuracy.

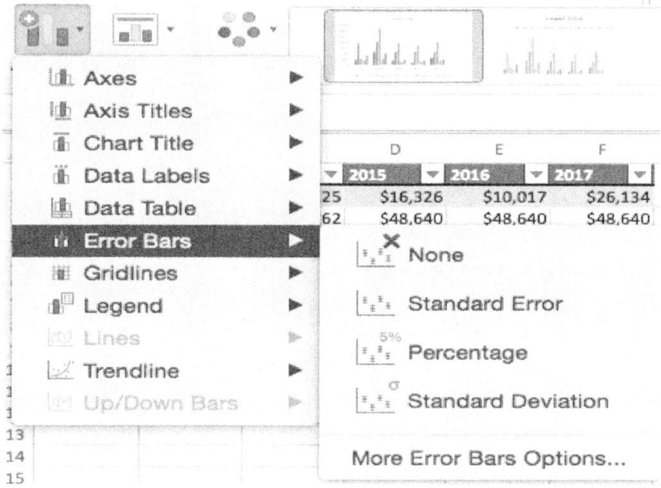

Several alternatives are available, and if you choose Standard Error, you get a chart like this.

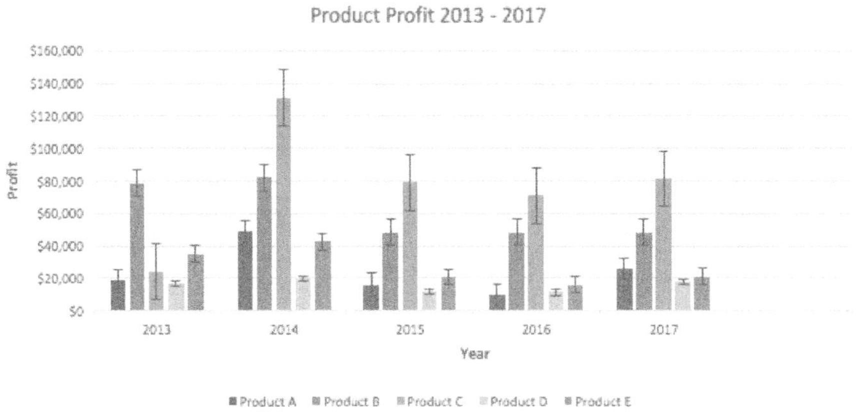

To Add the Gridlines:

You'll see Gridlines once you click Add the Chart Element. Additionally, there are 4 options: primary major horizontals, primary minor horizontals, primary major verticals, & primary minor verticals.

Excel automatically adds the Primary Major Horizontal gridline when creating a column chart.

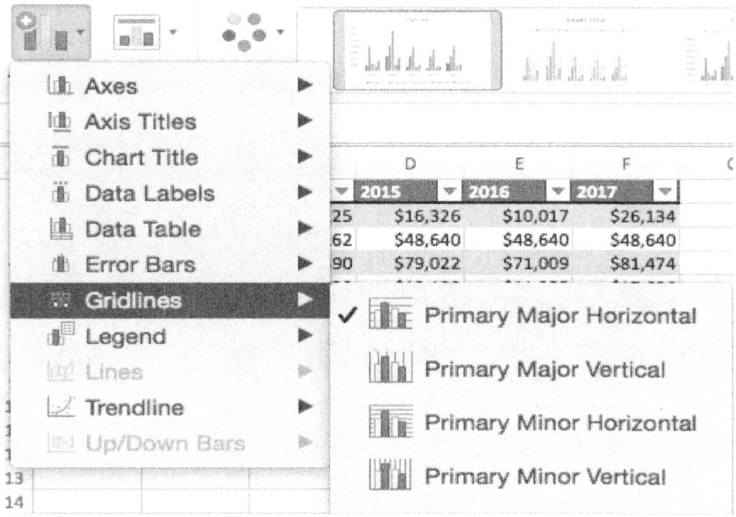

You may pick as many gridlines as you want by choosing the choices. Your chart appears when all 4 gridline choices are used, for example.

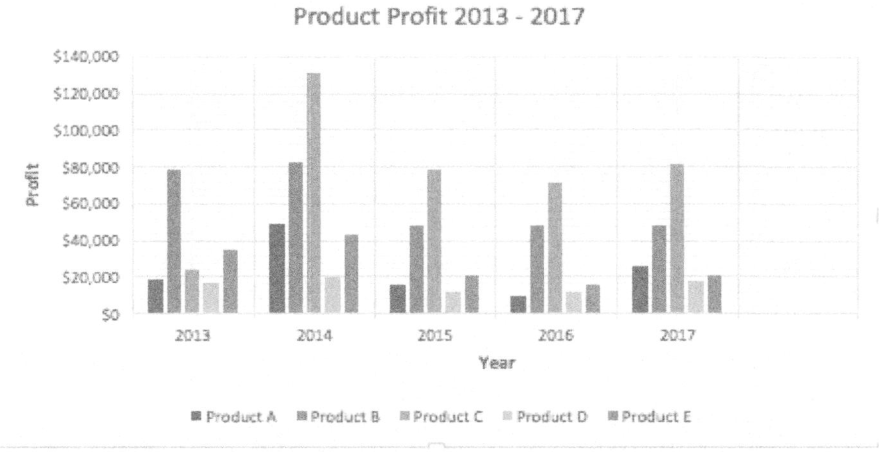

To Add the Legend:

Then choose Legend from the drop-down menu under Add Chart Element. You may choose from one of five placements for the legends: none; right; left; top; or bottom.

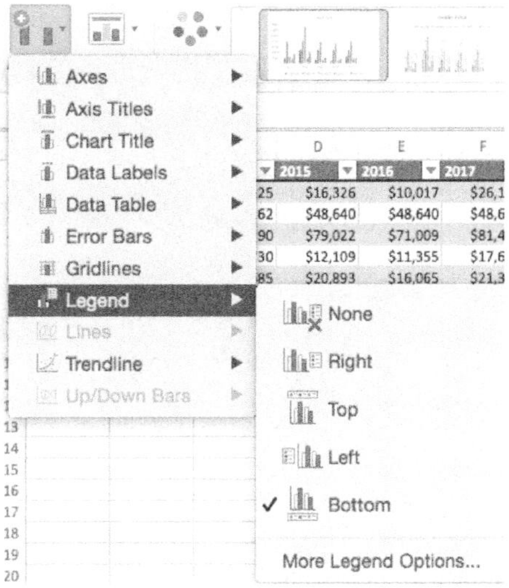

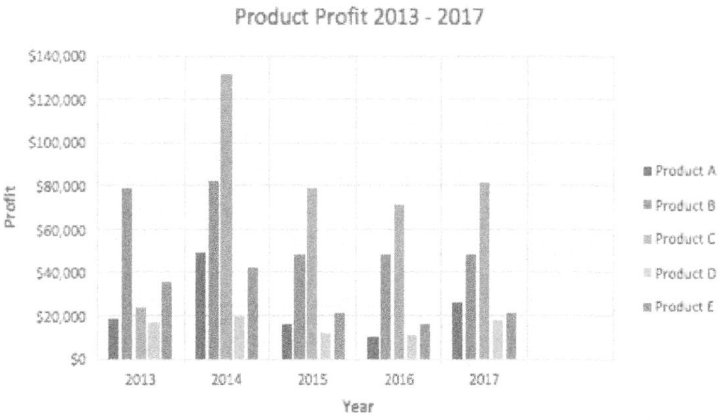

Chart type and format dictate where the legend should be placed. Use your chart to choose the option that seems to be the most visually appealing. This is the chart you get when you choose the Right legend position.

For Cluster Column Charts, Lines are not accessible. However, you may add lines (e.g., goal, reference, average, etc.) to the chart by choosing the relevant option in other chart styles where you just compare two variables.

To Add the Trendline:

Add a trendline by clicking the Add Chart Element button and selecting Trendline.

Other choices include None (the default), Linear Forecast, Linear, Exponential, & Moving Average in adding to Some more Trendline Alternatives. Verify that the one you've chosen is suitable for the collected data. Linear will be used here.

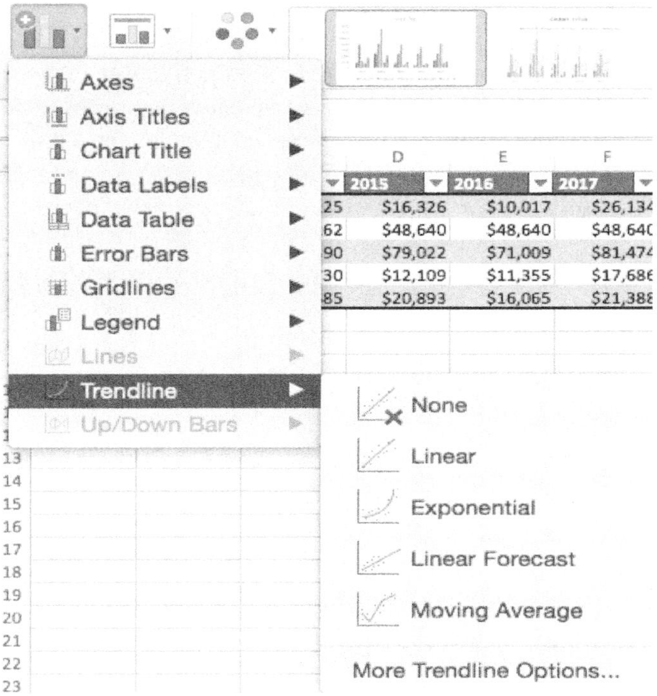

Excel constructs the trendline for five items you're comparing over time. Click Product A and then the blue OK icon to generate a linear trendline of Product A.

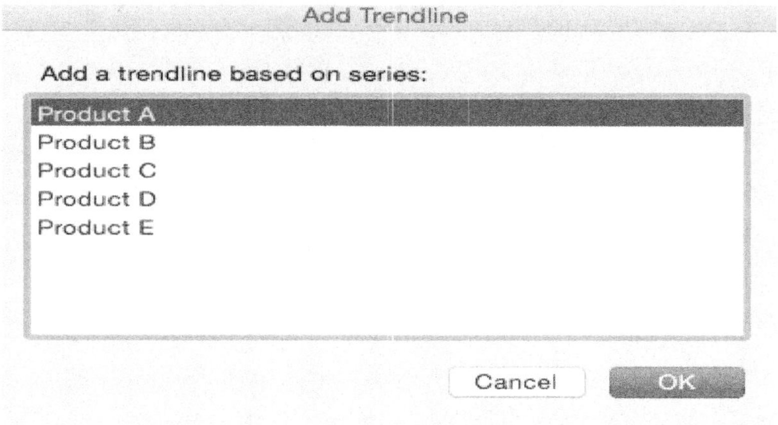

Product A's linear evolution will now be represented as a dotted trendline on the graph. Excel has additionally included a legend entry for Linear (Product A).

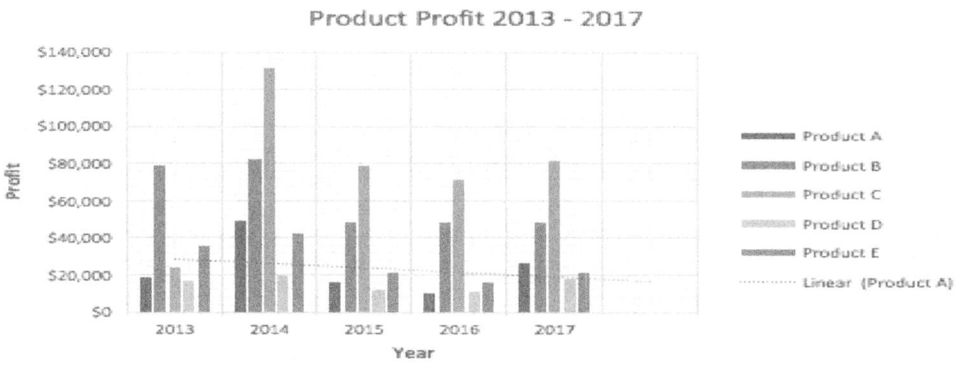

Double-click the trendline to see the equation on your chart. Right-click the Format Trendline window and choose Open. Display equation onto chart may be enabled by checking a box at the window's very bottom. Your graph now shows the solution to the problem.

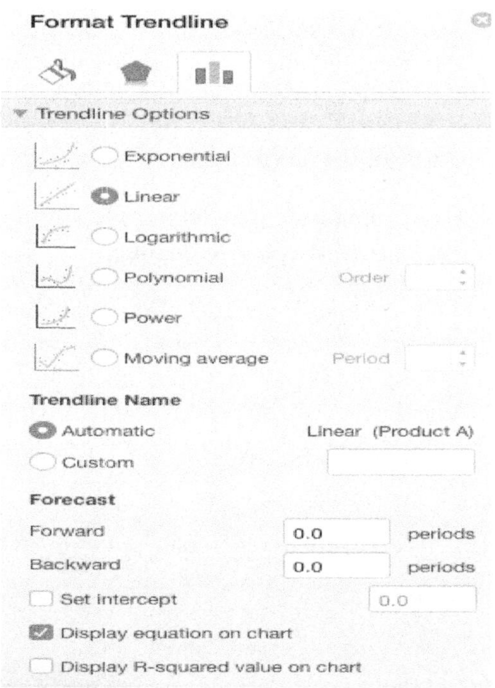

Please remember that you may add as many different trendlines as you like on your chart. In this example, you've plotted the trendlines for Products A and C on a graph.

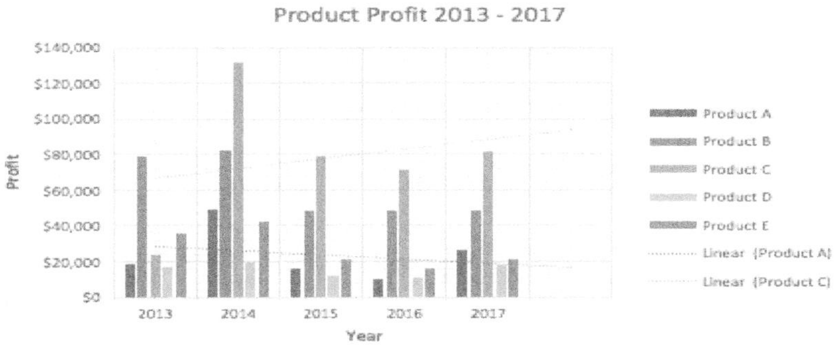

The Up/Down Bars feature is not accessible in the column chart, but you may use them inside a line chart to display changes in data points.

Step 4: Adjusting the Quick Layout

Changing the arrangement of items in your chart is a snap using the Quick Layout option available from the toolbar's second dropdown menu (legend, titles, clusters etc.).

There are eleven rapid layout alternatives. To learn more about each choice, move your mouse over it. Then select the one you wish to use.

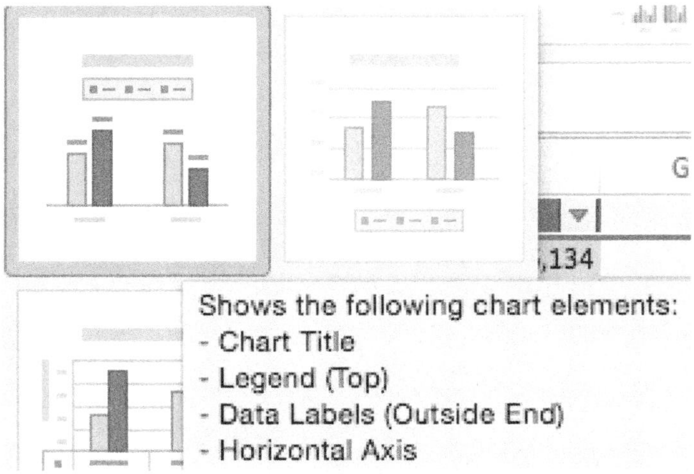

Step 5: Change the Colors

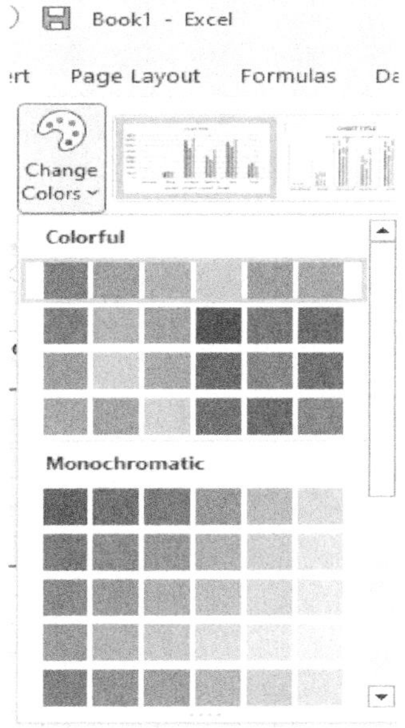

Change Colors is the next drop-down option in the toolbar. To match your brand's colors and style, click on the icon & choose the color scheme you like.

Step 6: Change the Style

There are a total of 14 cluster column chart styles to choose from. Excel will use Style 1 by default, but you may vary the chart's look by selecting one of the other styles. Other alternatives may be shown by clicking the right arrow in the picture bar.

Step 7: Switch the Row/Column

Flip the axis by clicking the Switch Row/Column toolbar button. Switching the axes in charts with more than two variables may be a bit of a mystery.

By rearranging the columns and rows, we may change the product & year (profit remains over the y-axis). Color-coded legends have been added to show which products are grouped by year (not product). To prevent any misunderstanding, click just on legend and convert the series names to years.

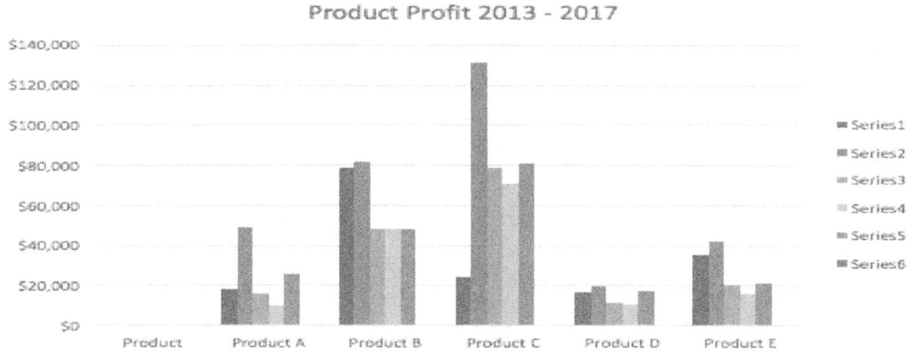

Step 8: Selecting the Data

Click the Select Data button on the toolbar to alter the data range.

Click "Ok" once you've typed in the range of cells you wish to work with. This fresh set of data will be reflected in the graphic.

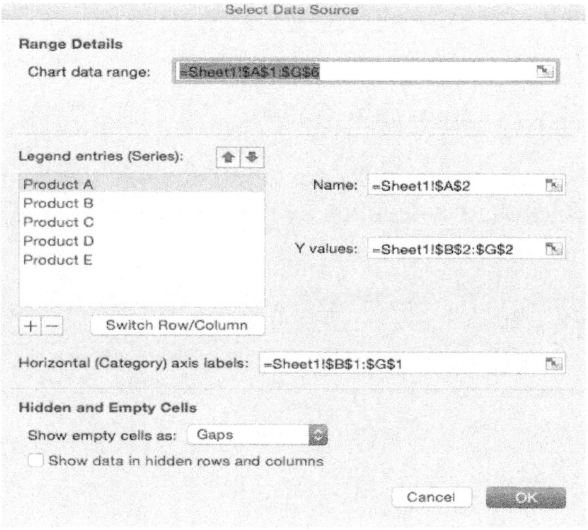

Step 9: Changing the Chart Type

Select a new chart type from the drop-down list.

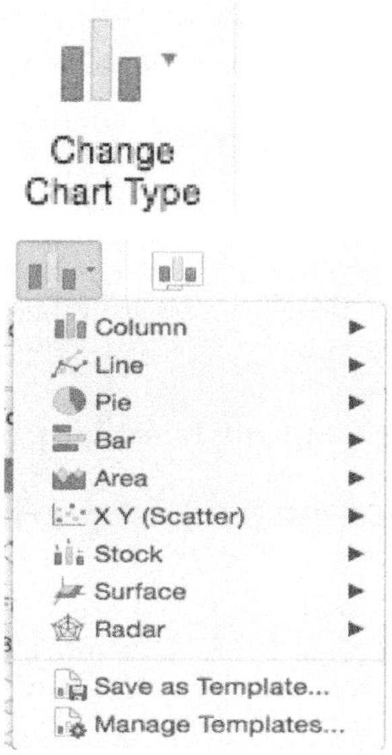

Excel has nine different chart types for you to choose from. Your data must be suitable for the chart type you select.

If you want to save the chart as a template, you may do so by choosing Save as Template.

In the new window, you'll be able to give your template a name. To simplify, Excel creates a folder just for your template files. Go ahead and click the Save button.

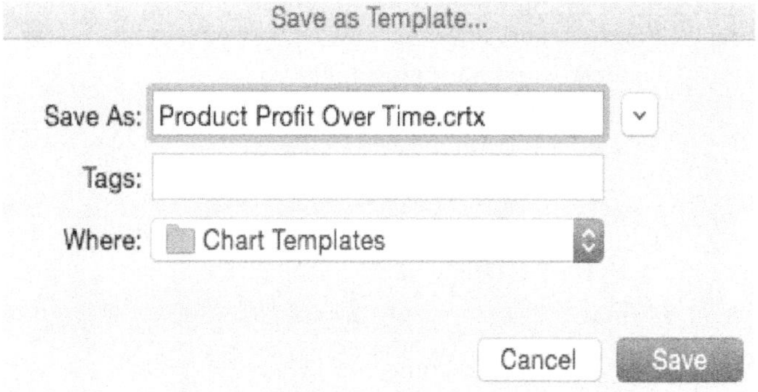

Step 10: Moving the Chart

Right-click the toolbar's Move Chart icon and choose it from the drop-down menu.

Charts may be positioned in several ways in the open dialogue box. Create the new sheet and include this chart in it (New sheet) or use it as an item in another sheet (Place this chart in another sheet) (Object in). Right-click and choose "OK."

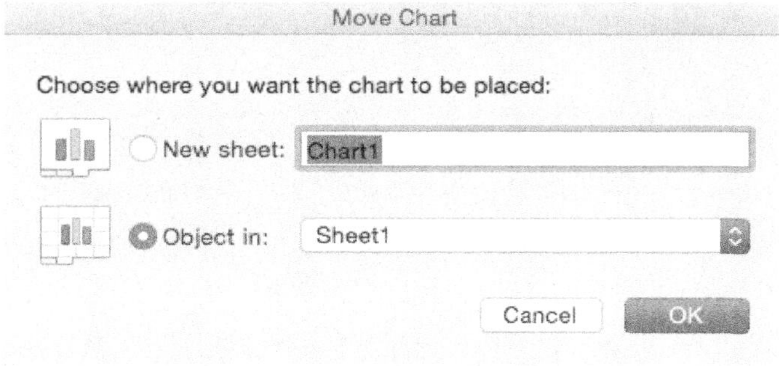

Step 11: Change the Formatting

Formatting the chart's components and text is easy thanks to the Format tab, which lets you adjust color, shape, fill, size, & alignment and insert shapes. Use the shortcuts in the Format tab to build a chart that fits your company's identity (images, colors, etc.).

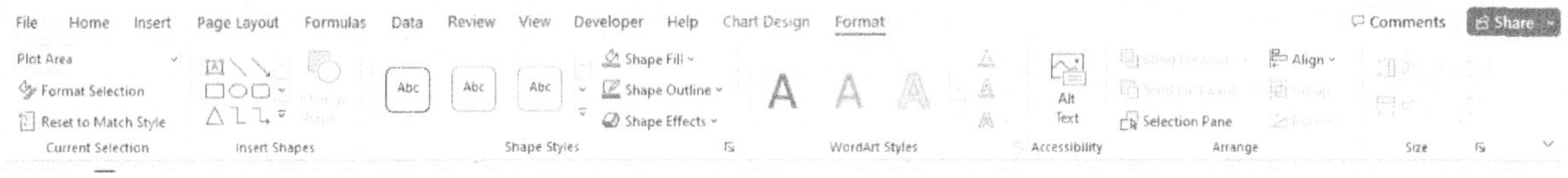

To alter a specific chart element, click the drop-down menu on the top left of your toolbar and choose it.

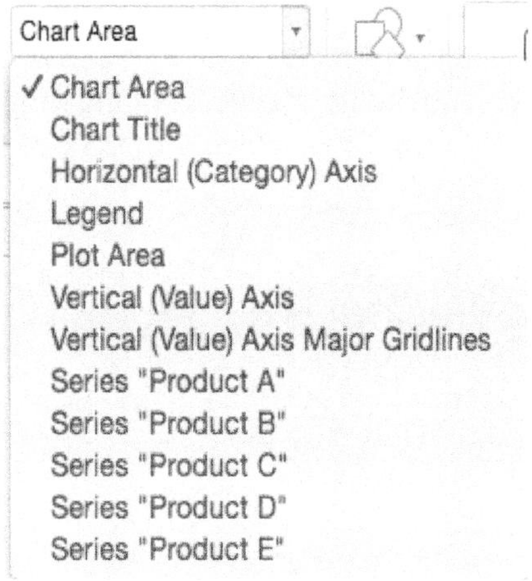

Step 12: Deleting the Chart

The simplest way to remove a chart is to select it and then press the Delete key.

How can you make the Graph into Excel

Excel categorizes all graphs as "charts" because they perform similar duties. If you want to create a graph in Excel, follow these instructions.

Select Range for Creating Graph from the Workbook Data

By clicking & dragging the mouse over the cells, you may choose the data you wish to include in the graph.

It's now easier to see your cell range.

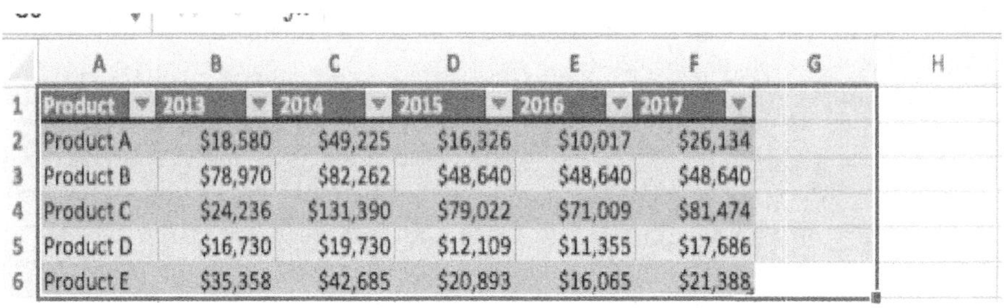

	A	B	C	D	E	F	G	H
1	Product	2013	2014	2015	2016	2017		
2	Product A	$18,580	$49,225	$16,326	$10,017	$26,134		
3	Product B	$78,970	$82,262	$48,640	$48,640	$48,640		
4	Product C	$24,236	$131,390	$79,022	$71,009	$81,474		
5	Product D	$16,730	$19,730	$12,109	$11,355	$17,686		
6	Product E	$35,358	$42,685	$20,893	$16,065	$21,388		

There are many graphs to choose from after the text has been highlighted (which Excel refers to as the chart).

Select the Recommended Charts toolbar option from the Insert tab. Then choose the kind of graph you like by clicking on it.

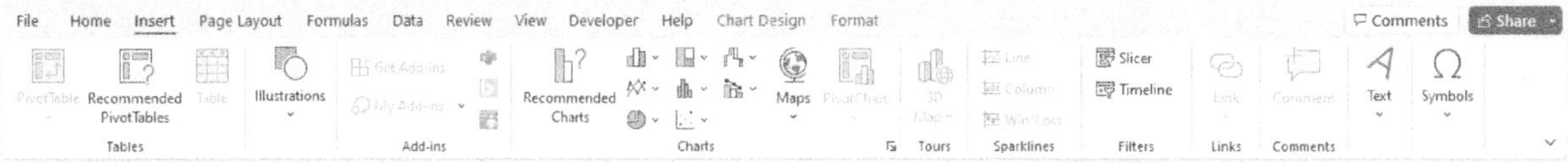

You now have a chart. You may use the same procedures outlined within the previous section to personalize your graph. When constructing a graph, all the functionality for producing a chart stays the same.

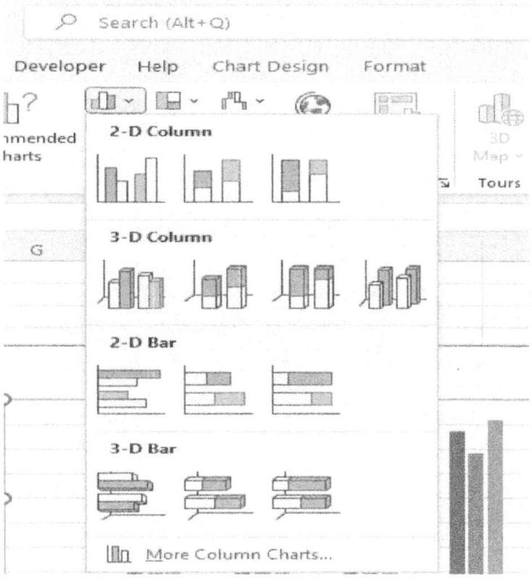

CHAPTER 5

INTERMEDIATE FORMULAS

Intermediate formulae including IF, SUMIF, COUNTIF, IFERROR, and concatenate formulas are covered in this chapter.

5.1 IF FUNCTION

When a statement is true, the IF function, which is a check function, returns one value; when a statement is false, it returns a different value. The whole functionality helps you compare a value and your prediction.

The IF function accepts the following inputs.

=IF (Logical_text, [Value_if_true], [Value_if_false])

- Logical text is the value or logical expression that must be evaluated and classified as TRUE or FALSE (Required Argument).
- (Probable Defense) Value if accurate When the outcome of the reasonable evaluation is TRUE, this value will be shown.
- Value if false (Possible Argument) will be returned if the rational assessment yields a FALSE result.

These logical operators can be used for this function:

Equal to (=)
Greater than (>)
Greater than or equal to (≥)
Less than (<)
Less than or equal to (≤)
Not equal (≠)

Verify that the value in cell A2 is more than 500. =IF (Yes" and "No"; A2>500)

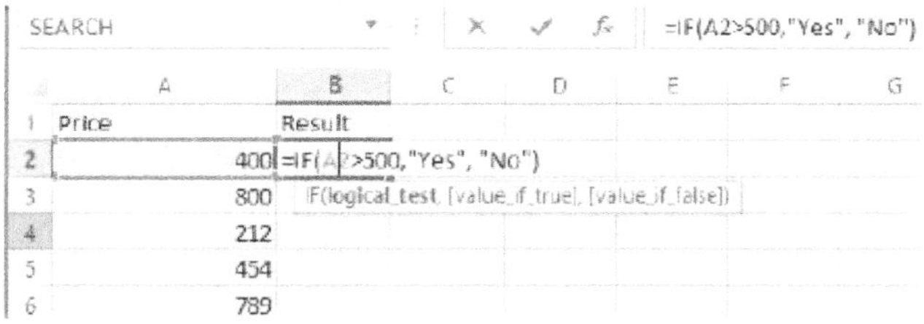

Follow the instructions above to get the value of A3 to B6: A3>500, "Yes", "No," A4>500, "Yes," "No," A5>500, and A6>500, "Yes," "No," respectively.

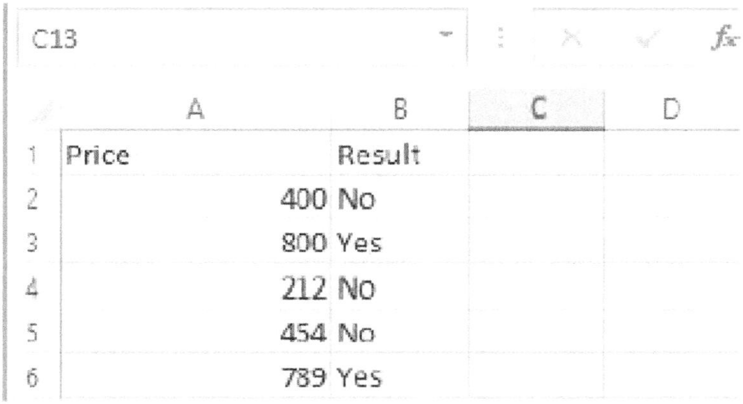

5.2 SUMIF FUNCTION

The SUM function adds up cells based on a set of parameters.

The criteria or requirements are created using dates, statistics, and sentences.

This work also uses logical operators like > and wildcards (*,)

=SUMIF (range, criteria, [sum_range]

The SUMIF method takes the following inputs.

The range of cells against which the criteria are expanded (Mandatory Argument).

Criteria (Required Argument): It determines which cells may be combined. Criteria arguments may be presented in several ways.

- Numerical values include things like numbers, integers, and times.
- Text strings include terms like Monday, East, Price, etc.
- Expressions >11 and <3 are examples of expressions.

Sum_range (Optional Argument): This is the cell to sum if there are any further cells to sum than those specified in the range argument.

Application of SUMIF

Let's examine whether the SUMIF function is utilized to calculate revenue in January and the United States.

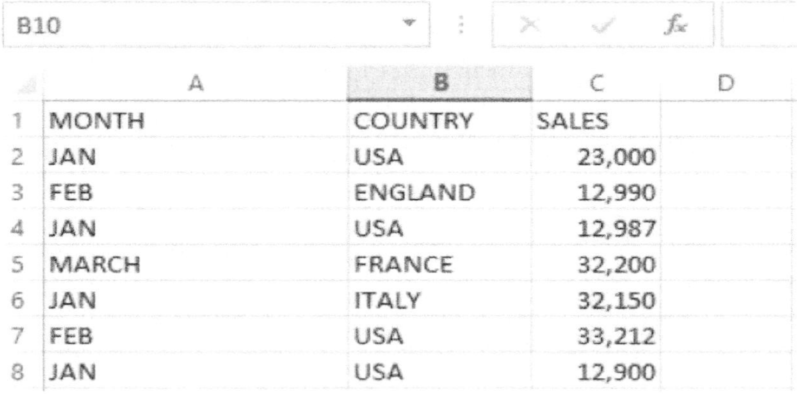

B10

	A	B	C	D
1	MONTH	COUNTRY	SALES	
2	JAN	USA	23,000	
3	FEB	ENGLAND	12,990	
4	JAN	USA	12,987	
5	MARCH	FRANCE	32,200	
6	JAN	ITALY	32,150	
7	FEB	USA	33,212	
8	JAN	USA	12,900	

First, find out how much money you earned in January using the techniques listed below.

Fill in the role with an empty cell for the cell set to be rounded up. SUM (A2:A8)

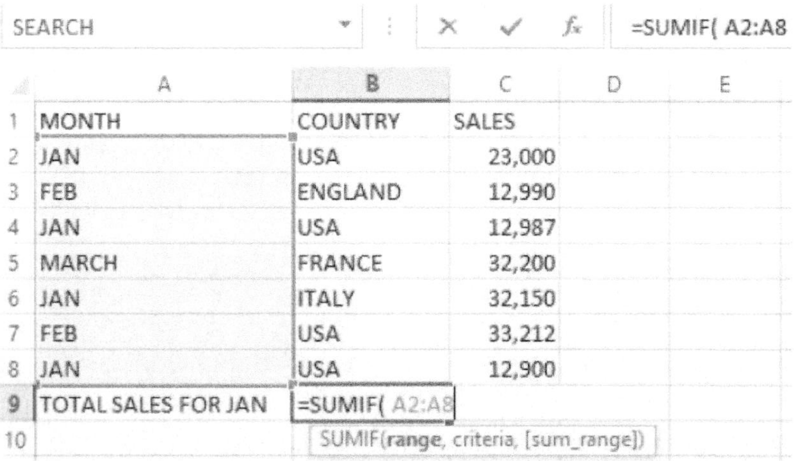

SEARCH =SUMIF(A2:A8

	A	B	C	D	E
1	MONTH	COUNTRY	SALES		
2	JAN	USA	23,000		
3	FEB	ENGLAND	12,990		
4	JAN	USA	12,987		
5	MARCH	FRANCE	32,200		
6	JAN	ITALY	32,150		
7	FEB	USA	33,212		
8	JAN	USA	12,900		
9	TOTAL SALES FOR JAN	=SUMIF(A2:A8			
10		SUMIF(range, criteria, [sum_range])			

- Fill up the blanks for January's criteria. SUM (JAN, A2:A8,)

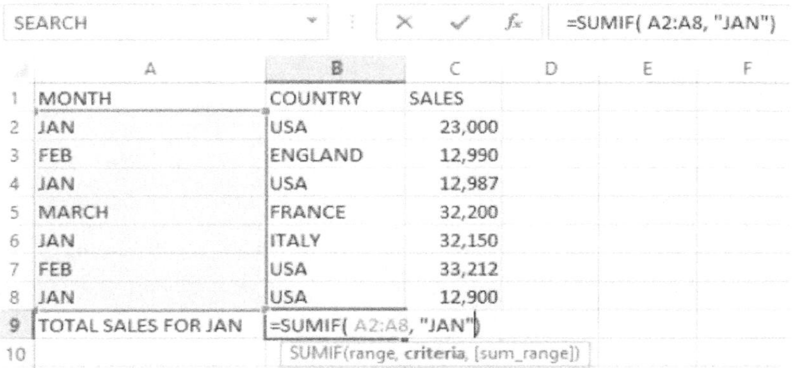

SEARCH | =SUMIF(A2:A8, "JAN")

	A	B	C	D	E	F
1	MONTH	COUNTRY	SALES			
2	JAN	USA	23,000			
3	FEB	ENGLAND	12,990			
4	JAN	USA	12,987			
5	MARCH	FRANCE	32,200			
6	JAN	ITALY	32,150			
7	FEB	USA	33,212			
8	JAN	USA	12,900			
9	TOTAL SALES FOR JAN	=SUMIF(A2:A8, "JAN")				
10		SUMIF(range, criteria, [sum_range])				

Then put in the sum_range; **SUM (A2:A8, “JAN”, C2;C8)**

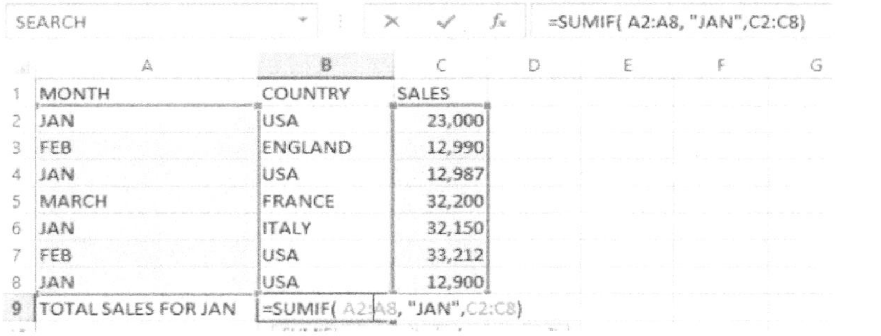

SEARCH | =SUMIF(A2:A8, "JAN",C2:C8)

	A	B	C	D	E	F	G
1	MONTH	COUNTRY	SALES				
2	JAN	USA	23,000				
3	FEB	ENGLAND	12,990				
4	JAN	USA	12,987				
5	MARCH	FRANCE	32,200				
6	JAN	ITALY	32,150				
7	FEB	USA	33,212				
8	JAN	USA	12,900				
9	TOTAL SALES FOR JAN	=SUMIF(A2:A8, "JAN",C2:C8)					

- According to the data below, there were 81,037 sales in January.

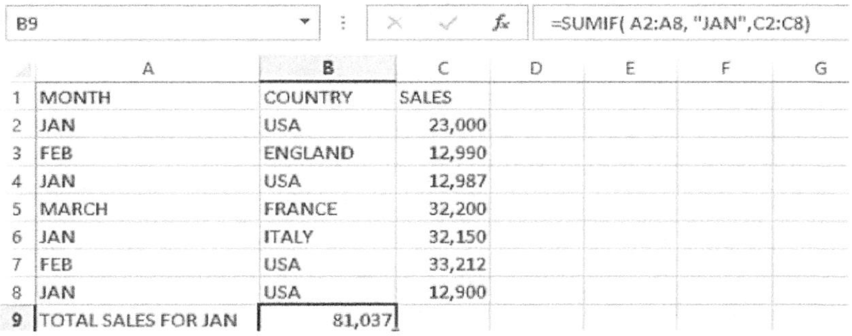

B9 | =SUMIF(A2:A8, "JAN",C2:C8)

	A	B	C	D	E	F	G
1	MONTH	COUNTRY	SALES				
2	JAN	USA	23,000				
3	FEB	ENGLAND	12,990				
4	JAN	USA	12,987				
5	MARCH	FRANCE	32,200				
6	JAN	ITALY	32,150				
7	FEB	USA	33,212				
8	JAN	USA	12,900				
9	TOTAL SALES FOR JAN	81,037					

To calculate the total number of sales in the United States.

- With an empty cell, fill the role with the cell set to be summed =SUM (B2:B8).

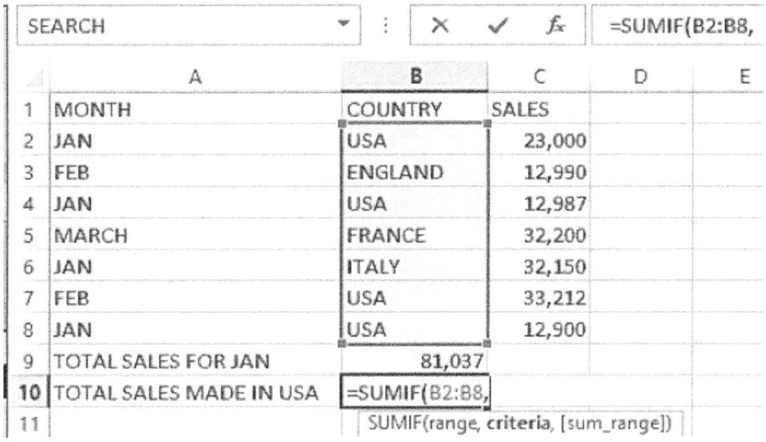

SEARCH | =SUMIF(B2:B8,

	A	B	C	D	E
1	MONTH	COUNTRY	SALES		
2	JAN	USA	23,000		
3	FEB	ENGLAND	12,990		
4	JAN	USA	12,987		
5	MARCH	FRANCE	32,200		
6	JAN	ITALY	32,150		
7	FEB	USA	33,212		
8	JAN	USA	12,900		
9	TOTAL SALES FOR JAN	81,037			
10	TOTAL SALES MADE IN USA	=SUMIF(B2:B8,			
11		SUMIF(range, criteria, [sum_range])			

Put in the criteria which are **USA; SUM(B2:B8 "USA"**

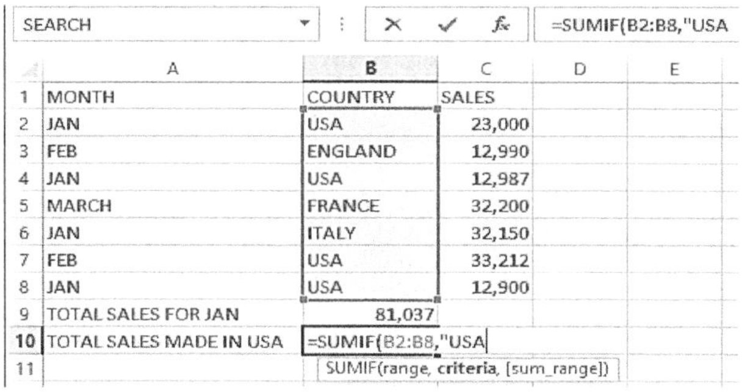

SEARCH | =SUMIF(B2:B8,"USA

	A	B	C	D	E
1	MONTH	COUNTRY	SALES		
2	JAN	USA	23,000		
3	FEB	ENGLAND	12,990		
4	JAN	USA	12,987		
5	MARCH	FRANCE	32,200		
6	JAN	ITALY	32,150		
7	FEB	USA	33,212		
8	JAN	USA	12,900		
9	TOTAL SALES FOR JAN	81,037			
10	TOTAL SALES MADE IN USA	=SUMIF(B2:B8,"USA			
11		SUMIF(range, criteria, [sum_range])			

Then put in the sum_range; **SUM(B2:B8, "USA", B2:B8)**

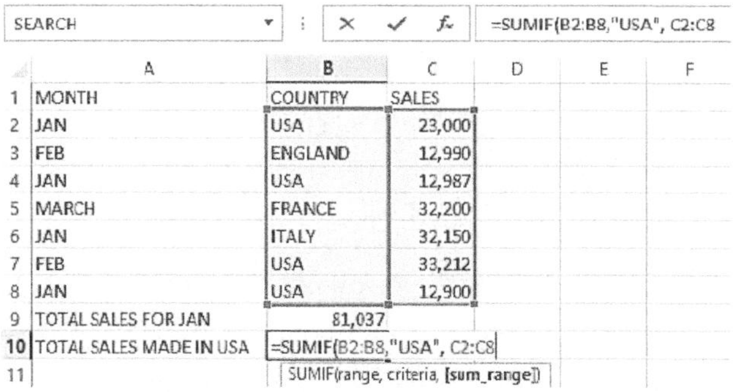

SEARCH | =SUMIF(B2:B8,"USA", C2:C8

	A	B	C	D	E	F
1	MONTH	COUNTRY	SALES			
2	JAN	USA	23,000			
3	FEB	ENGLAND	12,990			
4	JAN	USA	12,987			
5	MARCH	FRANCE	32,200			
6	JAN	ITALY	32,150			
7	FEB	USA	33,212			
8	JAN	USA	12,900			
9	TOTAL SALES FOR JAN	81,037				
10	TOTAL SALES MADE IN USA	=SUMIF(B2:B8,"USA", C2:C8				
11		SUMIF(range, criteria, [sum_range])				

The gross sales in the United States are shown in the table below.

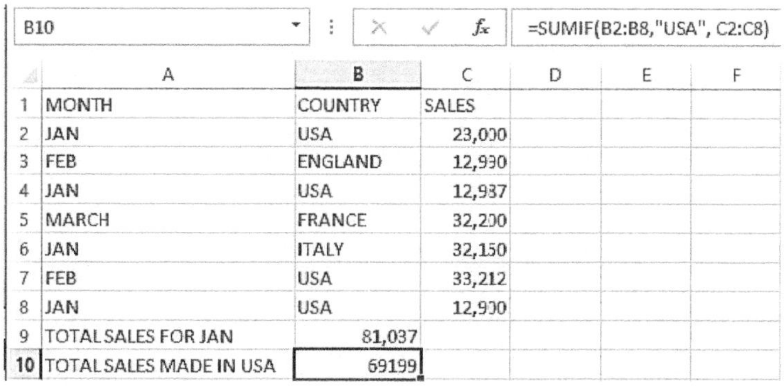

B10 | =SUMIF(B2:B8,"USA", C2:C8)

	A	B	C	D	E	F
1	MONTH	COUNTRY	SALES			
2	JAN	USA	23,000			
3	FEB	ENGLAND	12,990			
4	JAN	USA	12,987			
5	MARCH	FRANCE	32,200			
6	JAN	ITALY	32,150			
7	FEB	USA	33,212			
8	JAN	USA	12,900			
9	TOTAL SALES FOR JAN	81,037				
10	TOTAL SALES MADE IN USA	69199				

Take this into account when using the SUMIF FUNCTION.

- A VALUE! error occurs if the criteria supplied are greater than 255 characters.
- The cells in range would be automatically summed since the total range is not specified.
- It won't fit if you don't use double quotes around text strings in parameters.
- The wildcards in the SUMIF function? It's also possible to use the symbol *.

5.3 COUNTIF FUNCTION

The COUNTIF function may count how many cells are "true" for a certain condition. Cells containing text, numbers, or dates may all be counted using this approach. You can also use logical operators and wildcards if you use this feature.

The following are the parameters that may be sent into the COUNTIF method:

=COUNTIF (Range, criteria)

Range (Required Argument): This outlines the range of cells that will be listed.

Criteria (Compulsory Argument): This requirement must be met by each cell in the worksheet. Several examples of criteria are as follows, for example:

- Numerical values include decimal, temporal, integer, & logical values.
- The text string "Monday, East, Price" is an example of a text string that contains wildcard characters like asterisks or question marks.

Application of COUNTIF

Let's use the COUNTIF function to determine how many times James' name appears in the column that is shown below.

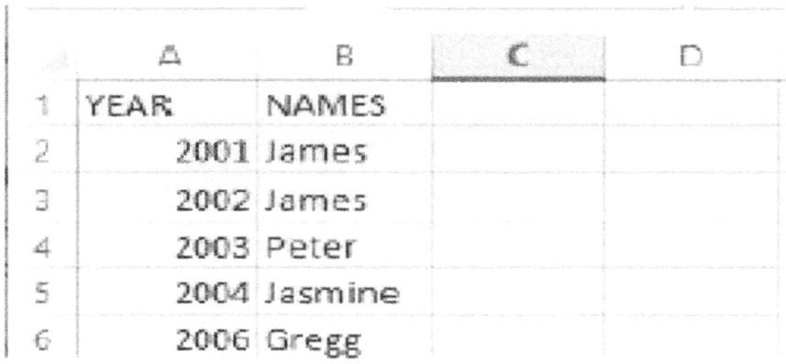

	A	B	C	D
1	YEAR	NAMES		
2	2001	James		
3	2002	James		
4	2003	Peter		
5	2004	Jasmine		
6	2006	Gregg		

To find out how many times James' name occurs on this page, follow the methods provided below.

Choose a currently empty cell and then enter the name of the function and the arguments that will be used. =COUNTIF (B2:B6, "James") =COUNTIF (B2:B6, "James") =COUNTIF (B2:B6, "James") =COUNTIF (B2

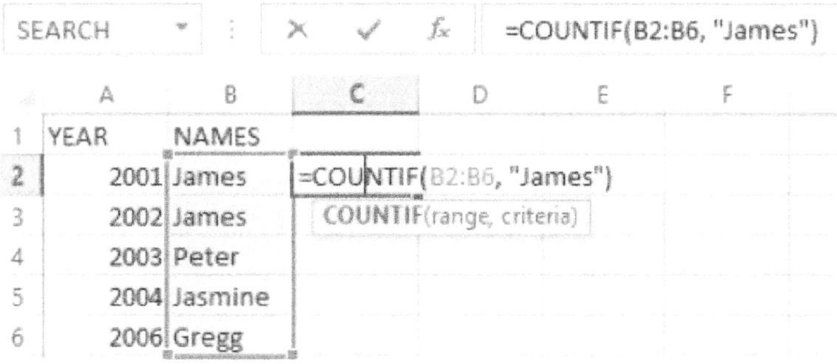

SEARCH | =COUNTIF(B2:B6, "James")

	A	B	C	D	E	F
1	YEAR	NAMES				
2	2001	James	=COUNTIF(B2:B6, "James")			
3	2002	James	COUNTIF(range, criteria)			
4	2003	Peter				
5	2004	Jasmine				
6	2006	Gregg				

When working with the COUNTIF tool, keep the following in mind.

- Please use the COUNTIF function to check that the criterion statement is included in quotation marks, such as "James."
- An instance of #VALUE ERROR occurs if the supplied criterion statement is a text string longer than 255 characters.
- When a formula in a closed workbook refers to a cell or range of cells, a #VALUE error will occur in the collection of cells where the formula is located.

5.4 ROUND FUNCTION

Rounding a number to a pre-specified number of digits is done with the ROUND function.

The following formula may be used to round the value 23.7825 in cell A1 to the closest two decimal places:

=ROUND (A 1, 2)

This method returns a value of 23.78.

Syntax

ROUND (number, number_digits)

The following are the parameters of the ROUND function:

A specific number is needed. The number you'd want to round up or down.

Number_digits Required. Some decimal places to round the argument's value to.

Remarks

The integer is round to the provided number of the decimal places if the num digits are larger than 0 (zero). To round to the closest integer, num digits must be zero. The integer is rounded to a left of a decimal point if num digits are below zero.

You may use this ROUNDUP function to ensure that your results are always rounded upwards.

Use this ROUNDDOWN function to always round down (to zero).

Round an integer using the MROUND function (for example, rounding to the closest 0.5).

Example

Cell A1 on a new Excel workbook should be filled up using the sample data from the table below.

Selecting the formulae, pressing F2, and then pressing Enter will display the results.

To view all the data, you may widen the columns if necessary.

SUM =ROUND(2.15, 1)

	A	B	C
1	Formula	Description	Result
2	=ROUND(2.15, 1)	Rounds 2.15 to one decimal place	2.2
3		Rounds 2.149 to one decimal place	2.1
4		Rounds -1.475 to two decimal places	-1.48
5		Rounds 21.5 to one decimal place to the left of the decimal point	20
6		Rounds 626.3 to the nearest multiple of 1000	1000
7		Rounds 1.98 to the nearest multiple of 10	0
8		Rounds -50.55 to the nearest multiple of 100	-100

5.5 CONCATENATE FUNCTION

You may use the text function CONCATENATE to combine many text strings. This function has been superseded by the CONCAT function in Excel 2019, Excel Mobile, & Excel for the Web. Even though the CONCATENATE function is still supported for backward compatibility, you should use CONCAT instead.

This is due to the possibility that CONCATENATE may be removed from Excel.

Syntax: CONCATENATE (text 1, [text 2], …)

For example:

- =CONCATENATE ("Stream populations for ", A 2, " ", A 3, " is ", A 4, "/ mile.")
- =CONCATENATE (B 2, "“", C 2)

Argument name	Description
text1 (required)	The first item to join. The item can be a text value, number, or cell reference.
Text2, ... (optional)	Additional text items to join. You can have up to 255 items, up to a total of 8,192 characters.

Examples

For Excel, just copy the data from the table below & paste it into cell A1 on a new worksheet.

Data		
brook trout	Andreas	Hauser
species	Fourth	Pine
32		
Formula	**Description**	
=CONCATENATE ("Stream population for ", A 2, " ", A 3, " is ", A 4, "/mile.")	The data inside column A is joined with additional material to form a sentence. The brook trout population is 32/miles in this stream.	
=CONCATENATE (B 2, " ", C 2)	It connects the string inside cell B2 with a space letter and the cell C2 value with a single space character. Andreas Hauser is the product.	
=CONCATENATE (C2, ", ", B2)	It combines the text in cell C 2, a string including a comma or a space character, & the value into cell B 2. Andreas, Hauser is the product.	
=CONCATENATE (B3, " & ", C3)	A space with an ampersand & another space is joined to the value into cell C 3 and the string into cell B 3. Fourth & Pine is the product of this collaboration.	
=B 3 & " & " & C3	The ampersand (&) calculating operator is used before CONCATENATE function for joining the same elements as in the preceding example. Fourth & Pine is the product of this collaboration.	

Common Problems

Problem	Description
Quotation marks appeared in the result string.	Commas should separate the text. Because there was no comma between the text parameters, Excel will show =CONCATENATE ("Hello "World") as Hello "World with an additional quotation mark. No quotation marks should be used around numeric values.
Words are also jumbled together.	The text will flow together if no specific spaces are used to separate it. As part of a CONCATENATE formula, add additional spaces. Either of these approaches will work. The gap between the two quote marks " " should be included. =CONCATENATE ("Hello", " ", "World!") is an illustration of this. After the Text parameter, a new line should be added. =CONCATENATE ("Hello," "World!"") is an example. Additional space has been added to the string "Hello."
The #NAME? An error appeared rather than an expected result.	#NAME? a Text argument may lack quotation marks if this is the case.

Best practices

Do this	Description
Use the character & ampersand rather than a CONCATENATE function.	You may connect text strings without a function using the ampersand (&) operator. Because =A 1 + B 1 yields the same result as =CONCATENATE (A 1, B 1). Use the ampersand operator instead of CONCATENATE to produce strings in many circumstances.
Use your TEXT function four combine & format strings.	In the TEXT function, integers and symbols may be combined into a single numeric value. If the value in cell A 1 is 23.5, you may format it as a dollar amount using the following formula: =TEXT (A 1,"$0.00") Result: $ 23.50

5.6 IFFEROR FUNCTION

When a formula fails, the IFFEROR function creates a unique answer. The IFERROR records and manages errors instead of nested IF statements.

These are the parameters that the IFERROR utilizes.

=IFFERROR (value, value_if_error)

Value (required argument). It's a concept or utterance that has been examined or faults found.

If there is a mistake in the formula, the value will be returned (Required Argument).

Let's use the IFFEROR function to add a customized message that reads "invalid data" instead of the errors in the table below.

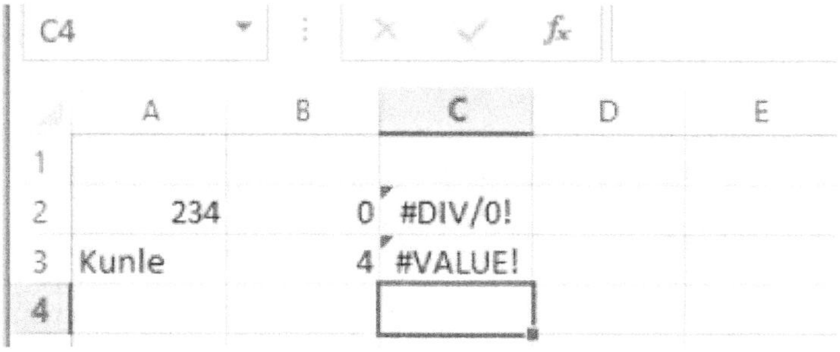

To fix the issue in cell C2, adhere to the methods listed below.

- Write the function's name and its arguments in a blank cell.

=IFERROR (A2/B2, "invalid data")

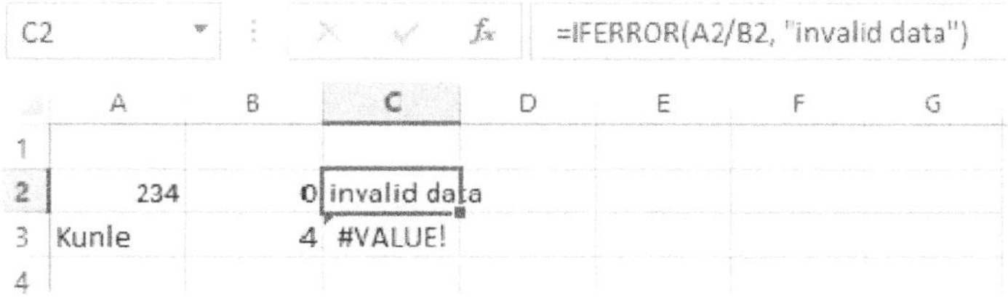

CHAPTER 6

PIVOT TABLES

There are several strong options for creating Pivot Tables inside Excel. Analyze up to a million data rows with mouse clicks, display the findings in a simple table that can be "pivoted"/changed by moving fields around, highlight essential information for management, and incorporate Charts and Slicers for the monthly presentations with the Pivot Table.

Some examples of those who utilize pivot tables are project managers and financial analysts; auditors; sales analysts; sales managers; and even human resources managers and statisticians. A broad range of people utilizes Excel Pivot Table!

For your convenience, a few fundamental Pivot Table concepts are discussed below.

6.1 INSERT THE PIVOT TABLE

A Pivot Table will be built using the data that you provide. You're in for a treat!

STEP 1: Select the dataset you want to work with. You have a list of sales figures.

CUSTOMER	REGION	ORDER DATE	SALES	MONTH	YEAR
Acme, inc.	NORTH	13/04/2014	$24,640	April	2014
Widget Corp	SOUTH	21/12/2014	$24,[illegible]40	December	2014
123 Warehousing	EAST	15/02/2014	$29,923	February	2014
Demo Company	WEST	14/05/2014	$66,901	May	2014
Smith and Co.	NORTH	28/06/2015	$63,116	June	2015
Foo Bars	SOUTH	15/01/2015	$38,281	January	2015
ABC Telecom	EAST	22/08/2015	$57,650	August	2015
Fake Brothers	WEST	31/12/2015	$90,967	December	2015

STEP 2: Go to the Insert ➔ Pivot Table

It's time for your first Pivot Table, so do this now!

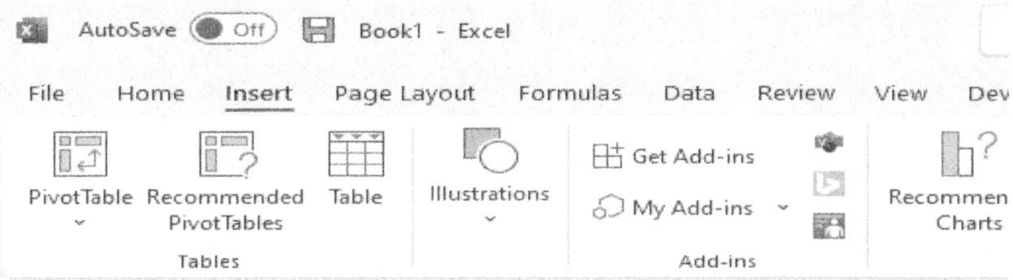

You may either create a new workbook or use one that already exists.

Determine the position of your pivot table by using this method of locating it.

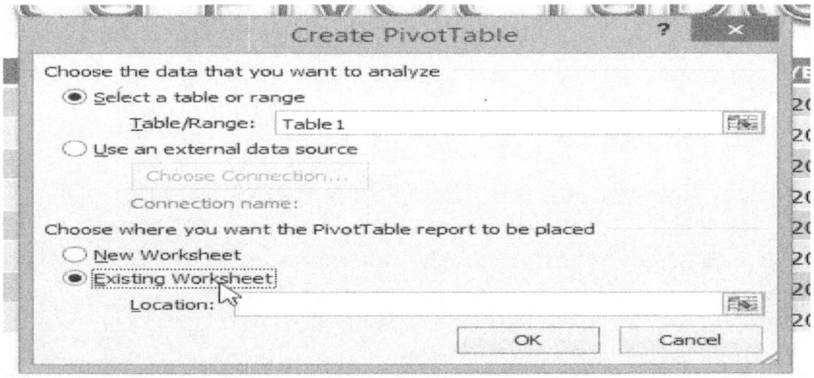

The fields may be dragged and dropped. In this example, you have the following setup:

Column ➔ YEAR

Row ➔ Region

Values ➔ Sum of the SALES

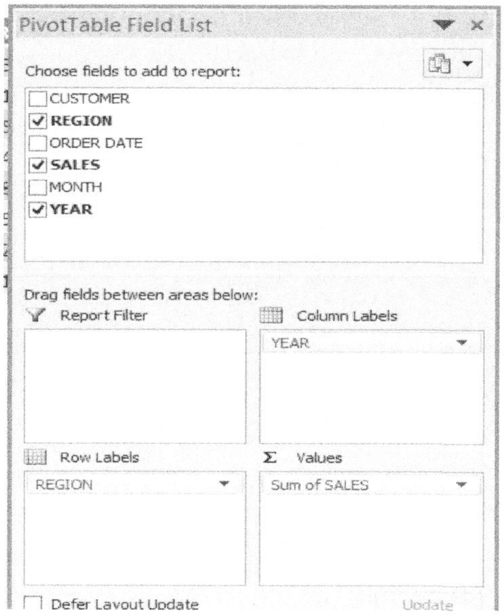

Create a report in which the rows are the regions, and the columns are the years; the numbers within a pivot table will be sums of sales for each area (depending upon the groupings of year & region)

The Pivot Table is now yours! Finally, there were no manual computations. Excel crunches your data into rows and columns, which uses magic to figure out how many values are in each column.

You'll find this invaluable resource when dealing with huge data. This is a wonderful time to look for patterns, trends, outliers, and anomalies.

Sum of SALES	Column Labels		
Row Labels	2014	2015	Grand Total
EAST	29923	57650	87573
NORTH	24640	63116	87756
SOUTH	24640	38281	62921
WEST	66901	90967	157868
Grand Total	**146104**	**250014**	**396118**

6.2 REFRESHING YOUR PIVOT TABLES

You must refresh the Pivot Table whenever you make changes to your data set to view those changes within Pivot Table. Occasionally, you may question why the pivot table values don't represent your new data set.

Three methods are available, and all of them are simple.

Start by clicking on the Pivot Table.

1. From your Ribbon, select: PivotTable Tools ➔ Options ➔ Refresh
2. Then Press ALT + F5
3. Right-click on the Pivot Table & choose Refresh

That means that your Excel Pivot Table has already been constructed.

The first step is to alter some of the data in your database. When you reload your Excel Pivot Table, you'll see a dramatic difference if you alter one variable to a large amount.

CUSTOMER	REGION	ORDER DATE	SALES	MONTH	YEAR
Acme, inc.	NORTH	13/04/2014	$1,000,000	April	2014
Widget Corp	SOUTH	21/12/2014	$1,500,000	December	2014
123 Warehousing	EAST	15/02/2014	$2,000,000	February	2014
Demo Company	WEST	14/05/2014	2500000	May	2014
Smith and Co.	NORTH	28/06/2015	$63,116	June	2015
Foo Bars	SOUTH	15/01/2015	$38,281	January	2015
ABC Telecom	EAST	22/08/2015	$57,650	August	2015
Fake Brothers	WEST	31/12/2015	$90,967	December	2015

STEP 2: Select Pivot Table from the list. Any cell may be selected.

Sum of SALES	Column Labels		
Row Labels	2014	2015	Grand Total
EAST	29923	57650	87573
NORTH	24640	63116	87756
SOUTH	24640	38281	62921
WEST	66901	90967	157868
Grand Total	**146104**	**250014**	**396118**

STEP 3: Right-click and choose Refresh from the context menu that appears.

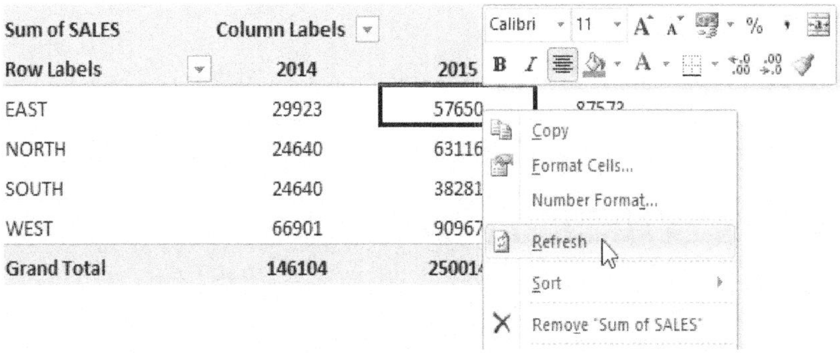

You can now change the Pivot Table data with just a single click! As you can see in the 2014 figures, your revised data set has been reflected in the changes.

Sum of SALES	Column Labels		
Row Labels	2014	2015	Grand Total
EAST	2000000	57650	2057650
NORTH	1000000	63116	1063116
SOUTH	1500000	38281	1538281
WEST	2500000	90967	2590967
Grand Total	**7000000**	**250014**	**7250014**

6.3 GROUP DATES USING YOUR PIVOT TABLE

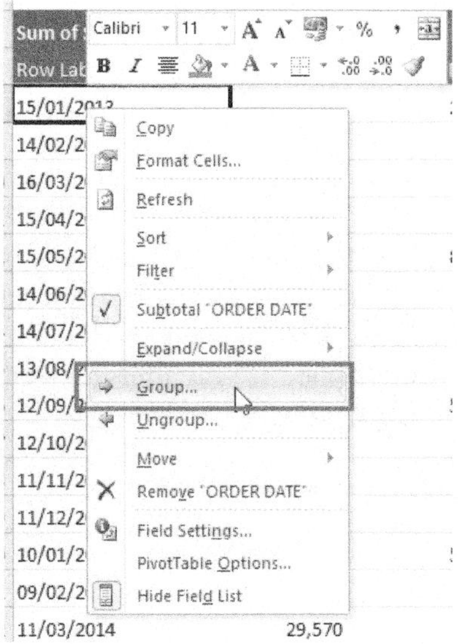

Using the Pivot Table, you may create groups of related data. Among the most often utilized features is the ability to aggregate dates.

A Pivot Table makes it simple to group dates. To create a group, you only need to Right Click over the Date values (within Column or Row Labels of the Pivot Table). And that's all there is to it!.

You may select to group by quarter, day, month, or a year from the drop-down menu in the dialogue box. Let's have a look at an example.

Group your data values by right-clicking and selecting Group from the context menu.

STEP 2: Decide on the groupings you want to use. To finish, click the OK button. In this case, you'd like to organize the data by quarter & year.

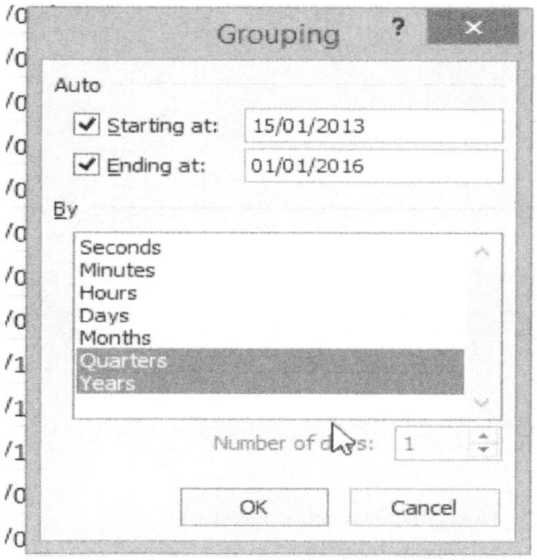

The dates in your pivot table have now been grouped! Excel has once again saved the day for you!

Sum of SALES	Column Labels				
Row Labels	EAST	NORTH	SOUTH	WEST	Grand Total
⊟ 2013					
Qtr1	44,802	26,884	46,174		117,860
Qtr2		80,369	53,522	49,049	182,940
Qtr3	67,320	58,146		66,663	192,129
Qtr4	22,024		83,288	64,750	170,062
⊟ 2014					
Qtr1	29,570	53,586	14,333		97,489
Qtr2		25,263	68,797	83,468	177,528
Qtr3	49,562	23,798		13,964	87,324
Qtr4	78,715		16,843	80,780	176,338
⊟ 2015					
Qtr1	37,544	56,959	47,189		141,692
Qtr2		20,816	85,607	53,413	159,836
Qtr3		56,959		43,216	114,834
Qtr4		20,816	47,189	53,413	158,962
Grand Total		**423.596**	**462.942**	**508.716**	**1.776.994**

Sum of SALES
Value: No value
Row: 2015 - Qtr2
Column: EAST

6.4 INSERTING SLICERS WITHIN PIVOT TABLE

Let's briefly look at how to utilize the Pivot Table with slicers. Pivot Tables get a new level of engagement with this feature. The report's author didn't say it had to be static.

Using Slicers in Excel, you may view which rows of a Pivot Table have been selected using interactive buttons or visual filters.

To wow your employer with interactive reports, they are a must-have! Below, you can see how to put a Slicer inside a Pivot Table.

STEP 1: To begin, locate your Pivot Table and click on it. After that, all you must do is choose a cell.

Sum of SALES	Column Labels		
Row Labels	2013	2014	2015
123 Warehousing	66,826	49,562	75,088
ABC Telecom	67,320	108,285	14,659
Acme, inc.	85,030	25,263	113,918
Demo Company	113,799	13,964	106,826
Fake Brothers	66,663	164,248	43,216
Foo Bars	53,522	31,176	85,607
Smith and Co.	80,369	77,384	41,632
Widget Corp	129,462	68,797	94,378
Grand Total	**662,991**	**538,679**	**575,324**

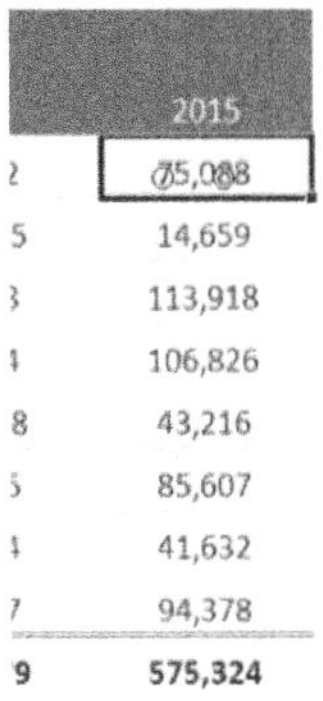

STEP 2: Go to the Options (Excel 2010) / Analyze (Excel 2013, 2016 &2019) ➔ Insert Slicer

Click the Month & Year Fields.

Now Click the OK.

You may now use your slicer! Click, slice, and dice your data to your heart's content!

Filtering your data based on choices is possible just by using this. Finding the exact combination you or your supervisor needs is much simpler today.

Hold down your CTRL key if you want to pick numerous things in your Slicer.

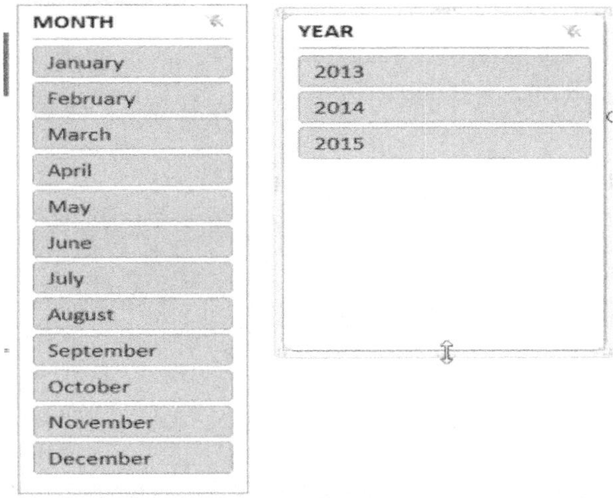

CHAPTER 7

ADVANCED FUNCTIONALITY

Several of Excel's more complex features, such as AND, OR, XOR, VLOOKUP, and Text Functions, are covered in this chapter.

7.1 AND FUNCTION

In a data set, the AND function checks to see whether the specified conditions are true, and it returns a result of FALSE if all the requirements are not satisfied; for instance, B1 is more than 50 but less than 100. The AND function is called with the following arguments as its parameters.

=AND (logical1, [logical2},)

1 logical (Necessary Argument) The first criterion, often known as the logical quality, must first be determined, is logical2 (Optional Argument). A logical value is the second state being evaluated in this process.

To get the result of the table as described before.

- Write the name of the function and the arguments in a currently empty cell.

=AND(A2>67, A2<A3)

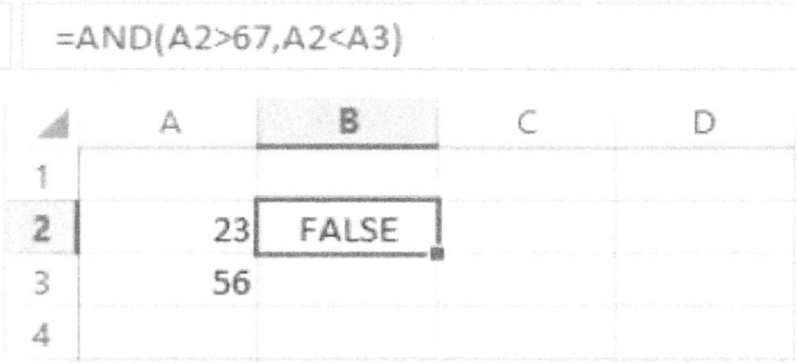

The AND function in the table above returns the value FALSE because one of the conditions in the data set was not satisfied; specifically, A2 does not have a value greater than 67.

The following table demonstrates that when all the criteria in the dataset are met, the AND feature will return TRUE.

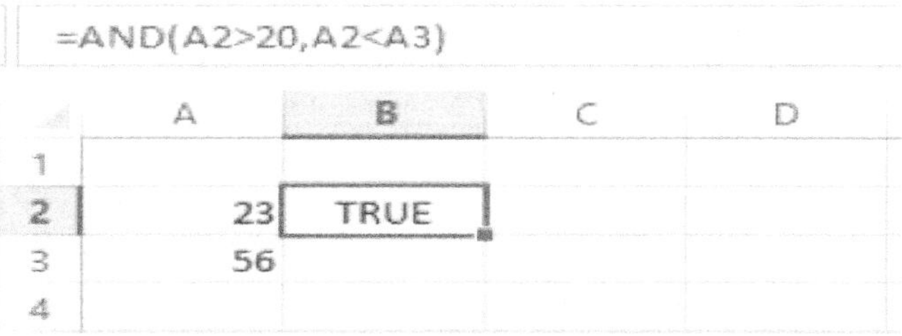

7.2 OR FUNCTION

The OR function will return the value TRUE if all conditions are met; otherwise, it will return the value FALSE. In contrast to the AND function, the value will be returned as false if any of the conditions are false. The OR function takes the following arguments for its parameters:

=OR (logical1, [logical2} ...)

The first logical value or condition must be determined logical1 (Required Argument).

(Important counterargument) Establishing logical validity is the second need that must be met.

To accomplish the result shown in the table just described.

- =OR(A2>30, B2>50, B3=45) Complete the missing cell with the function's name and the arguments it accepts.

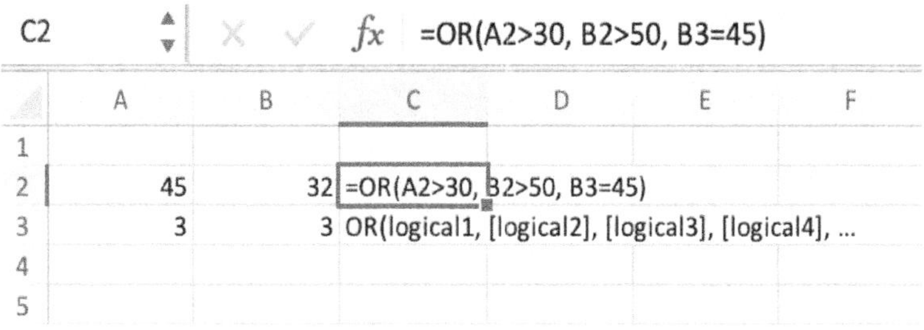

- When you press enter, the response will be FALSE, as seen in the next paragraph.

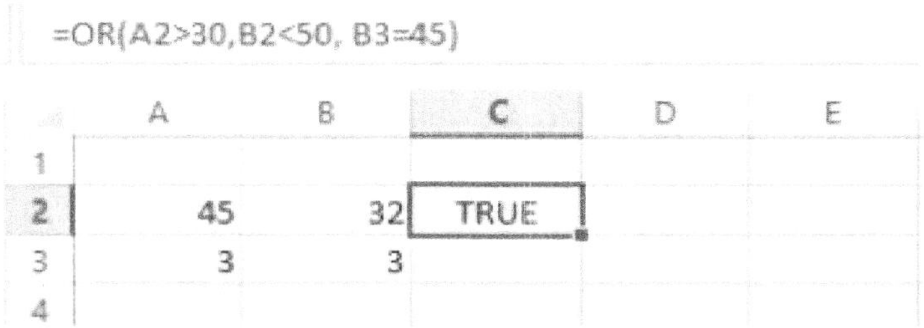

7.3 EXCEL TEXT FUNCTION

Excel contains numeric, text, and string data. Text functions ease text management and processing.

Excel offers text(), Len(), left(), right(), Replace(), concatenate(), & trim(). Text dropdown list on Formula tab. Excel text manipulation tools.

Excel's TEXT() function converts numbers to text. In this chapter, we'll cover Excel's TEXT() function.

TEXT() function

Excel's TEXT() function converts numbers to text. It's in Excel. Excel's number-to-text feature may be used.

"Text-formatted TEXT() data cannot be utilized for calculations. Keep the original values in another cell if you want to calculate them."

This method is for text/strings. This method converts numbers to text.

Syntax

TEXT() requires 2 parameters: value & formatting text. TEXT() formula:

= TEXT (value, formating_text)

Return Value

The TEXT() method returns text-formatted data.

Basic Example: Format numbers

You formatted numbers using TEXT().

A2 contains a float. Use TEXT() to convert to a percentage.

=TEXT (A 2, "0.0%")

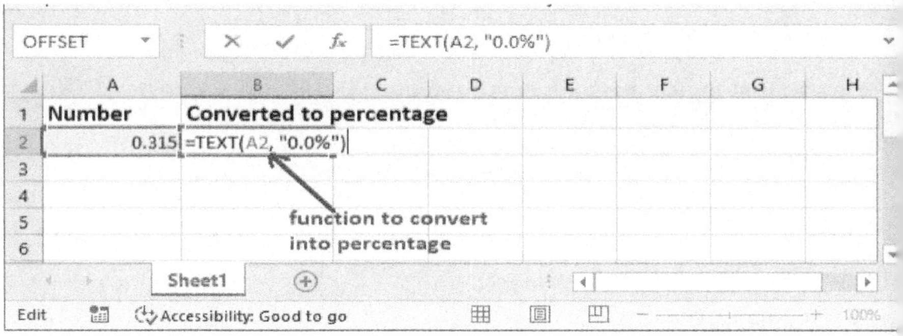

It converts to percentile. Look.

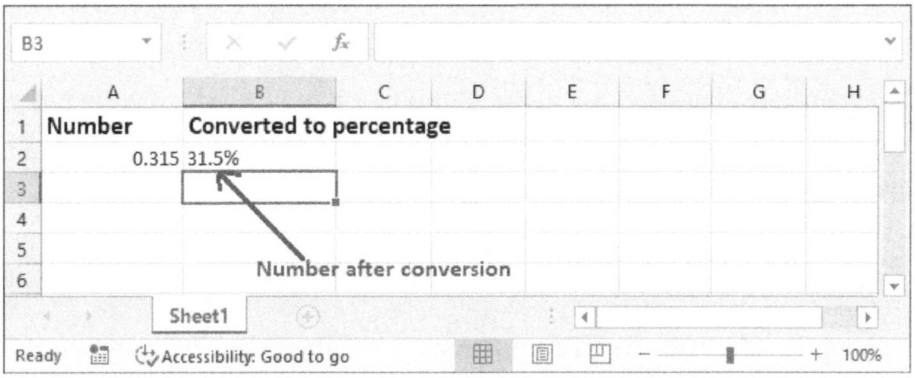

But your number type is now text and not a number.

See another TEXT number conversion:

=TEXT (A 5, "$#,##0.00")

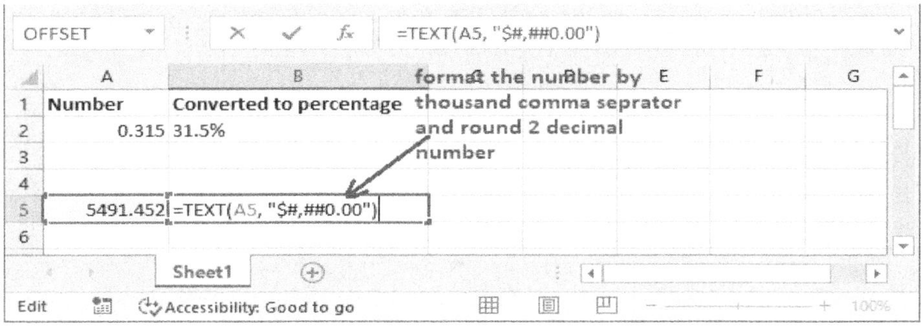

It separates the number by a thousand commas & rounds to the right.

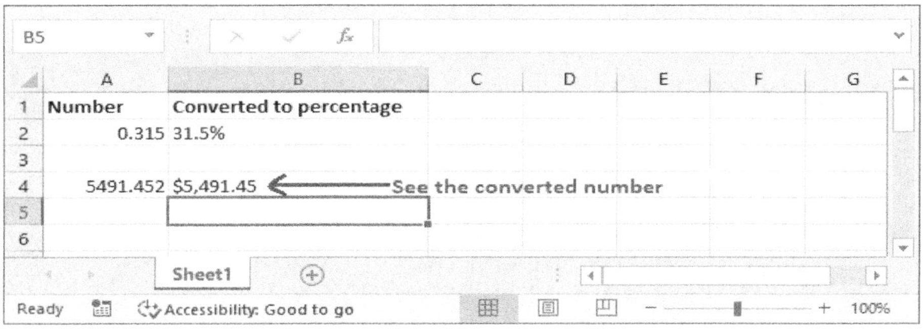

This function also formats numbers.

Formatting codes

Excel's TEXT() function supports formatting codes. These codes format text numerals.

Code	Description	Example
# (hash)	It hides the extra zero/numbers from numeric values.	It helps to display such numbers like #.# to display a single decimal point. For example, 5.374 as 5.3
0 (zero)	It displays irrelevant zero from numbers if you add.	#.00 - It would display two zeros after the decimal point in a numeric value. For example, A number 2.4 will be 2.40
, (comma)	It is used as a thousand separator in numbers.	For example, ##,### it will put a thousand separator. A number 23548 will be displayed as 23,548.

Use them in TEXT() to prepare Excel worksheet data.

7.4 XOR FUNCTION

Programming often uses exclusive OR. In English, we may say, "I'll study Electronics or Computer Science at a reputable university." The phrase shows that the speaker can't take both classes.

They can only choose one. True if they take any course. False if they do neither or both. Programming uses XOR (Exclusive OR).

What is XOR Function?

"Exclusive OR" is Excel's XOR function. This method returns all arguments' Exclusive OR."

XOR yields TRUE if one of the two logical propositions is true but FALSE if both are true. It returns FALSE if both assertions are false. If the XOR function includes two or even more logical variables, this method returns TRUE if a count is odd, else FALSE.

Excel OR function is a common mistake. They're different. The OR method evaluates to true if some assertion is true, whereas XOR() does not.

Syntax

=XOR (logical 1, [logical 2], ...)

Return

Excel's XOR() function returns:

- False despite both conditions being true
- IF the condition is TRUE, the output is TRUE
- IF one condition is FALSE and another is TRUE, the output is TRUE
- FALSE is returned if both criteria are FALSE.

Condition 1	Condition 2
1>0	2>9
2 >= 3	5 == 6
5 < =4	7 > 6
2 > 4	4 < 3
4 < = 3	2 > 1

Example Solve the following criteria using Excel's XOR function.

Above, you're provided 2 conditions. To use Excel's XOR() function, follow these steps:

Insert your Column helper

Next to condition 2, you'll add an 'XOR' column.

Image below:

Condition 1	Condition 2	XOR Output
1>0	2>9	
2 >= 3	5 == 6	
5 < =4	7 > 6	
2 > 4	4 < 3	
4 < = 3	2 > 1	

You'll utilize Excel's XOR() function within the XOR helper column.

Type your XOR function

Start typing in the next column. =, formula name, open parenthesis. = XOR (

Condition 1	Condition 2	XOR Output
1>0	2>9	=XOR (
2 >= 3	5 == 6	
5 < =4	7 > 6	
2 > 4	4 < 3	
4 < = 3	2 > 1	

Insert both your parameter

First, enter the first condition. Refer to condition1 for exclusive OR output. You'll use a B4 cell. = XOR (B 4

Condition 1	Condition 2	XOR Output
1>0	2>9	=XOR (B4
2 >= 3	5 == 6	
5 < =4	7 > 6	
2 > 4	4 < 3	
4 < = 3	2 > 1	

The second condition follows. You'll use the D4 cell. Close bracket to end function.

Formula is: = (B4, C4)

Drag your XOR formula around cells.

Condition 1	Condition 2	XOR Output
1>0	2>9	=XOR (B4,C4)
2 >= 3	5 == 6	
5 < =4	7 > 6	
2 > 4	4 < 3	
4 < = 3	2 > 1	

Pick a cell for the formula. Move the mouse to the rectangle's end. The mouse cursor turns into a black cross. Copy & auto-fill your formula by dragging this icon below the cells.

Image below:

Condition 1	Condition 2	XOR Output
1>0	2>9	=XOR (B4,C4)
2 >= 3	5 == 6	
5 < =4	7 > 6	
2 > 4	4 < 3	
4 < = 3	2 > 1	

Drag the icon

Result

The data's Boolean output is returned. Results are based on:

- Since 1>0 is True & 2>9 is False, the output is TRUE.
- Both requirements are false; thus, the output is likewise false.
- 5=4: FALSE, 7>6: TRUE; Condition1 is False, condition2 is True; hence the outcome is True.

- Both requirements are false; thus, the output is likewise false.
- 4=3: FALSE, 2>1:TRUE; first condition True, second condition False, output False

See the outcome below.

Condition 1	Condition 2	XOR Output
1>0	2>9	TRUE
2 >= 3	5 == 6	FALSE
5 < =4	7 > 6	TRUE
2 > 4	4 < 3	FALSE
4 < = 3	2 > 1	FALSE

7.5. VLOOKUP FUNCTION

The VLOOKUP function, which stands for "vertical lookup," is a straightforward method to look up a piece of data in the first column of a table or dataset, as well as retrieve or return equal information and data from a different column of the data set or table in the same row.

With the following parameters, the VLOOKUP function performs its operation:

=VLOOKUP (col_index_num, table_array, lookup_value, [range_lookup])

Look-up_value (Required argument): The value to search for in the first column of the table or dataset.

Table_array (Required argument): The data array that the lookup value in the column's left portion may search through.

Col_index_num (Needed argument): The table lists column numbers or integers where equivalent statistics are returned.

Range_lookup (optional argument): This code component decides whether VLOOK can find an exact or good match. The statement's value is either TRUE or FALSE. The next highest value is returned if a satisfactory match cannot be discovered. FALSE denotes a precise match; if none is found, #N/A is returned as an error.

To use this function to determine the value of yam in the table above, follow the steps below:

- Select an empty cell and type the lookup value method, i.e., the cell holding the data to be searched for. In this example, the lookup cell is A12, which includes Yam =VLOOKUP (A12)

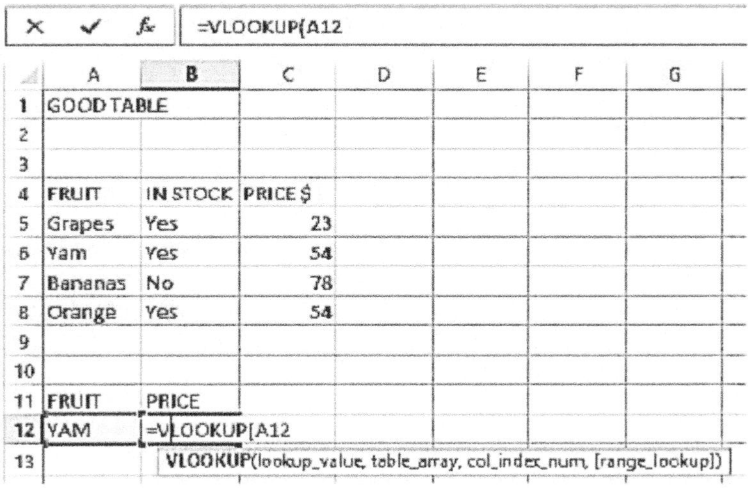
=VLOOKUP(A12

	A	B	C	D	E	F	G
1	GOOD TABLE						
2							
3							
4	FRUIT	IN STOCK	PRICE $				
5	Grapes	Yes	23				
6	Yam	Yes	54				
7	Bananas	No	78				
8	Orange	Yes	54				
9							
10							
11	FRUIT	PRICE					
12	YAM	=VLOOKUP(A12					
13		VLOOKUP(lookup_value, table_array, col_index_num, [range_lookup])					

7.6 HLOOKUP FUNCTION

The HLOOKUP function, which stands for "horizontal lookup," is a tool for searching up a value or a piece of data within a top row of a table array or dataset and then returning the item or value from another row specified in the table array or dataset in the same column.

The HLOOKUP function uses the following inputs to accomplish its action.

=HLOOKUP (table_array, lookup_value, row_index_num, [range_lookup])

To determine your total Joy in Mathematics score, follow the steps below.

- Choose an empty cell and type the lookup value method, the cell holding the data to be searched for.

In this situation, B1 is the lookup cell and includes the name. Joy; =HLOOKUP (B1

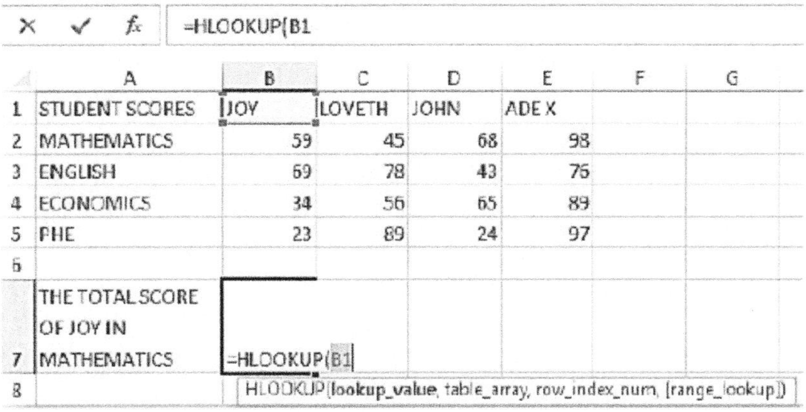
=HLOOKUP(B1

	A	B	C	D	E	F	G
1	STUDENT SCORES	JOY	LOVETH	JOHN	ADE X		
2	MATHEMATICS	59	45	68	98		
3	ENGLISH	69	78	43	76		
4	ECONOMICS	34	56	65	89		
5	PHE	23	89	24	97		
6							
7	THE TOTAL SCORE OF JOY IN MATHEMATICS	=HLOOKUP(B1					
8		HLOOKUP(lookup_value, table_array, row_index_num, [range_lookup])					

Finally, by putting TRUE or FALSE, you may tell Excel whether you're searching for an exact or perfect match.

= HLOOKUP (B1, A1:E5,3, FALSE) or =HLOOKUP (B1, A1:E5,3, TRUE)

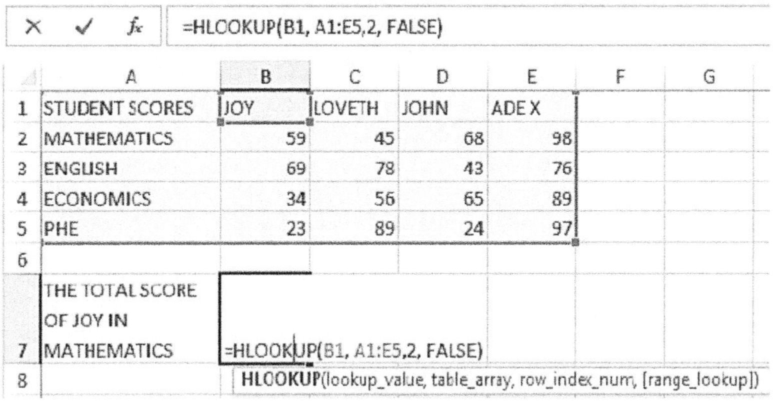
=HLOOKUP(B1, A1:E5,2, FALSE)

	A	B	C	D	E	F	G
1	STUDENT SCORES	JOY	LOVETH	JOHN	ADE X		
2	MATHEMATICS	59	45	68	98		
3	ENGLISH	69	78	43	76		
4	ECONOMICS	34	56	65	89		
5	PHE	23	89	24	97		
6							
7	THE TOTAL SCORE OF JOY IN MATHEMATICS	=HLOOKUP(B1, A1:E5,2, FALSE)					
8		HLOOKUP(lookup_value, table_array, row_index_num, [range_lookup])					

CHAPTER 8

ADVANCED FORMULAS

In this chapter, you will go through some most advanced formulas in excel.

8.1 TXT. JOIN FUNCTION

The TEXTJOIN Function combines the text of two or more strings by using a delimiter between the values. TEXTJOIN is an Excel String/Text function that was first introduced there.

Syntax

= TEXTJOIN (delimiter, ignore-empty, text 1, [text 2], … text_n)

TEXTJOIN accepts the following parameters:

- The string to use as a delimiter between individual text values in the output string. A comma or even a space is often used as a delimiter.
- If you want to exclude or include empty cells in the output string, use the Ignore empty (mandatory) option. Empty values are disregarded if an argument is TRUE. The blank values in the output are only an issue if it is set to FALSE.
- The input strings that will be concatenated are denoted by [Text1, Text2..., Text n]. Up to 252 strings may be joined using the TEXTJOIN function.

How can you use a TEXTJOIN Function in Excel?

Let's look at several samples to see how this operation is implemented.

Example 1

Let's pretend you've successfully retrieved some data from an address & that it's being sent as follows:

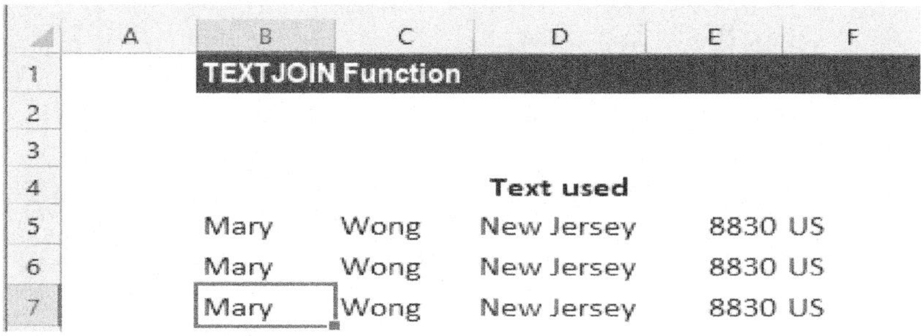

Using this formula =TEXTJOIN (“, “, TRUE, B 5, C 5, D 5, E 5, F 5), you can join your text strings as seen below:

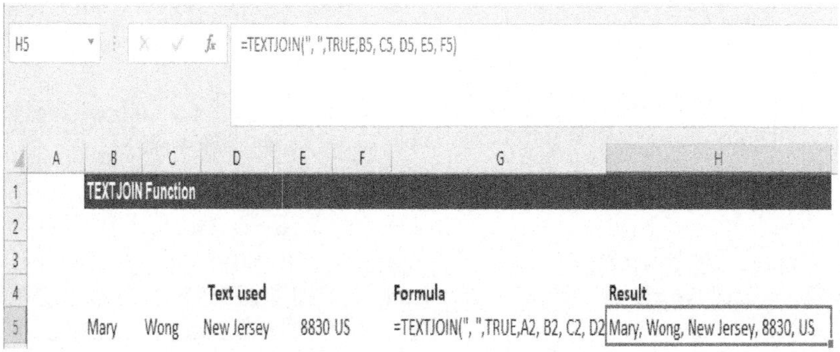

Let's pretend you want to insert "Country" before "US" now. If this were to happen, the formula would shift to = TEXTJOIN (” “, TRUE, B 6, C 6, D 6, E 6,” Country”, F 6).

The following is what you get if you enter these figures into the formula:

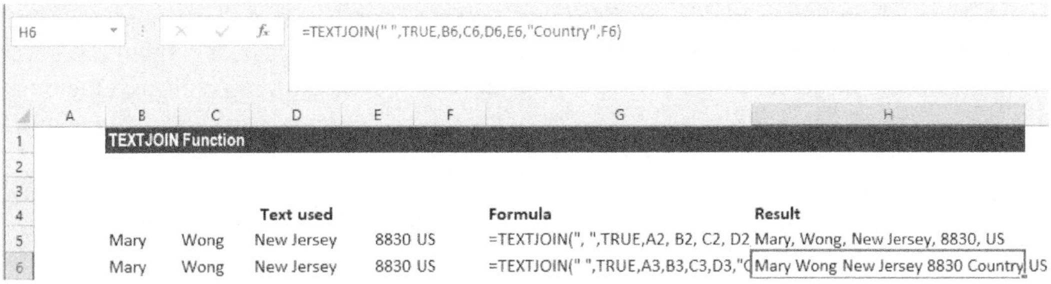

Let's pretend you need a separator and decide to use a space. The appropriate formula in this case is = TEXTJOIN (" ", TRUE, B 7, C 7, D 7, E 7, F 7).

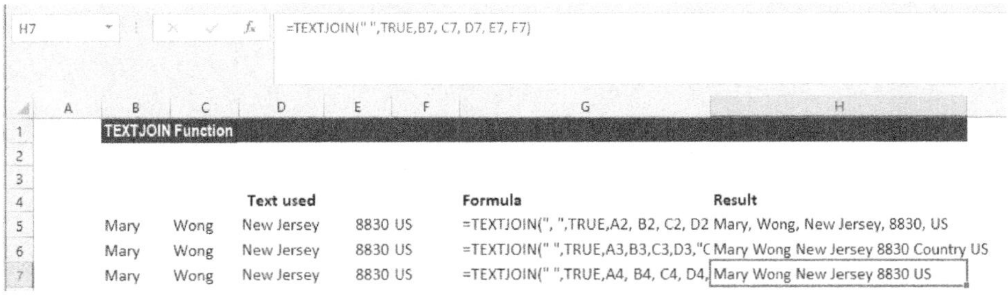

Example 2

For illustration, let's look at a scenario where more than two columns need to be joined (using any data in the columns below).

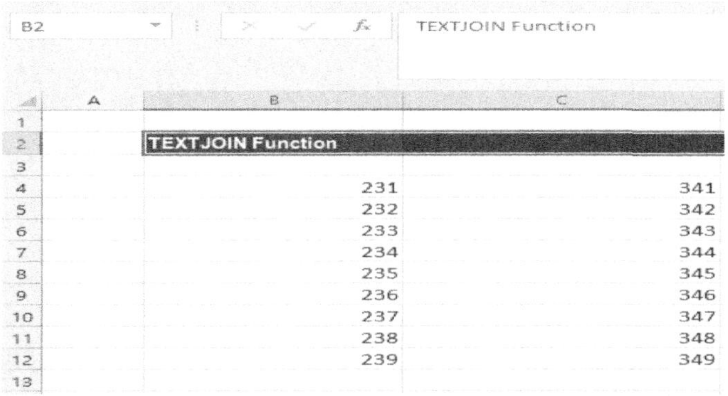

If you use this formula = TEXTJOIN (", ", TRUE, B 4:C 12), then you will see the following results:

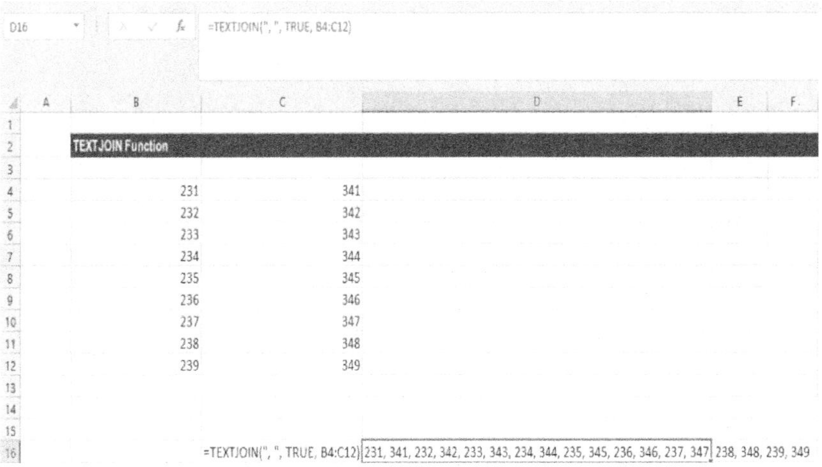

Example 3

Let's say you have a list of anniversaries, each with a name, a surname, & the year, and you want to combine the columns so that the names and anniversaries appear together. In this case, it's important to remember that since Excel stores data in numerical format, entering the date directly would result in a numeric value being returned.

Please use the below date:

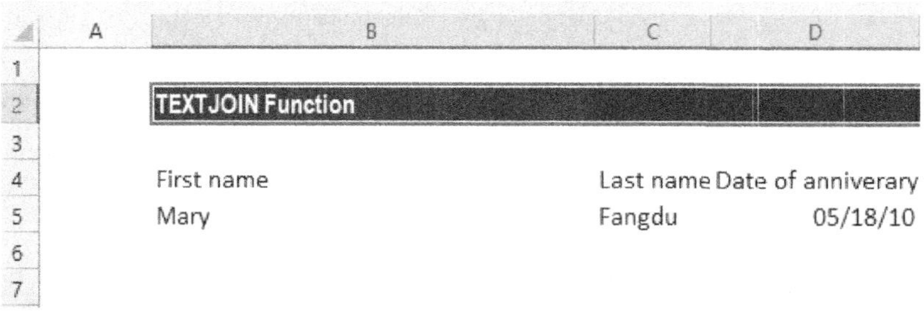

If for such data, you enter this formula = TEXTJOIN (" ", TRUE, B 5: D 5,)

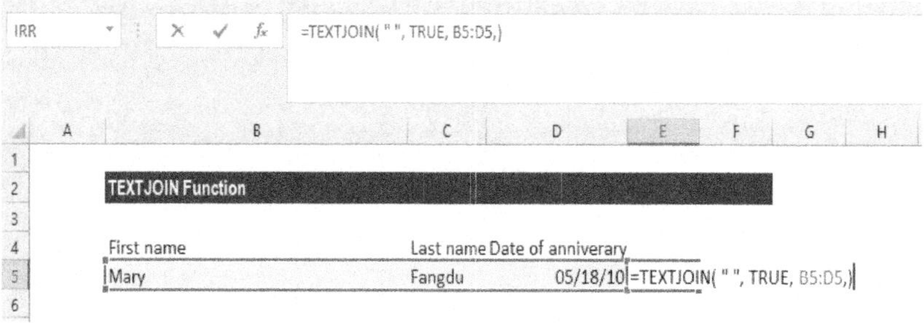

The following is the output from Excel:

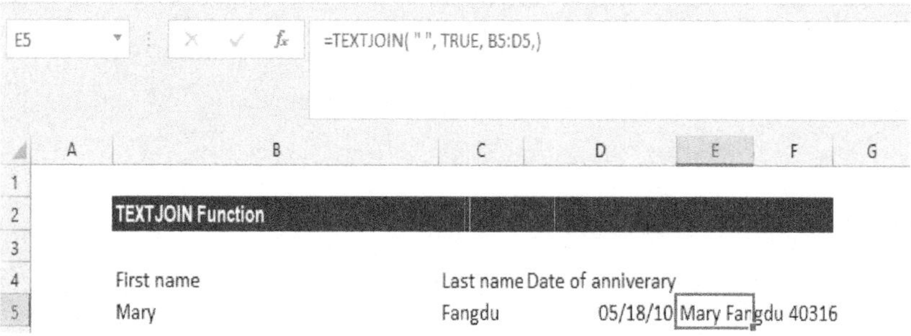

Consequently, you must first transform the date into a string of text. For this reason, the appropriate formula is = TEXTJOIN (" ", TRUE, B 5: D 5, TEXT (C 2, "mm /dd /yyyy")). You will get the following result:

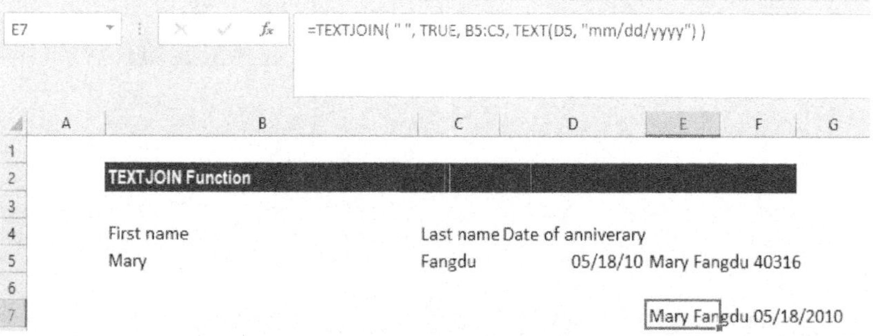

More regarding TEXTJOIN Function

- When the final string is more than 32767 characters, Excel will throw the #VALUE! Error.
- There is enough for 252 text parameters in the function.
- This operation is quite close to the CONCAT operation. As opposed to CONCAT, TEXTJOIN allows for a delimiter to be used.
- Using an unsupported version of Excel (an earlier version) will result in the #NAME? Error.
- Mistakenly omitting a comma while trying to concatenate strings results in a #NULL! Error.
- It allows the user to specify a range of cells rather than specific ones.

8.2 STRING.EXTRACT FUNCTION

Excel's string (text) functions make it easy to work with textual data in several ways. Altering the case of text, finding a string, calculating its length, etc., are all possible with the assistance of these built-in functions. Top text operations are discussed in this section. (Example Data)

FIND Function

When you use the FIND function on a string, it will return a number that indicates where in the string the beginning of the substring may be found. Simply said, the find function allows you to locate the beginning of a string inside another string (case-insensitively).

Syntax

FIND (find_text, within_text, [start_num])

Arguments

find_text: the part of another text that you need to locate.

within_text: Where in the source text do you want to find it?

[start_num]: Number indicates the initial location from which to begin the search.

SEARCH Function

The SEARCH function finds the beginning of a substring inside a string and returns a number. Simply put, the SEARCH function allows you to find the first occurrence of a string of text inside another without regard to the case.

Syntax

AD

SEARCH (find_text, within_text, [start_num])

Arguments

find_text: A piece of text sought for utilizing another.

within_text: Some written material inside which the target language is hidden. Two ways to enter data into a function are by referencing a cell or typing in the data directly.

Example

Below is an example where you begin your search for the letter "P" by setting the start num to 1. When you plug the text's location into your algorithm, you get the value 1.

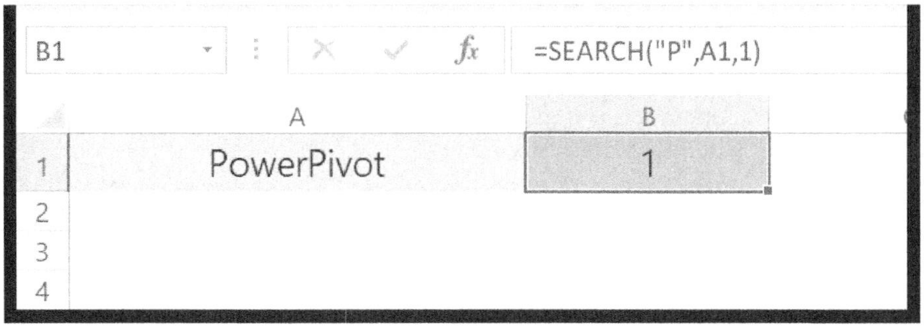

However, the sixth letter of the word is a "P," as can be seen by careful examination. Due to this, the SEARCH function may only return the starting position if you seek the first occurrence of a phrase or if you supply the starting position yourself.

LEFT Function

To get characters from the left side of a string, use a function called LEFT (starting). Put another way, using the LEFT function allows you to take characters off the left side of a string.

Syntax

LEFT (text, num_chars)

Arguments

text: Characters to be taken from another string or numerical value.

[num_char]: The total number of characters to be taken out.

Example

In the following example, you use LEFT to remove the first five numbers from a text string by setting the set of characters to remove as input.

AD

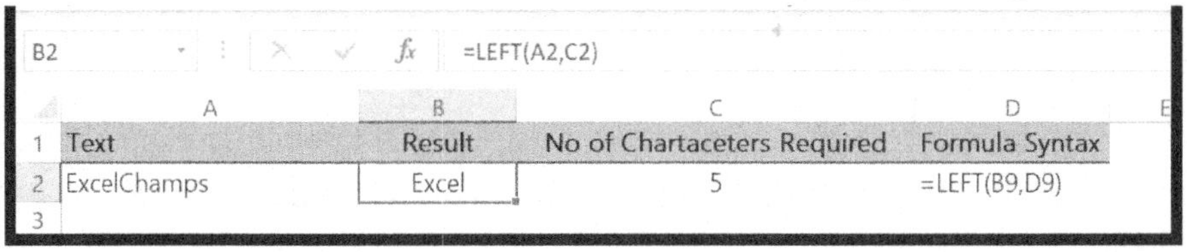
B2 =LEFT(A2,C2)

Text	Result	No of Chartaceters Required	Formula Syntax
ExcelChamps	Excel	5	=LEFT(B9,D9)

Below is an example of a formula that uses LEN, FIND, & LEFT to get the name out of the cell.

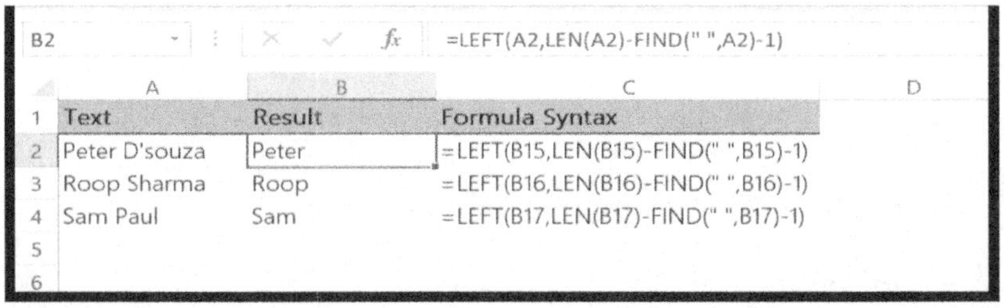
B2 =LEFT(A2,LEN(A2)-FIND(" ",A2)-1)

Text	Result	Formula Syntax
Peter D'souza	Peter	=LEFT(B15,LEN(B15)-FIND(" ",B15)-1)
Roop Sharma	Roop	=LEFT(B16,LEN(B16)-FIND(" ",B16)-1)
Sam Paul	Sam	=LEFT(B17,LEN(B17)-FIND(" ",B17)-1)

RIGHT Function

The RIGHT function takes a string and returns its rightmost characters in order (ending). To put it another way, the RIGHT function allows you to take the leftmost characters from a string.

Syntax

RIGHT (text, num_chars)

Arguments

text: Characters to be taken from another string or numerical value.

[num_char]: Specify the number of characters you want to retrieve.

Example

You successfully retrieved 6 characters using the appropriate extraction function in the code snippet below. You can use a number to extract a certain number of characters from a string if you know how many letters you need.

B2 =RIGHT("ExcelChamps",6)

	A	B	C	D
1	Text	Result	No of Chartaceters Required	Formula Syntax
2	ExcelChamps	Champs	6	=RIGHT("ExcelChamps",6)
3				
4				
5				

Consider the following example: you need to get the last word from a cell but don't know how many characters it contains.

B2 =RIGHT(A2,LEN(A2)-FIND(" ",A2))

	A	B	C
1	Text	Result	Formula Syntax
2	Peter D'souza	D'souza	=RIGHT(A2,LEN(A2)-FIND(" ",A2))
3	Roop Sharma	Sharma	=RIGHT(A3,LEN(A3)-FIND(" ",A3))
4	Sam Paul	Paul	=RIGHT(A4,LEN(A4)-FIND(" ",A4))
5			

To obtain the name, you will use LEN & FIND.

First, you used LEN to determine how long the whole string of text was, and then you used FIND to pinpoint the precise location of the separating space between the first and final names.

To arrive at the surname, you combined the two digits.

Arguments

value1: A direct numeric input, an array reference, or a cell reference.

[value2]: A reference to an array, a cell, or a numerical value supplied to the function.

MID Function

MID extracts a substring from the string using a given offset and length and returns it. With MID, you can easily extract the substring from a string by providing a beginning character and the desired length of the extracted substring.

Syntax

MID (text, start_num, num_chars)

Arguments

text: An input that may be either textual or numeric, from which characters will be retrieved.

start_char: The index within the string from which you want to get characters.

num_chars: The desired length of the start char data to be extracted.

Example

A variety of values are used in the illustrative example below:

From the sixth character forward, including the following six.

The following 10 characters after the sixth one.

You tried to utilize a negative character's initial position and got an error.

When the number of characters extracted was set to 0, the result was a blank.

Returning an error message when the number of characters for extracting is negative.

An error has been returned because the initial value is 0.

Simply input the string of text into the procedure.

Text String	Result	Formauls Syntax	Remarks
ExcelChamps.com	Champs	=MID(A2,6,6)	A Valid Syntax
ExcelChamps.com	Champs.com	=MID(A3,6,10)	A Valid Syntax
ExcelChamps.com	#VALUE!	=MID(A4,-1,6)	start_num is negative
ExcelChamps.com		=MID(A5,6,0)	num_char is zero
ExcelChamps.com	#VALUE!	=MID(A6,6,-1)	num_char is negative
ExcelChamps.com	#VALUE!	=MID(A7,0,6)	start_num is Zero
ExcelChamps.com	Champs	=MID("ExcelChamps",6,6)	Text defined with in the function

LOWER Function

The string is returned by LOWER after being converted to a tiny case.

Put it another way; it takes a string of text where all letters are little and capitalizes them while leaving the numbers alone.

Syntax

LOWER (text)

Arguments

text: The text that must be made lowercase.

Example

Compare and contrast lower case, proper case, upper case, & sentence case with one another in the following example.

When compared to other fonts, lower case text features smaller characters.

A4 =LOWER(A3)

	A	B	C
1	The quick brown fox jumps over the lazy dog	Sentence Case	
2	THE QUICK BROWN FOX JUMPS OVER THE LAZY DOG	Upper Case	
3	The Quick Brown Fox Jumps Over The Lazy Dog	Proper Case	
4	the quick brown fox jumps over the lazy dog	Lower Case	
5			
6			
7			

PROPER Function

The PROPER function converts the given text string into a proper case and returns it. With a correct function, where the initial letter is capitalized, and the other letters are tiny (proper case).

Syntax

PROPER (text)

Arguments

text: The text you would like to convert into a proper case.

Example

In an appropriate case, just the first letter of a word is capitalized; the rest of the letters are written in lowercase.

A3 =PROPER(A2)

	A
1	The quick brown fox jumps over the lazy dog
2	THE QUICK BROWN FOX JUMPS OVER THE LAZY DOG
3	The Quick Brown Fox Jumps Over The Lazy Dog
4	
5	

Case-conservative regularization using the PROPER function is shown below.

E11 =PROPER(E10)

	A	B
1	Text	Proper Text
2	STEPHANIE KAYE	Stephanie Kaye
3	amy janota	Amy Janota
4	Kimber WIGGS	Kimber Wiggs
5	NAT devo	Nat Devo
6	jim pruitt	Jim Pruitt

UPPER Function

After the UPPER function has been called, the string will be returned with all the characters capitalized. Let's simplify things and say it accepts a string of text where all the letters are capitals and keeps the numbers while doing nothing else to it.

Syntax

UPPER (text)

Arguments

text: The text that should be capitalized.

Example

Below is an example of using UPPER to change all lowercase names in a string of text to uppercase ones.

B2 =UPPER([@Text])

	A	B
1	Text	UPPER TEXT
2	STEPHANIE kate	STEPHANIE KATE
3	amy janota	AMY JANOTA
4	Kimber WIGGS	KIMBER WIGGS
5	NAT devo	NAT DEVO
6	jim pruitt	JIM PRUITT

REPT Function

Repeatedly, the REPT function will return a text value. The REPT function allows you to supply a text or an integer to repeat.

Syntax

REPT (value1, [value2], …)

Example

Below is an example of REPT being used to repeat distinct types of text.

A REPT function is most useful for making in-cell charts, and it can replicate any combination of text, numbers, & symbols that you provide in the function.

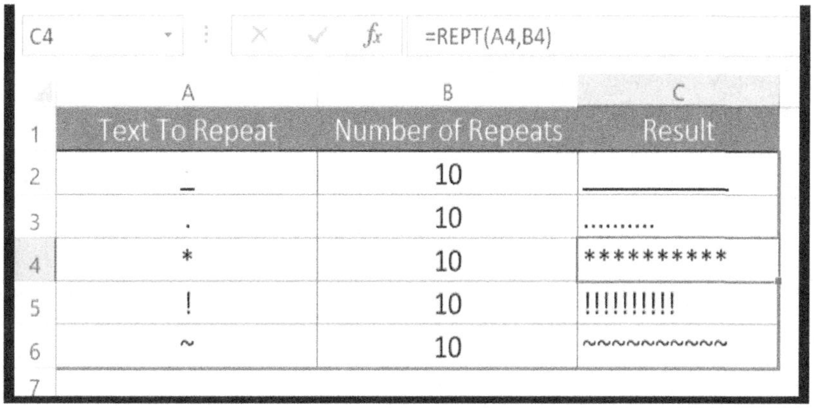

C4 =REPT(A4,B4)

	A	B	C
1	Text To Repeat	Number of Repeats	Result
2	_	10	__________
3	.	10	....
4	*	10	**********
5	!	10	!!!!!!!!!!
6	~	10	~~~~~~~~~~
7			

8.3 DATE, DATE.MONTH, DATE.VALUE FUNCTIONS

WEEKDAY Formula into Excel

So, what is the function of this thing?

A date's appropriate day this week is returned. The day is stated as an integer between 1 (Sunday) & 7 (Saturday).

Formula breakdown:

= WEEKDAY (Serial-Number, [Return-Type])

Means:

= WEEKDAY (Date, [Numbers 1 (Sunday) through 7 (Saturday)])

Your WEEKDAY function computes and returns the weekday associated with a given date. The day is shown as an integer between 1 (Sunday) and 7 (Saturday). For this reason, the WEEKDAY function may determine the day of the week a person was born.

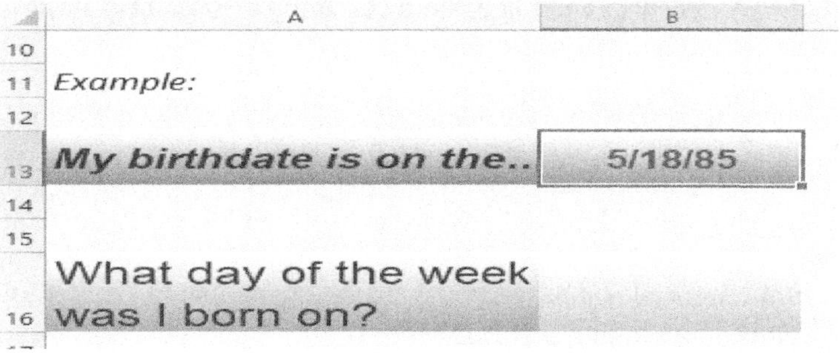

FIRST STEP: Pick any date you want and enter it here.

STEP 2: The reasons for the WEEKDAYS

Choose the date that you have written down.

=WEEKDAY (B13,

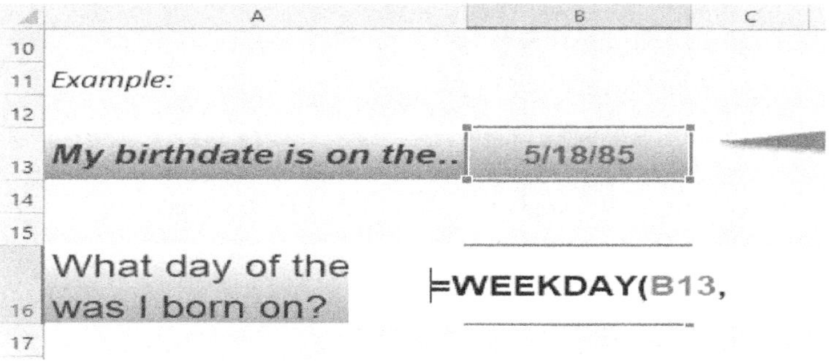

Return_Type

Simply entering 1 will give you the day of the week as its corresponding number. A figure of 7 is obtained here, which indicates that it is a Saturday. Since Type 1 denotes days spanning from 1 (Sunday) through 7 (Saturday).

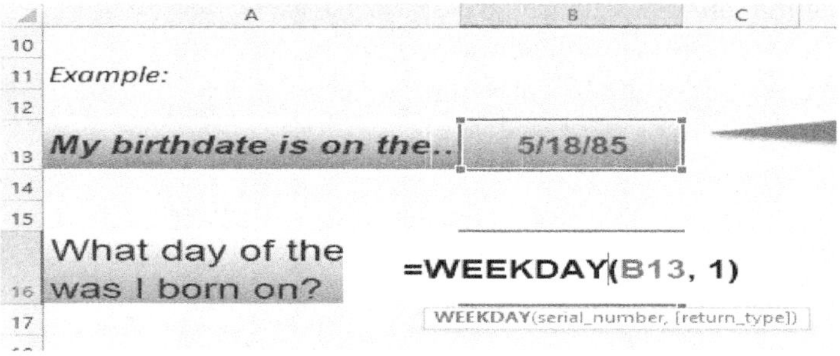

=WEEKDAY (B 13, 1)

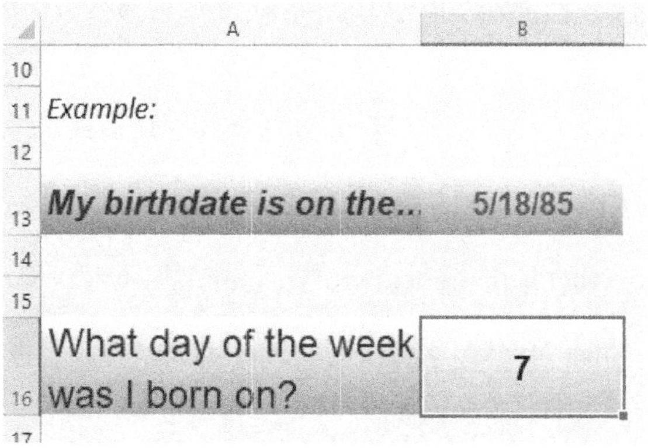

Now, in a single second, you are aware of the day!

WEEKNUM Formula into Excel

Calculates the week number based on the current date.

Formula breakdown:

= WEEKNUM (serial-number, [return-type])

Means:

=WEEKNUM (date from which the week number is going to be retrieved, [day on which the next week will start])

Do you need to calculate the week number based on the provided date? Excel's WEEKNUM Formula is an excellent choice for this purpose!

There are a few noteworthy aspects of a WEEKNUM Formula that are worth bringing to your attention:

The value of the return statement parameter indicates which day next week serves as the basis for the beginning week number.

In the examples that follow, you shall make use of the default. However, there are a variety of options at your disposal, including the following:

- 1 (default) –Sunday
- 2 –Monday
- 11 –Monday
- 12 –Tuesday
- 13 –Wednesday
- 14 –Thursday
- 15 –Friday
- 16 –Saturday
- 17 –Sunday
- 21 –Monday, The European weekly numbering system is used here instead of the American one; ISO 8601 designates the first week of the year as the week that includes January 1st. The key distinction is here.

To begin, copy and paste the WEEKNUM function into an empty cell:

=WEEKNUM (

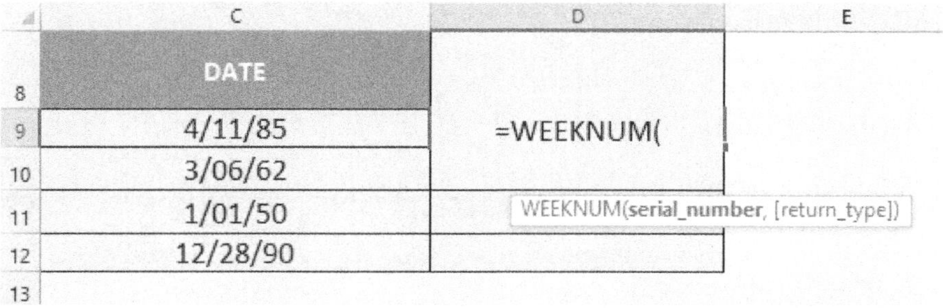

STEP 2: All arguments about the WEEKNUM:

serial_number

Where can you get the date that will determine the week number?

Find the cell that contains the date and select it:

=WEEKNUM (C9)

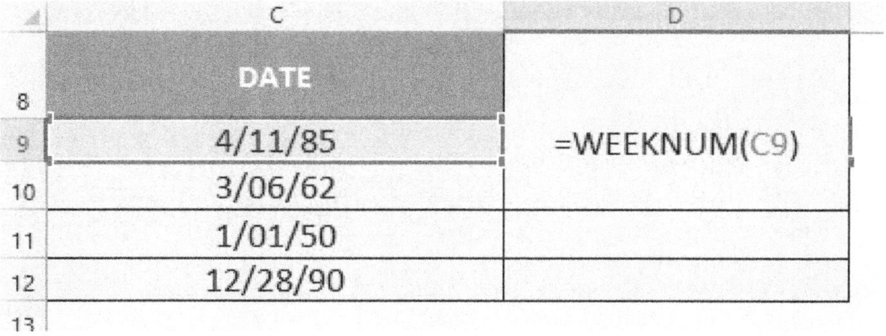

Moving the cell's upper right corner toward the bottom may apply a similar formula to the remaining cells.

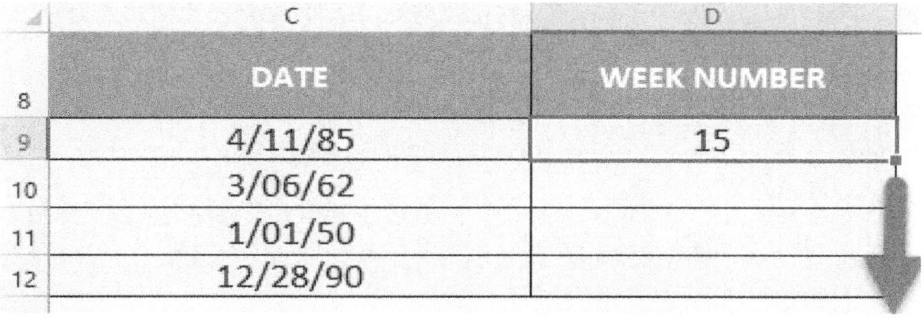

You may now calculate your weekly totals!

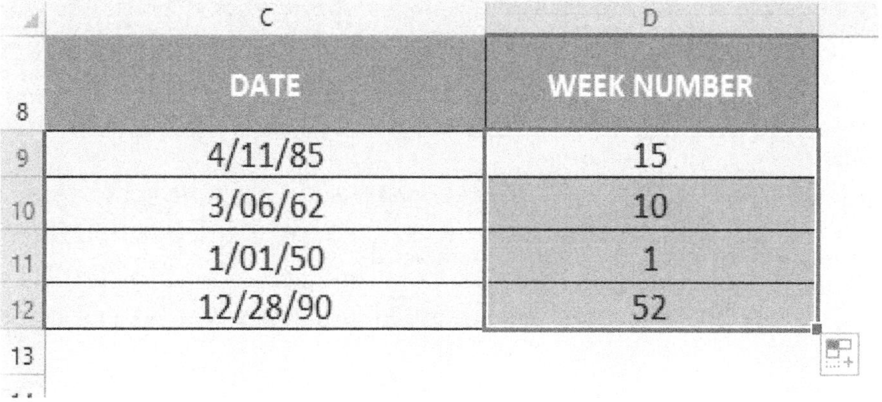

WORKDAY Formula into Excel

So, what is the function of this thing?

Appends or removes the provided number of business days to the date, resulting in a new date in the future or a date in the past.

Formula breakdown:

=WORKDAY (start_date, days, [holidays])

DATE	# OF WORKDAYS ADDED	RESULT
2/12/10	10	2/26/10
1/15/18	150	8/13/18
3/05/09	23	4/07/09
5/15/15	55	7/31/15

What this means:

=WORKDAY (Special date, num of workdays for adding/subtracting, [holidays for consideration])

It is tedious to manually compute the future date by adding a certain number of business days.

The long and arduous way: ordinarily, you would pull out a calendar and tally the days.

Use Excel's WORKDAY formula; that's the simple way to do it!

First, in a new, empty cell, type the WORKDAY function:

=WORKDAY (

DATE	# OF WORKDAYS ADDED	
2/12/10	10	=WORKDAY(
1/15/18	150	
3/05/09	23	WORKDAY(start_date, days, [holidays])
5/15/15	55	

STEP 2: All WORKDAY arguments:

start_date

When is the date due exactly?

Choose the cell that contains the date to which you'd want to apply the additional working days:

DATE	# OF WORKDAYS ADDED	
2/12/10	10	=WORKDAY(C9,
1/15/18	150	
3/05/09	23	WORKDAY(start_date, days, [holidays])
5/15/15	55	

=WORKDAY (C9,

DAYS

Just how many more workdays are needed?

Find the cell containing the number of additional workdays (i.e., the number of days following the start date, not weekends or holidays) and click on it.

=WORKDAY (C9, D9)

DATE	# OF WORKDAYS ADDED	
2/12/10	10	=WORKDAY(C9,D9)
1/15/18	150	
3/05/09	23	
5/15/15	55	

Moving the rightmost corner down may apply a similar formula to the remaining cells.

Timetables for the near future have been updated to include working days.

8.4 VAL.ERROR FUNCTION

Excel would throw a VALUE error if the cell referenced by the formula is incorrect or the variable given in the formula isn't a supported type. This is Excel's method of indicating that the incorrect kind of argument has been supplied.

Excel may show this error for several reasons; to resolve the issue; you'll need to track down the root cause.

What's a #VALUE error in Excel?

An #VALUE! Error may appear in a formula if you input invalid data. There are a few potential triggers for this Excel error:

- A cell has concealed gaps; the Date is recorded as text; Numerical Operations are Performed Using Text

Let's look at some real-world situations to dissect these root reasons and figure out a solution.

How can you fix the #VALUE error in Excel?

Example 1: Text is utilized in Arithmetic Operations

Here, you aim to determine overall sales by summing results from both areas on separate days.

As can be seen, a #VALUE! Error is generated in cell D7 when the values in cells B7 and C7 are added. That's because there's some writing in cell B7 rather than a number.

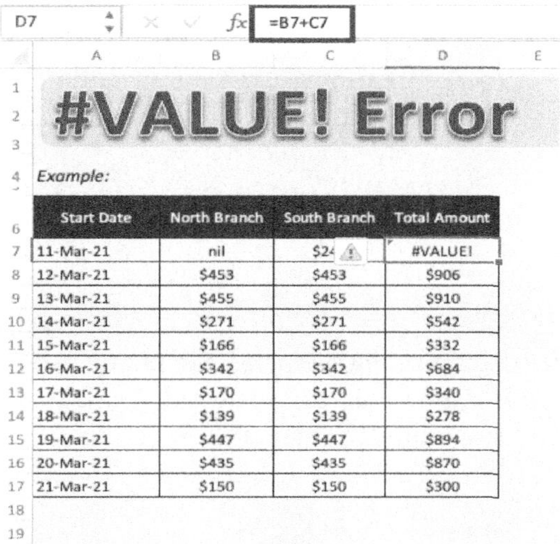

Start Date	North Branch	South Branch	Total Amount
11-Mar-21	nil	$24	#VALUE!
12-Mar-21	$453	$453	$906
13-Mar-21	$455	$455	$910
14-Mar-21	$271	$271	$542
15-Mar-21	$166	$166	$332
16-Mar-21	$342	$342	$684
17-Mar-21	$170	$170	$340
18-Mar-21	$139	$139	$278
19-Mar-21	$447	$447	$894
20-Mar-21	$435	$435	$870
21-Mar-21	$150	$150	$300

Put an end to this!

The word "nil" should be replaced by the digit 0.

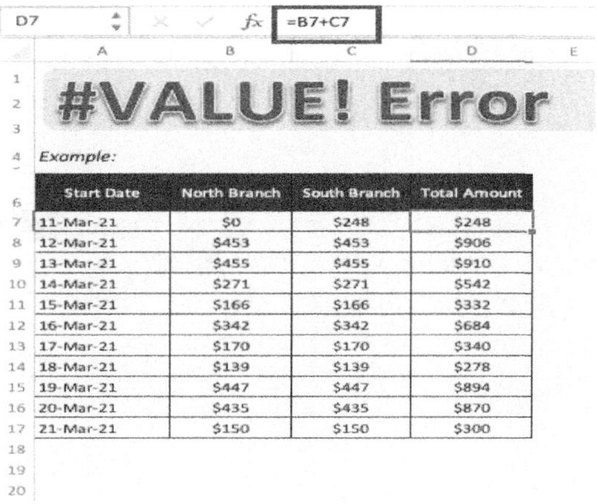

Start Date	North Branch	South Branch	Total Amount
11-Mar-21	$0	$248	$248
12-Mar-21	$453	$453	$906
13-Mar-21	$455	$455	$910
14-Mar-21	$271	$271	$542
15-Mar-21	$166	$166	$332
16-Mar-21	$342	$342	$684
17-Mar-21	$170	$170	$340
18-Mar-21	$139	$139	$278
19-Mar-21	$447	$447	$894
20-Mar-21	$435	$435	$870
21-Mar-21	$150	$150	$300

In addition to the plus sign (+), the function SUM may be used to do addition. If you try to use an operator in a cell containing text, you will get a VALUE error instead of the expected result.

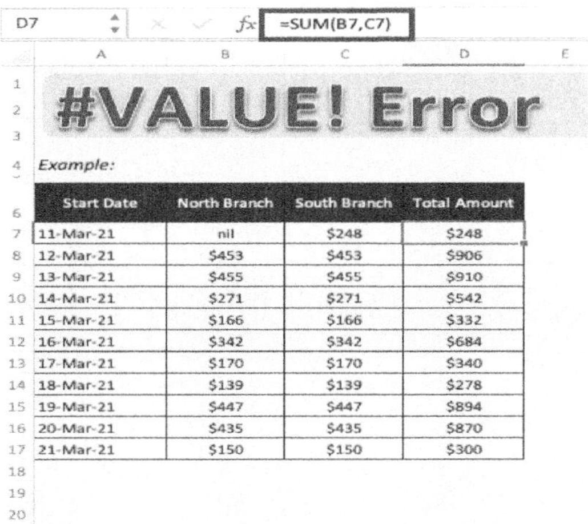

Start Date	North Branch	South Branch	Total Amount
11-Mar-21	nil	$248	$248
12-Mar-21	$453	$453	$906
13-Mar-21	$455	$455	$910
14-Mar-21	$271	$271	$542
15-Mar-21	$166	$166	$332
16-Mar-21	$342	$342	$684
17-Mar-21	$170	$170	$340
18-Mar-21	$139	$139	$278
19-Mar-21	$447	$447	$894
20-Mar-21	$435	$435	$870
21-Mar-21	$150	$150	$300

Functions will just disregard text values and compute everything else.

Example 2: Cells contain hidden space

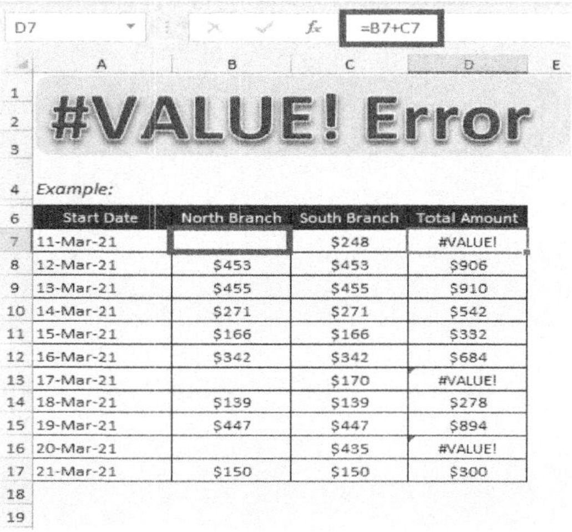

Start Date	North Branch	South Branch	Total Amount
11-Mar-21		$248	#VALUE!
12-Mar-21	$453	$453	$906
13-Mar-21	$455	$455	$910
14-Mar-21	$271	$271	$542
15-Mar-21	$166	$166	$332
16-Mar-21	$342	$342	$684
17-Mar-21		$170	#VALUE!
18-Mar-21	$139	$139	$278
19-Mar-21	$447	$447	$894
20-Mar-21		$435	#VALUE!
21-Mar-21	$150	$150	$300

The VALUE error message will be shown when a cell includes invisible spaces.

These gaps make it seem like the cell is empty while including a space.

Even if cell B7 seems empty, the error message in cell D7 indicates otherwise. This is because there is extra room in cell B7.

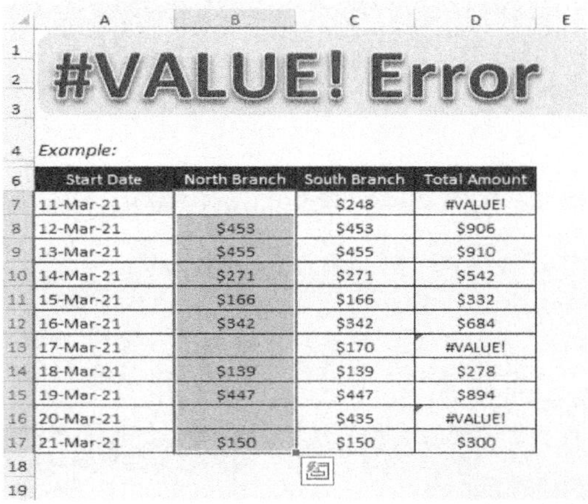

Start Date	North Branch	South Branch	Total Amount
11-Mar-21		$248	#VALUE!
12-Mar-21	$453	$453	$906
13-Mar-21	$455	$455	$910
14-Mar-21	$271	$271	$542
15-Mar-21	$166	$166	$332
16-Mar-21	$342	$342	$684
17-Mar-21		$170	#VALUE!
18-Mar-21	$139	$139	$278
19-Mar-21	$447	$447	$894
20-Mar-21		$435	#VALUE!
21-Mar-21	$150	$150	$300

Finding and eliminating the hidden voids inside the many cells that make up a living organism may be challenging. The following instructions will help you locate and eliminate unnecessary gaps. First, zero in on the range where you want to insert spaces.

Second, pick the Replace tab in the Find and Replace dialogue box (accessed through Ctrl + F).

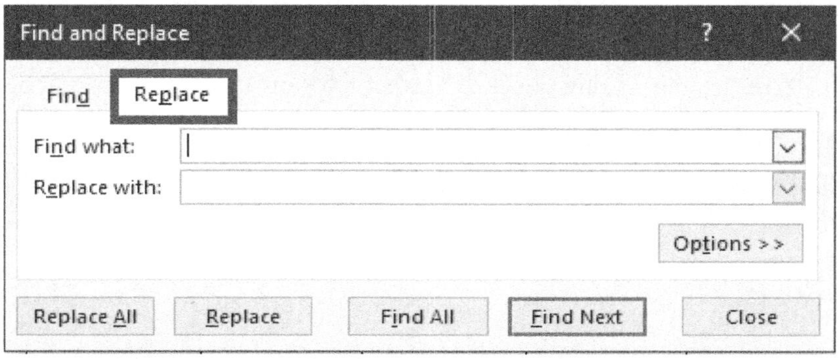

Insert a blank space after Keep the Replace box blank and use the Find What field to locate the information.

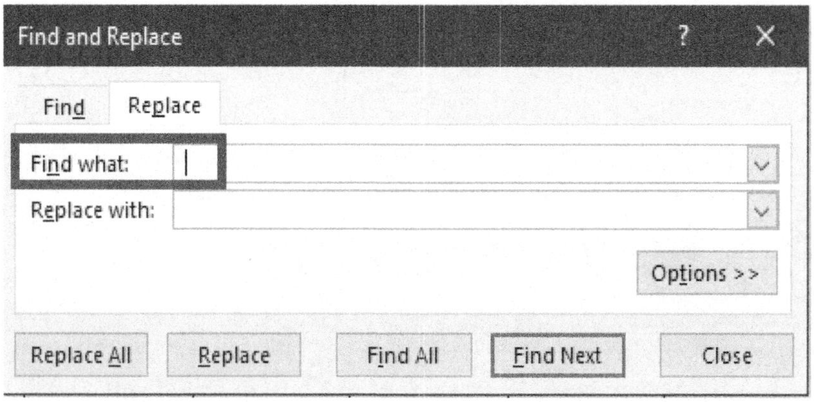

3rd - Use the Replace All button to make all the changes.

This will delete any spaces or tabs in the chosen cells, leaving them blank.

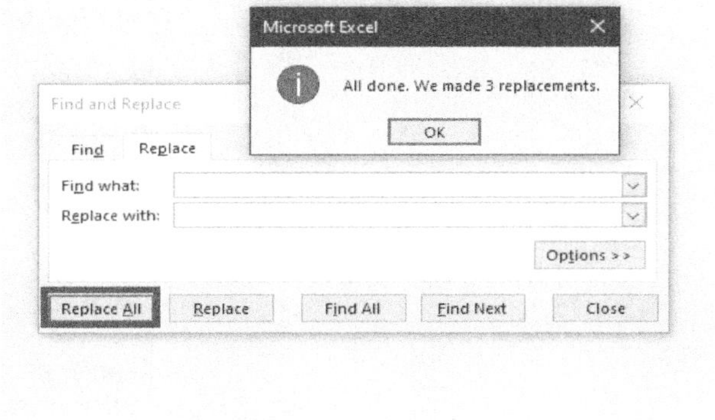

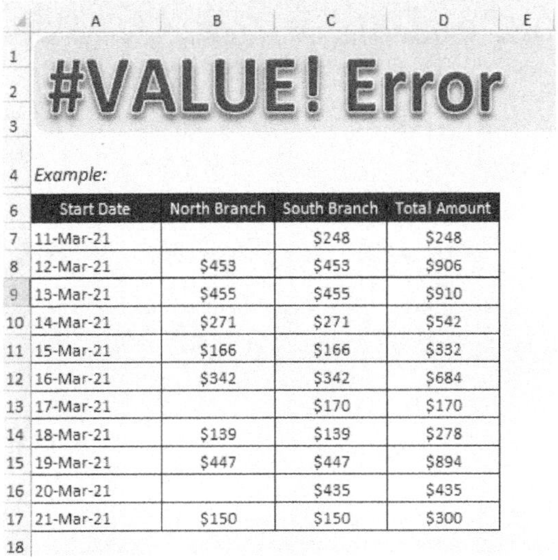

Start Date	North Branch	South Branch	Total Amount
11-Mar-21		$248	$248
12-Mar-21	$453	$453	$906
13-Mar-21	$455	$455	$910
14-Mar-21	$271	$271	$542
15-Mar-21	$166	$166	$332
16-Mar-21	$342	$342	$684
17-Mar-21		$170	$170
18-Mar-21	$139	$139	$278
19-Mar-21	$447	$447	$894
20-Mar-21		$435	$435
21-Mar-21	$150	$150	$300

There will be no more mistakes.

Example 3: Dates stored like the text

Here, you want to calculate the project's end date by adding the duration to the day it began.

If you try to enter this number into cell C7 or C11, you will get a #VALUE! Error because Excel does not recognize it as a date. The reason for this is that the decimal places are used to distinguish the digits of a date.

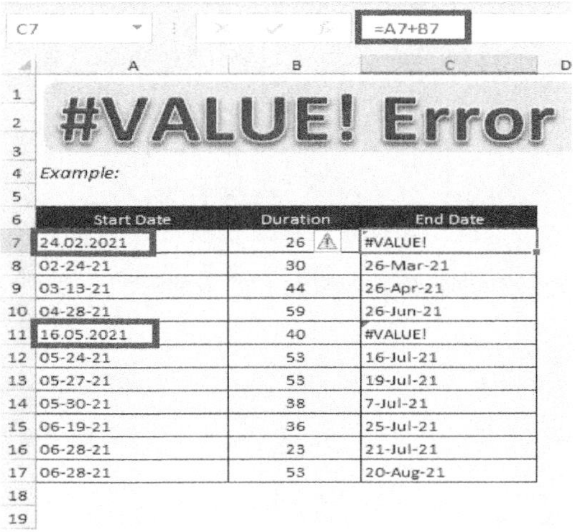

Start Date	Duration	End Date
24.02.2021	26	#VALUE!
02-24-21	30	26-Mar-21
03-13-21	44	26-Apr-21
04-28-21	59	26-Jun-21
16.05.2021	40	#VALUE!
05-24-21	53	16-Jul-21
05-27-21	53	19-Jul-21
05-30-21	38	7-Jul-21
06-19-21	36	25-Jul-21
06-28-21	23	21-Jul-21
06-28-21	53	20-Aug-21

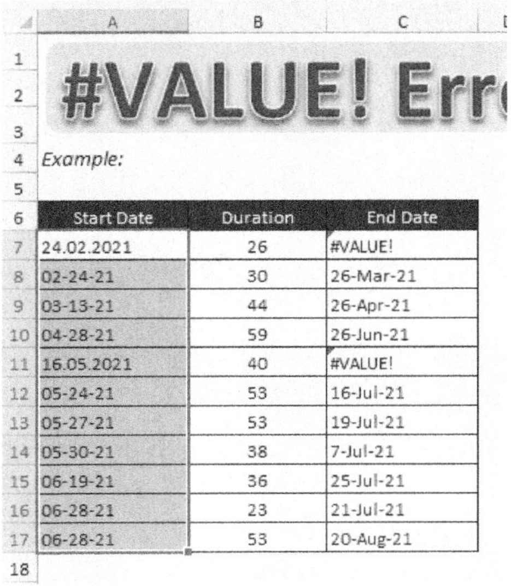

Start Date	Duration	End Date
24.02.2021	26	#VALUE!
02-24-21	30	26-Mar-21
03-13-21	44	26-Apr-21
04-28-21	59	26-Jun-21
16.05.2021	40	#VALUE!
05-24-21	53	16-Jul-21
05-27-21	53	19-Jul-21
05-30-21	38	7-Jul-21
06-19-21	36	25-Jul-21
06-28-21	23	21-Jul-21
06-28-21	53	20-Aug-21

Let's swap the dot with a hyphen as the separator!

First, find the cells that contain dates and select them.

Second, launch the Find and Replace dialogue box by pressing Ctrl+H.

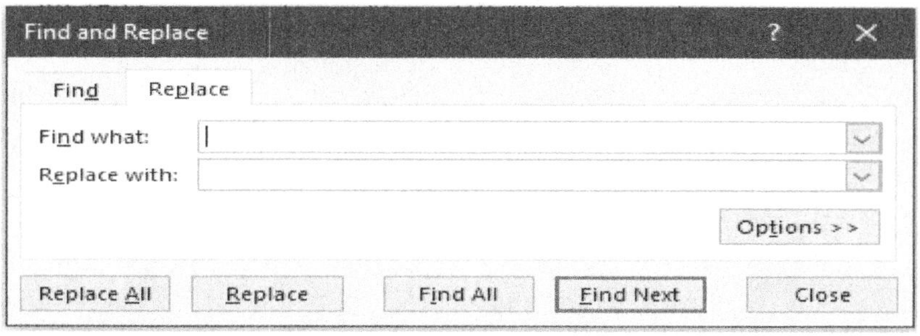

The third step is to enter a hyphen in the Replace With box and a decimal point in the Find What field.

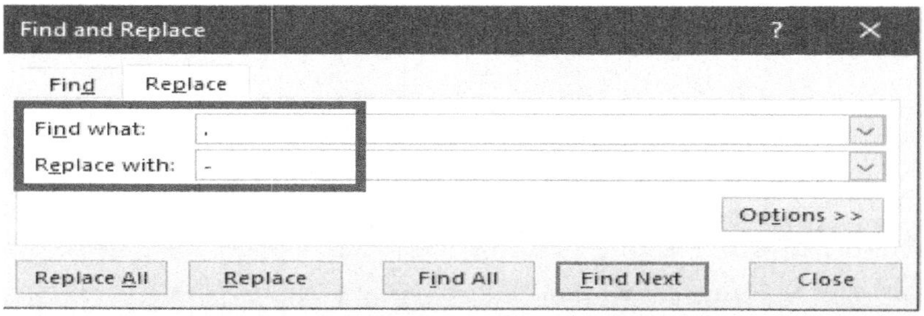

To go to STEP 4, click the Replace All option.

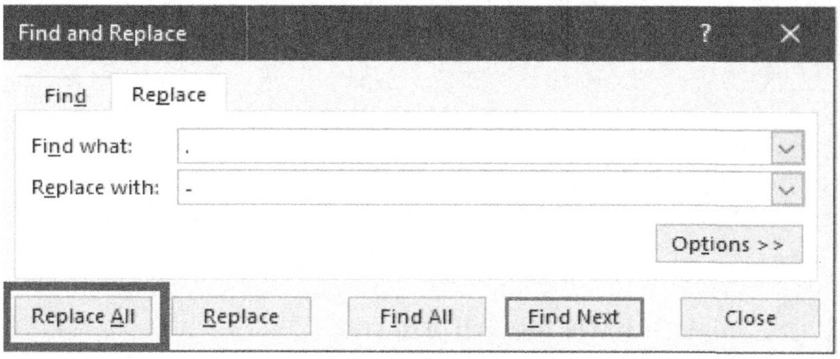

The hyphen will be used instead of the decimal point.

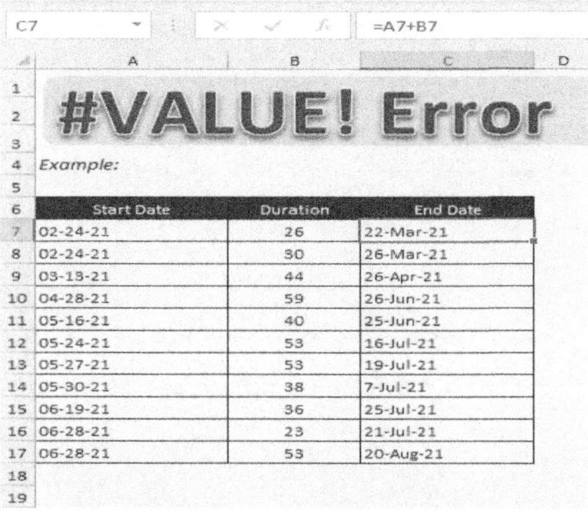

Start Date	Duration	End Date
02-24-21	26	22-Mar-21
02-24-21	30	26-Mar-21
03-13-21	44	26-Apr-21
04-28-21	59	26-Jun-21
05-16-21	40	25-Jun-21
05-24-21	53	16-Jul-21
05-27-21	53	19-Jul-21
05-30-21	38	7-Jul-21
06-19-21	36	25-Jul-21
06-28-21	23	21-Jul-21
06-28-21	53	20-Aug-21

Your calculation will now function flawlessly since Excel is treating them as dates.

In Excel, a value error occurs when the type of the value supplied in the calculation does not match the intended type. And after that value is corrected, the mistake will be gone.

8.5 EXCEL PMT FUNCTION

The PMT function calculates loan payments. Excel users utilize the PMT function to calculate loan payments based on a loan amount, interest rate, and several cycles.

Simple implementation. Enter the PMT() function, your interest rate reduced by 12 (1 year including 12 months), your Term (cycle of the monthly payments), and the Loan Amount.

Consider a Rs 5,000,000 loan for 60 months at 7.8% APR. PMT can compute your monthly payments and how much principal and interest you pay each month.

Syntax

=PMT (rate, PV, [fv], nper, [type])

Example

You loaned XYZ firm $80,000 for two years in the scenario below. The monthly loan payment is 4.5% of the loan balance. PMT function retrieves monthly payments.

Formula:

=PMT (rate, PV, [fv], nper, [type])

The values are:

Amount= 80000

Time(nper) = 2*12 = 24

Rate of the Interest: 4.5 %

[type] = At the start of every period = 1

Applied Formula:

=-PMT (E 4/12, E 5, E 3)

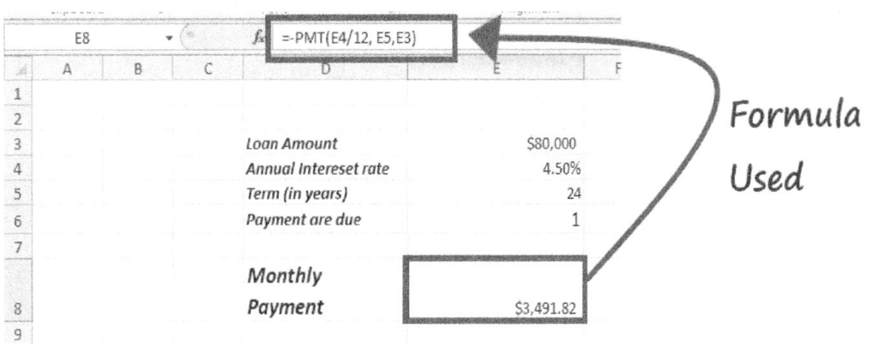

Invest monthly. 2 yrs x 12 (per year contains 12 months) Equals 24 months

The following description states that payments will be made at the start of each month. So [type]=1

Negative numbers reflect outgoing payments, while positive ones represent receiving payments.

Negative output means outgoing payment.

The fetched value includes the principal and interest rate but no stock payments, taxes, or fees.

8.6 XNPV FUNCTION

Excel's XNPV function calculates the net current value of irregular cash flows. Unlike the usual NPV calculation, XNPV lets users specify dates for discounted cash flows.

The XNPV function allows for more flexible date input than the NPV formula, resulting in one more exact computation. Using XNPV, the user specifies cash flows, discount rates, and dates.

XNPV formula:

=XNPV (cash flows, rate, dates of the cash flow)

XNPV Examples

Here are four XNPV Excel examples:

1. Use XNPV to calculate NPV

The XNPV function accounts for a project's net present value. The user wants to know whether the project's npv is higher than zero. A good net present value indicates a positive cash flow, which suggests investing in the project will be profitable. If the project's npv is less than zero, the investor might reject it.

2. Determine end-of-period cash flows

XNPV may also compute end-of-period cash flows. This function is used when a corporation gets its cash on the same day each year. The function requires two arguments. Discount rate and cash flow range are parameters. Since the program assumes organizations compute cash flows just at the end of a month, adapting the method is unnecessary.

3. Determine beginning cash flows

Use XNPV to determine cash flows just at the beginning of a period. For enterprises that gather cash flow annually but before the end of a period, multiply the NPV with one plus its discount rate. The program assumes enterprises get cash flows just at the end of the term; therefore, altering the function lets you compute cash flows from the start. This change improves function.

4. Calculate the cash flows using XNPV

XNPV calculates cash flows at various times. While a typical NPV calculation confines cash flow calculations to specified periods, an XNPV formula allows greater flexibility and accuracy. Applying XNPV to distinct cash flows requires three factors. Parameters include discount rate, cash flow series, and date range.

CHAPTER 9

EXCEL FOR BUSINESS

May you explain how Microsoft Excel can be helpful in a business setting? Microsoft Excel has a wide variety of commercial applications. However, we have simplified the issue by compiling a list of the top 10.

Microsoft Excel is used for basic data storage, analysis, and reporting. Spreadsheets are widely used in the corporate world because of their accessibility and visual nature.

Excel is globally used in the corporate world for various purposes, including data analysis, HR management, performance reporting, and inventory and supply chain administration. This is a proven truth based on examining employment records (using MS Excel).

9.1 BUSINESS ANALYSIS

Photo by Rawpixel.com - Freepik.com

Doing business analysis is by far MS Excel's most popular usage in the office.

The goal of any good business analysis is to help guide management in making informed choices. Every aspect of a company's operations generates data, whether it is about sales, internet traffic, supply costs, insurance claims, etc.

Performing a business analysis entails transforming information into a form that the company's management can use. For instance, you may break down your profits by day of the week. Decisions might be based on data like whether or if Sundays are consistently bad for business (including closing over Sundays).

Job examples: Finance Business Analysts, Claims Analysts, Investment Operation Portfolio Analysts, Collections Analysts, Junior Data Analysts, Senior Data Analysts, Senior Finance Analysts, Regional Finance Analysts, Senior Portfolio Analysts, Credit Officers, and many more.

9.2 PEOPLE MANAGEMENT

Photo by Rawpixel.com - Freepik.com

Human resource management is one of the most surprising ways Excel is used in a business. Data on individuals may be efficiently organized in Microsoft Excel, whether they are workers, clients, supporters, or training participants.

Information about yourself may be safely saved and quickly accessed using Excel. Each row or column in a spreadsheet represents a unique record, which could contain details such as a person's email address, name, hire date, subscription status, first purchase, and most recent contact.

Job example: client management and administrations, client growth coordinators, client service managers, client relationship managers, employer service consultants, HR administrators, client service specialists, HR administrative assistants, HR administrators, HR advisers, junior HR analysts, HR officers, reconciliation & payments officers, relationship manager.

9.3 MANAGING OPERATIONS

Photo by Dcstudio - Freepik.com

Excel plays a crucial role in the day-to-day management of many enterprises.

Managing the logistics of business operations is not always a simple task. Managing inventory flow is essential for ensuring the continuity of business operations and avoiding the needless accumulation of stock. That includes noting important dates, managing timeframes and schedules, and keeping a record of customer and supplier transactions.

While Amazon employs high-end, specialized software to run its operations, many small firms rely on Microsoft Excel (or part of the larger businesses).

It doesn't rely too much on cutting-edge technology, so a wide audience may use Excel without worrying about introducing any nagging flaws.

Job examples: data operations managers, business operations analysts, graduate programs – supply chain & operations, within market's supply chain analysts, operational enablement associates, operational business analysts, operational knowledge of management specialists, supply chain specialists, supply chain associates.

9.4 PERFORMANCE REPORTING

As a subset of business analysis, operation reporting and monitoring are well suited to the spreadsheet program Microsoft Excel.

Even though there is cloud-based accounting software, many accountants continue to utilize Excel. Creating a pivot table in Excel is a standard method for transforming raw data into a useful report on performance. If you connect your data to a pivot table, you may rapidly extract more insights. Many predefined operations, including counting & summing, are incorporated into pivot tables.

Job examples: forecast analysts / sales support, financial accountants, performance analysts, performance analysts – procurement, reporting analysts, professional service operation analysts, reporting development analysts, sales coordinators, and sales operations analysts.

9.5 OFFICE ADMINISTRATION

Office administrators recognize Excel's value since the program records and preserve crucial administrative information. Accounting, business analysis, financial reporting, & performance reporting may all benefit from using the same data. Office administration duties like invoicing, bill payment, or contacting customers and suppliers may all be facilitated using Excel, proving Excel's use beyond record keeping. Office activity management has never been easier with this all-in-one application.

Job example: administration officers, administration assistants, administration supervisors, administrative assistants, business operations & office managers, junior clerical & administrative officers, office admin managers, office support – general duties / maintenance.

9.6 STRATEGIC ANALYSIS

Photo by Rawpixel.com - Freepik.com

Strategic analysis is one use of Excel in which data and formulae play an essential role in corporate decisions. You use Excel as a reference for financial investments and portfolio distributions.

You may, for instance, choose to get foreign exchange insurance after analyzing several scenarios in an Excel spreadsheet. Analyzing data in a spreadsheet is intended to help with certain corporate decision-making.

Job examples: mergers & acquisitions valuations – analysts, membership & campaigns strategists, asset managers – realty management divisions, portfolio administration associates, portfolio analysts, portfolio associates – wealth management, portfolio management officers – asset finance.

9.7 PROJECT MANAGEMENT

While dedicated project management software is available, a project manager may find that a simple Excel Workbook does the job.

Business projects are endeavors planned out in advance and have defined beginning and ending points. A workbook may store project plans and subsequently monitor and maintain adherence to those plans and deadlines. The project worksheet may be readily shared with other individuals, even those who are not acquainted with or do not have access to specialized PM software, which is one of the many benefits of utilizing Excel.

Job example: project analysts, project assistants / officers (IT), project business analysts.

9.8 MANAGING PROGRAMS

It's easy to organize and keep track of several apps using Excel. Depending on the requirements of certain software, it may be modified accordingly.

In addition, since MS Excel is so common, several individuals may manage program documentation at once and, when the time comes, transfer to new management with no difficulty. A program is like a project, except it may execute indefinitely and often relies on input from its target audience. Managers may use Microsoft Excel to distribute funds, monitor progress, & keep track of employees.

Job examples: learning & development officers, event coordinators, learning & development coordinators, managers – internships, programs & office coordinators, records & results coordinators, and training administrators.

9.9 CONTRACT ADMINISTRATION

Contract administrators often use Microsoft Excel because it allows for an easy method of documenting the many aspects of a contract, such as the dates of key events, major deliverables, and payments.

There are several contract management templates to choose from, and each may be modified to fit a unique set of circumstances.

Job example: building contract administrators, contracts administrators, estimators / contracts administrators, graduate contracts administrators, lease administrators, quote & tender administrators.

9.10 ACCOUNT MANAGEMENT

Account managers are expected to have a solid grasp of Microsoft Excel since they will be the recipients and custodians of sensitive client data.

An account manager's primary responsibility is maintaining connections with the company's current clientele. Loyalty and return business from existing clients are two objectives worth focusing on. The job requires marketing skills and is a common choice for MBA graduates.

Excel is often used in account administration since it facilitates easy file sharing and upkeep.

Job example: account coordinators, advertising managers, design studio account managers, digital account managers, and junior account managers.

9.11 REASONS WHY YOU REQUIRE TO KNOW EXCEL FOR WORK

Skills in Microsoft Excel are highly sought after by employers, as this list should have shown.

The usage of Excel is not ubiquitous, and the occupations that use it are often those that require a "middle-skill" level of proficiency. However, Excel has widespread use. Therefore, you may do a wide variety of things if you know how to use a spreadsheet well. Information provided in workbooks is also easier to extract value from. Learning Excel will lead to increased productivity once you begin using it. It's a user-friendly system capable of handling elementary and complex corporate operations.

9.12 BONUS 1: WHY READING THIS BOOK CAN HELP YOU GET A BETTER JOB AND ADVANCE IN YOUR CAREER

A common question is why so many of you rely on Excel. There comes a moment in every professional's life when they must utilize Excel. Excel is a necessary tool for filling out job applications, writing job descriptions, and meeting employment requirements. However, Excel stands out from the crowd, and here are seven reasons you must improve your Excel skills now more than ever.

- **One, Many businesses and private organizations are seeking someone with advanced Excel knowledge and expertise.**

Major corporations shell out a lot of cash to get Microsoft operating system licenses & Microsoft office suite software licenses. It's excellent that Windows tools provide the foundation for so many professional productivity skills. You live in the technological era, and Excel plays a significant role in this period.

- **Two, Excel is the universal language**

Excel is a need in every professional setting. Spreadsheets are used at all levels of the company for decision-making. Excel may be used internally, externally, across international boundaries, and globally.

To solve problems, Excel is more than simply a spreadsheet. Many professions benefit from its use, including accounting, financial analysis, science, and others. In what ways does it differ from a standard spreadsheet? There's nothing wrong with that but remember that this just scratches the surface of its potential. Can you imagine without using Excel's incredible capabilities?

- **Three: make more time**

In the end, you can't get that time back. More may be accomplished by those who invest time and effort into improving their Excel skills. You can cut hours off your daily responsibilities and get more done with the help of Excel once you start utilizing it to solve issues and discover answers. More time for personal growth and contributing to team growth is a nice side effect.

- **Four, Excel will be around to stay**

Excel has a lengthy life expectancy. Large organizations will find switching to other spreadsheet software difficult and expensive. And what will be a decent replacement for that? Excel is deeply embedded in your work culture & can communicate with a wide variety of other programs.

Data, Both Small and Large The term "data" describes a set of numerical or tally-based facts and figures for reference or analysis. Companies are investing heavily in Content Relationships Management (CRM)

& database systems to keep up with the massive data growth in the previous several years. Collecting information, examining it thoughtfully, and arriving at a conclusion that can be presented to decision-makers is essential. The capacity to organize, analyze, evaluate and present data is crucial to the success of any business. Information may be found everywhere and in infinite quantities. Avoid falling behind.

- **Five, As an analytical sketchpad**

Excel is a very sophisticated program for statistical analysis and data management. Excel may be adapted to accommodate every imaginable reporting need related to metrics, inventory, finances, or budgeting.

- **Six, Connecting for mutual benefit**

The greatest approach to networking and getting relevant information is via a spreadsheet. Yes, you can learn Excel on the job, but many employers either don't care or don't have the time to educate their staff. You'll be more desirable as an employee and save your company a ton of time if you arrive prepared with advanced Excel skills. With your Excel skills, you may significantly contribute to the company.

Being proficient in Excel increases your marketability.

Having expertise in Excel is a significant plus for any resume since it exemplifies a wide range of relevant abilities. Do you ever question whether learning Excel is worth it? Can you use your skills in different settings? The ability to work with spreadsheet formulas and functions is valuable.

Excel's Power Tools: Pivot Tables, VLOOKUP, Conditional Formatting, Macros, VBA, Charts, and Filters These demonstrate your skills far better than being able to write Excel in the eyes of a potential employer. A hiring manager's doubts about a candidate's analytical prowess may be allayed by examples of Pivot Table, VLOOKUP, & Filtering in the candidate's cover letter and resume. In the same way that including "Excel" on your resume demonstrates your proficiency with the program, listing "Pivot Table" demonstrates your ability to use Excel to analyze data automatically.

- **Seven, Income growth is positively correlated with increased proficiency in Excel**;

as one's ability to use Excel to contribute to an organization grows, so does one's ability to command a salary commensurate with that growth.

Excel is an immensely powerful program, yet it has certain limitations. Enhancing your Excel skills can help you stand out as an expert in any workplace and advance in your chosen field.

With the knowledge in this book, Excel has no more secrets, and it will be easier to get the career you want.

CHAPTER 10

EXCEL FOR THE FAMILY

Putting together a family budget may be daunting and time-consuming, but Excel's array of budgeting templates can ease the burden and help you stay on track.

If you don't use Excel daily, creating a budget in it may seem like a huge challenge. Thank goodness, a budget template may be easily created in Excel without the help of a professional accountant.

This detailed instruction will show you how to make a budget using Excel, which can be easily modified to fit your family's specific requirements, no matter how basic or complicated. Start by creating your budget spreadsheet by following these steps!

10.1 USING PRE-MADE TEMPLATES TO CREATE A BUDGET WITH EXCEL

It's no secret that rising inflation has made life a living hell for many people in terms of their finances. Since many individuals have lost their employment and others have seen a significant decrease in their monthly income, establishing a reliable budget is more crucial than ever.

Technology may be a big asset if used properly. Today, you can find hundreds of different pieces of software and applications that help you manage your finances. Finding a course of study tailored to your specific requirements might be difficult.

Excel, please. Making a spreadsheet for your budget in Microsoft Excel has always been a great option. If you're already paying for Microsoft services, you won't have to pay through the nose to get started.

Using one of Excel's many built-in budget templates is the quickest and most efficient method to create a budget in Excel. Using one of the software's budget templates is recommended as a jumping-off point if you're unsure what to put in your budget.

Upon launching the software, choose File ➔ New ➔ Budget. Several different budget templates in Excel, including family budgets, personal spending calculators, vacation budgets, and so on, will appear.

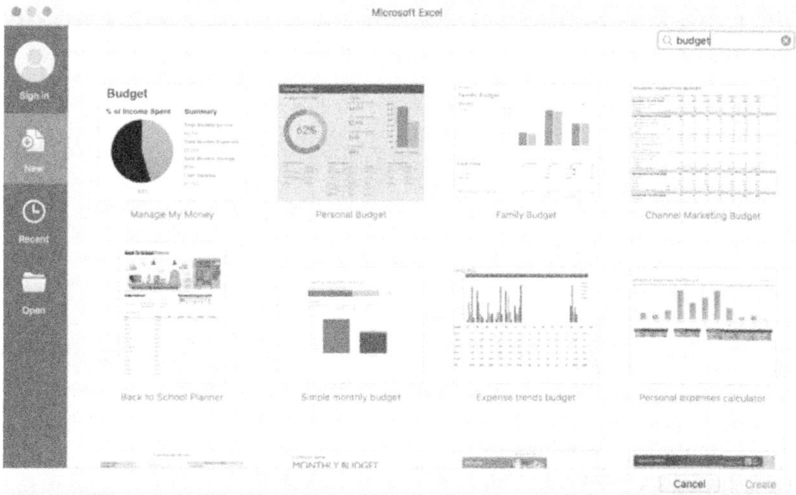

For illustration, if you use the family budget document, you would receive a preformatted spreadsheet with a Cash Flow diagram on the first tab. The family name & budget title may be updated here, but any formulas should be left alone. The fx input box will display "=Income[[#Totals], [Projected]]" if the "7,200" is selected. If you tinker with Excel's formulae, you might throw off the automated calculations that make the program so user-friendly.

The other two sections, "Monthly Income" & "Monthly Expenses," are where you'll fill in your information. Income and expenses are instantly updated in the Cash Flow section as you enter them here.

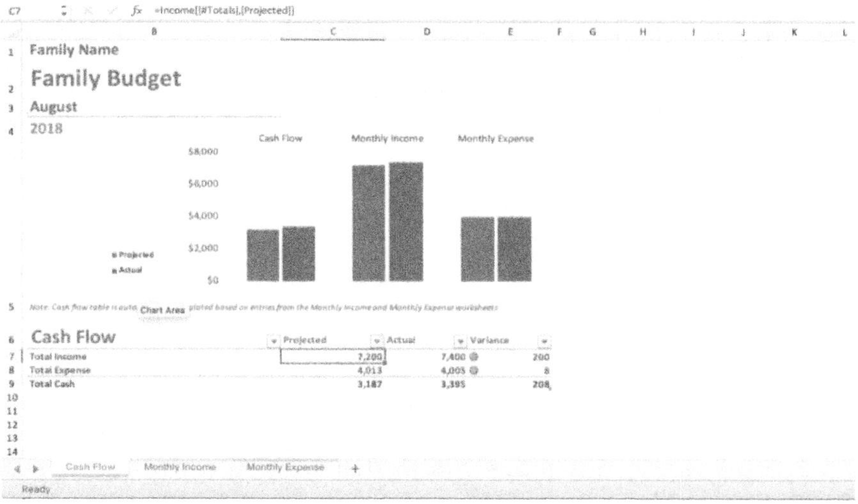

10.2 CUSTOMIZING THE PREMADE TEMPLATE

Right-click the area where you'd want to insert a new box into the current template. To insert a table, choose "Table Columns to the Left" or "Table Rows Above" from the Insert menu. New data should update itself in the current tabs mechanically. Assuming it doesn't, you may add the new columns to the projections by clicking the arrow keys next to the "Projected" column.

You may also remove unnecessary parts if you want to. Right-click your Monthly Expenses tab, pick "Delete," & then "Table Rows" if you no longer want to see the loans row.

This is as easy as it sounds!

10.3 CREATING THE BUDGET SPREADSHEETS: HELPFUL HINTS

Using Excel, you may create a monthly budget spreadsheet and store it as a template. If you have all your financial data in one place, such as earnings, expenditures, savings, etc., you may copy and paste the relevant boxes onto a new page. Change the sheet's name to reflect the new month. This is an excellent method for keeping track of one's financial transactions over a full year inside a single Excel spreadsheet. Make a fresh calculation at the year's end to total your income, expenses, and savings for the year.

Excel's built-in calculation capabilities make math a breeze. After discussing basic arithmetic operations, you will now provide the corresponding formulae for multiplication & division.

- **Multiplication:** To multiply a number in a particular cell, enter "=" and the cell's corresponding number. Follow that by clicking the cell containing the second number you would like to multiply it by, typing "*," and then clicking out. At last, press the enter key. That "=F5*H50" thing is just an example.
- **Division:** To divide a number, enter "=" and the cell number where the division should take place. Then, finish in the cell containing the other integer you want to divide by typing "/." At last, press the enter key. Use "=E15/A10" as an example.

Take the case of wanting the totals tallied on the bottom row. Dressing the formula across a row is faster than inputting it individually into each column. To achieve this, type the formula inside one cell, select the cell where the sum appears, and then drag a green box to include the rest of the worksheet. It is that easy.

Make Excel Your Own

Although I taught you how to create a budget using Excel in this chapter, you are not restricted to only those features. Every aspect of your financial life may be accounted for with a few clicks and keystrokes in Excel. If you want to track the vacation budget, debt repayment, holiday spending, and other financial goals, you shouldn't be frightened to make a brand-new budget spreadsheet.

Becoming acquainted with Excel is important since it may be a powerful tool for changing your spending patterns. After initial setup, the automated calculations in the Excel budget templates might be more convenient than budgeting with a pen and paper. Once you've entered the necessary information into the required fields, the remainder will populate automatically. Plus, with just some clicks, you may see your budget information for several months (or years).

Okay, now for the good part: If you don't want to, you can stop your education with this book. Don't feel like you need to become an Excel guru; sticking to a basic Excel budget template will do wonders for money management. You should be good if you only follow these instructions and ignore Excel's other features and settings. Still confused about where to begin with a budget. This comprehensive budgeting chapter will show you how to plan by projecting your monthly income and spending and creating a budget that costs you nothing. Click on the link to find out more.

In creating your Excel budget, this book might serve as a guide. Kind regards, and I appreciate you taking the time to read this.

CHAPTER 11

PROBLEM MANAGEMENT IN EXCEL

Several methods for problem management in databases are covered in this chapter. Hopefully, this guide will teach you some useful techniques for speeding up the process of removing duplicates, helper columns, password protection, and data validation in Excel.

11.1 DUPLICATE REMOVAL

Despite the program's widespread use, identifying and eradicating duplicate data in Microsoft Excel may be perplexing.

When dealing with large datasets, removing duplicates is an Excel operation. You may have duplicate entries in the spreadsheet if you merge several tables or if many persons have accessibility to the same document.

This information is thus redundant. There are more likely to be duplicated in a bigger dataset.

When they're not properly discovered and dealt with, they might cause problems.

We'll use a sample sports dataset to demonstrate how to eliminate duplicates in Excel.

The 2012 Olympic medal winners are documented in this data collection.

	A	B	C	D	E
1	Year	Sport	Athlete	Country	Medal
2	2012	Wrestling	Artur TAYMAZOV	UZB	Gold
3	2012	Wrestling	Davit MODZMANASHVILI	GEO	Silver
4	2012	Wrestling	Komeil GHASEMI	IRI	Bronze
5	2012	Volleyball	Martins PLAVINS	LAT	Bronze
6	2012	Volleyball	Julius BRINK	GER	Gold
7	2012	Volleyball	Alison CERUTTI	BRA	Silver
8	2012	Volleyball	Martins PLAVINS	LAT	Bronze
9	2012	Wrestling	Davit MODZMANASHVILI	GEO	Silver

Removing duplicate values within excel

Excel's built-in feature for removing duplicates from data collection is quite useful. Let's check out the Excel procedure for eliminating duplicates.

First, choose the data from which you wish to eliminate duplicates by clicking on a single cell or a range of cells. If you choose just one cell, Excel will figure out your range.

	A	B	C	D	E
1	Year	Sport	Athlete	Country	Medal
2	2012	Wrestling	Artur TAYMAZOV	UZB	Gold
3	2012	Wrestling	Davit MODZMANASHVILI	GEO	Silver
4	2012	Wrestling	Komeil GHASEMI	IRI	Bronze
5	2012	Volleyball	Martins PLAVINS	LAT	Bronze
6	2012	Volleyball	Julius BRINK	GER	Gold
7	2012	Volleyball	Alison CERUTTI	BRA	Silver
8	2012	Volleyball	Martins PLAVINS	LAT	Bronze
9	2012	Wrestling	Davit MODZMANASHVILI	GEO	Silver

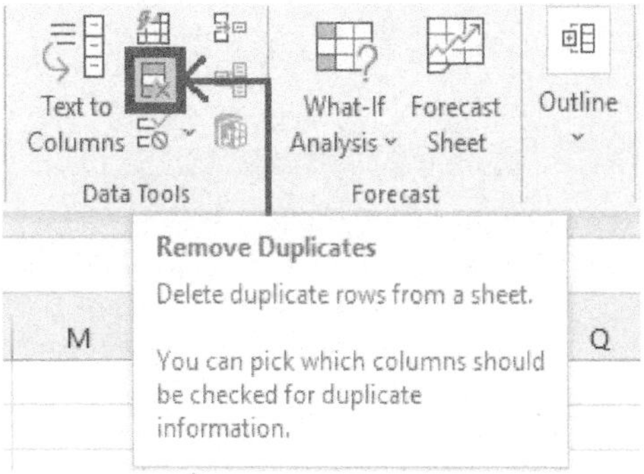

The second step is to find the "Remove Duplicates" option and click on it.

DATA tab ➔ Data Tool section ➔ Remove Duplicates

Third, you'll see a dialogue box like the one seen above. It's up to you to decide which columns to use for the comparison and whether to look for duplicates.

If your information contains column headings, check the box labeled "My data has headers" & then press the "OK" button.

Selecting the header option causes the first row to be ignored while searching for and deleting duplicates.

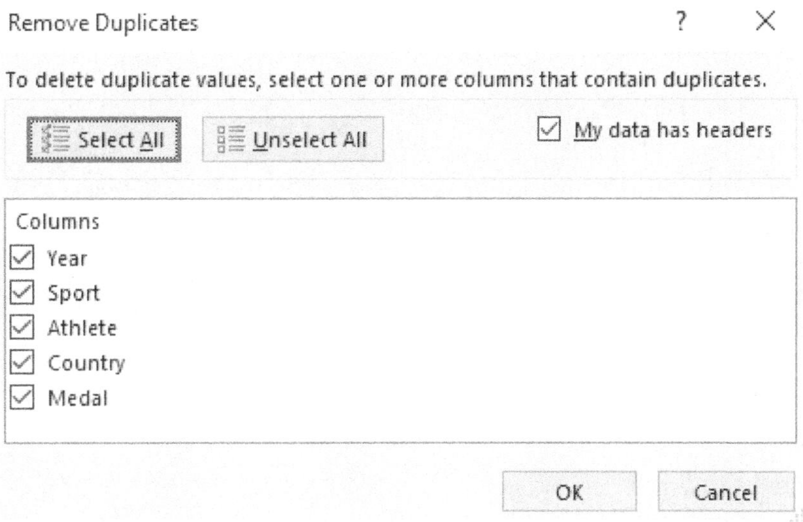

At this point, Excel will prompt you to confirm the deletion of the duplicate rows before removing them. The number of unique values and the total number of duplicates detected and deleted are both shown in the summary section of the dialogue box.

	A	B	C	D	E
1	Year	Sport	Athlete	Country	Medal
2	2012	Wrestling	Artur TAYMAZOV	UZB	Gold
3	2012	Wrestling	Davit MODZMANASHVILI	GEO	Silver
4	2012	Wrestling	Komeil GHASEMI	IRI	Bronze
5	2012	Volleyball	Martins PLAVINS	LAT	Bronze
6	2012	Volleyball	Julius BRINK	GER	Gold
7	2012	Volleyball	Alison CERUTTI	BRA	Silver
8					
9					
10					

In Step 5, you can see that the duplicates have been eliminated

Let's go on and learn how to use Excel's Advanced Filter to get rid of duplicates.

Using the Advanced Filter Options

By using Excel's Advanced Filter feature, you may eliminate duplicates and save just the relevant data. See the details below to learn how to use the Advanced Filter function.

To begin removing duplicates, choose the cells or range of cells in the dataset you wish to work with. When you choose Advanced Filter in Excel, the range is determined mechanically based on the cells you've clicked on.

	A	B	C	D	E
1	Year	Sport	Athlete	Country	Medal
2	2012	Wrestling	Artur TAYMAZOV	UZB	Gold
3	2012	Wrestling	Davit MODZMANASHVILI	GEO	Silver
4	2012	Wrestling	Komeil GHASEMI	IRI	Bronze
5	2012	Volleyball	Martins PLAVINS	LAT	Bronze
6	2012	Volleyball	Julius BRINK	GER	Gold
7	2012	Volleyball	Alison CERUTTI	BRA	Silver
8	2012	Volleyball	Martins PLAVINS	LAT	Bronze
9	2012	Wrestling	Davit MODZMANASHVILI	GEO	Silver

Find the menu item labeled "Advanced Filter."

DATA tab ➔ Filter & Sort section → Advanced & click on this option.

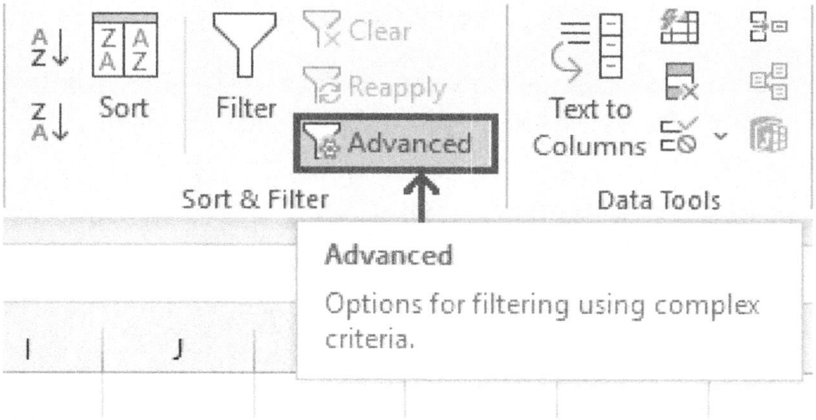

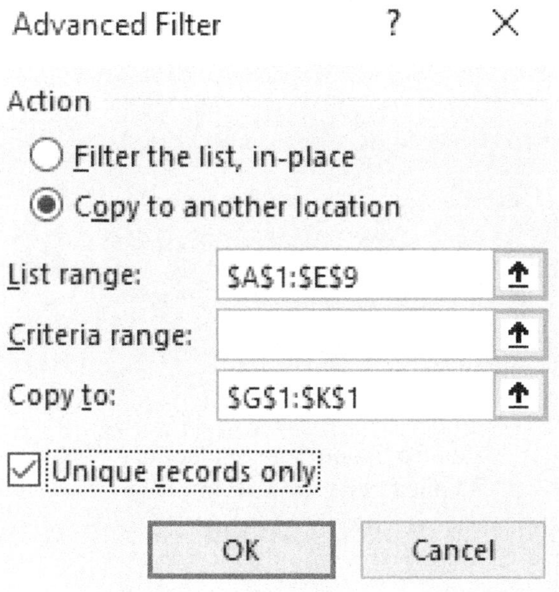

A dialogue window will pop up. There's a menu of refined filtering choices. Click the "Copy to another location" button to save the one-of-a-kind values in another area.

Be sure that the extent of the records matches the one you entered in the 'List Range' column.

Enter the range you want to copy the unique values generated in the 'Copy to:' box.

Make sure the option labeled "Unique records only" is checked. This is the most important stage.

It's safe to proceed by clicking OK.

Cell G1 will get the original values.

	A	B	C	D	E	F	G	H	I	J	K
1	Year	Sport	Athlete	Country	Medal		Year	Sport	Athlete	Country	Medal
2	2012	Wrestling	Artur TAYMAZOV	UZB	Gold		2012	Wrestling	Artur TAYMAZOV	UZB	Gold
3	2012	Wrestling	Davit MODZMANASHVILI	GEO	Silver		2012	Wrestling	Davit MODZMANASHVILI	GEO	Silver
4	2012	Wrestling	Komeil GHASEMI	IRI	Bronze		2012	Wrestling	Komeil GHASEMI	IRI	Bronze
5	2012	Volleyball	Martins PLAVINS	LAT	Bronze		2012	Volleyball	Martins PLAVINS	LAT	Bronze
6	2012	Volleyball	Julius BRINK	GER	Gold		2012	Volleyball	Julius BRINK	GER	Gold
7	2012	Volleyball	Alison CERUTTI	BRA	Silver		2012	Volleyball	Alison CERUTTI	BRA	Silver
8	2012	Volleyball	Martins PLAVINS	LAT	Bronze						
9	2012	Wrestling	Davit MODZMANASHVILI	GEO	Silver						
10											

These were the native features of Excel that assisted in eliminating duplicates. Let's go on and figure out how to implement our function that does the same thing.

Excel Duplicate Data Removal: How can you do this using formula?

To illustrate this method, you will use a sample data set with only three columns: athlete's name, sport, and medal count.

	A	B	C
1	Sport	Athlete	Medal
2	Wrestling	Artur TAYMAZOV	Gold
3	Wrestling	Davit MODZMANASHVILI	Silver
4	Wrestling	Komeil GHASEMI	Bronze
5	Volleyball	Martins PLAVINS	Bronze
6	Volleyball	Julius BRINK	Gold
7	Volleyball	Alison CERUTTI	Silver
8	Volleyball	Martins PLAVINS	Bronze
9	Wrestling	Davit MODZMANASHVILI	Silver

This approach includes utilizing an Excel formula to combine the columns and calculate the total.

Then, we'll exclude the paired data via filtering (ones with a count of more than 1).

You may join columns A, B, & C together by using the "&" concatenation operator. For this reason, the appropriate Excel formula is:

=A2&B2&C2

After entering the formula into cell D2, it will be duplicated down through each row.

D2 =A2&B2&C2

	A	B	C	D
1	Sport	Athlete	Medal	Combined
2	Wrestling	Artur TAYMAZOV	Gold	WrestlingArtur TAYMAZOVGold
3	Wrestling	Davit MODZMANASHVILI	Silver	WrestlingDavit MODZMANASHVILISilver
4	Wrestling	Komeil GHASEMI	Bronze	WrestlingKomeil GHASEMIBronze
5	Volleyball	Martins PLAVINS	Bronze	VolleyballMartins PLAVINSBronze
6	Volleyball	Julius BRINK	Gold	VolleyballJulius BRINKGold
7	Volleyball	Alison CERUTTI	Silver	VolleyballAlison CERUTTISilver
8	Volleyball	Martins PLAVINS	Bronze	VolleyballMartins PLAVINSBronze
9	Wrestling	Davit MODZMANASHVILI	Silver	WrestlingDavit MODZMANASHVILISilver

To identify the redundant entries in Column D, you need to add a new column labeled "Count." So, you'll implement the COUNTIF formula in E2. The equation is as follows:

=COUNTIF ($D$2: D2, D2)

Utilizing this technique, you can determine how many times each value appears in column D.

E2 =COUNTIF(D$2:D2,D2)

	A	B	C	D	E
1	Sport	Athlete	Medal	Combined	Count
2	Wrestling	Artur TAYMAZOV	Gold	WrestlingArtur TAYMAZOVGold	1
3	Wrestling	Davit MODZMANASHVILI	Silver	WrestlingDavit MODZMANASHVILISilver	1
4	Wrestling	Komeil GHASEMI	Bronze	WrestlingKomeil GHASEMIBronze	1
5	Volleyball	Martins PLAVINS	Bronze	VolleyballMartins PLAVINSBronze	1
6	Volleyball	Julius BRINK	Gold	VolleyballJulius BRINKGold	1
7	Volleyball	Alison CERUTTI	Silver	VolleyballAlison CERUTTISilver	1
8	Volleyball	Martins PLAVINS	Bronze	VolleyballMartins PLAVINSBronze	2
9	Wrestling	Davit MODZMANASHVILI	Silver	WrestlingDavit MODZMANASHVILISilver	2

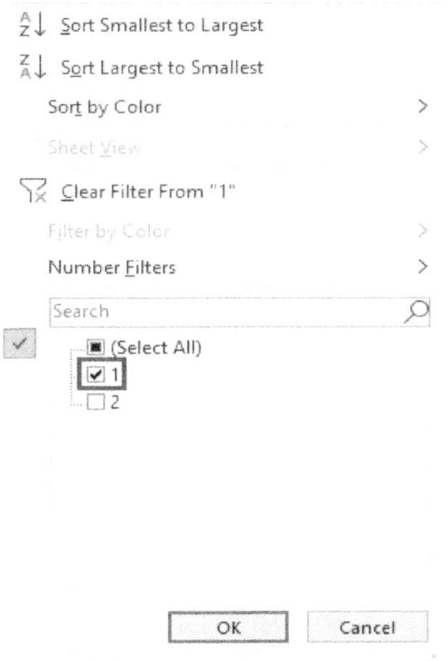

A count of "1" indicates that this item has only ever existed once. A duplicate value has a value of "2" or above.

Select the Filter option to apply a filter to a Count column.

On the DATA tab, under Sort & Filter, click Filter.

To apply a filter, choose it in Column E's header. Choose "1" to discard all except the unique entries.

The table's duplicate entries will be deleted when you click the OK button. The resulting one-of-a-kind records may be copied and pasted.

	A	B	C	D	E
1	Sport	Athlete	Medal	Combined	Count
2	Wrestling	Artur TAYMAZOV	Gold	WrestlingArtur TAYMAZOVGold	
3	Wrestling	Davit MODZMANASHVILI	Silver	WrestlingDavit MODZMANASHVILISilver	1
4	Wrestling	Komeil GHASEMI	Bronze	WrestlingKomeil GHASEMIBronze	1
5	Volleyball	Martins PLAVINS	Bronze	VolleyballMartins PLAVINSBronze	1
6	Volleyball	Julius BRINK	Gold	VolleyballJulius BRINKGold	1
7	Volleyball	Alison CERUTTI	Silver	VolleyballAlison CERUTTISilver	1
10					

The last method for eliminating duplicates is as follows. Power Query has been implemented.

Excel Duplicate Data Removal Using Power Query

When using Excel's Power Query feature, you may gather information from several sources, then modify, clean, & import it. Using this tool, removing duplicates in Excel is a breeze.

Select the cells or range you want to work with, then go to the Data tab and choose the From Table/Range option under the Get and Transform Data subheading.

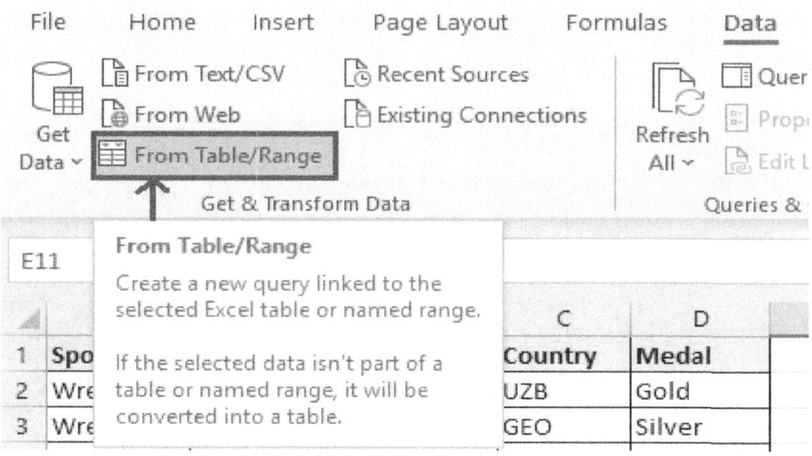

A window to create a "power query table" will pop up when you do this. Verify that the value range has been provided accurately. It's safe to proceed by clicking OK.

The Power Query editors window looks like this when you click the button.

You may choose one of two paths now. These criteria may be used to filter out duplicates:

- The use of any number of columns
- Complete table

Duplicates may be eliminated based on the contents of a single column or many columns by using the Delete Duplicates from... option in the context menu. Pressing the Control (CTRL) key simultaneously allows you to select several columns and efficiently eliminate duplicates.

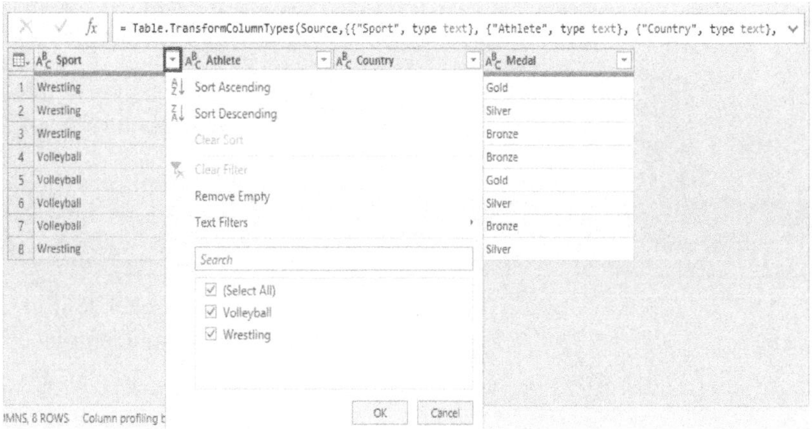

Select the button in the upper left corner of a data preview to eliminate any duplicates in the table. And after that, click the "Remove Duplicates" button.

Consequently, the information will be devoid of any occurrences of repetition.

= Table.TransformColumnTypes(Source,{{"Sport", type text}, {"Athlete", type text}, {"Country", type text},

	Sport	Athlete	Country	Medal
1	Wrestling	Artur TAYMAZOV	UZB	Gold
2	Wrestling	Davit MODZMANASHVILI	GEO	Silver
3	Wrestling	Komeil GHASEMI	IRI	Bronze
4	Volleyball	Martins PLAVINS	LAT	Bronze
5	Volleyball	Julius BRINK	GER	Gold
6	Volleyball	Alison CERUTTI	BRA	Silver
7	Volleyball	Martins PLAVINS	LAT	Bronze
8	Wrestling	Davit MODZMANASHVILI	GEO	Silver

Use the "Close & Load" button to transfer the information to your spreadsheet.

11.2 HELPER COLUMN

An Excel "helper column" is a column introduced to the data set for the sole purpose of streamlining the processing of certain computations or analyses. In Excel, a "helper column" is a column that is used to simplify formulae.

Illustration of a Criteria-Aided Column Vlookup

Find attached a table with a few of your staff members. You want to negotiate a pay comparable to that of Rahul, a senior analyst.

	A	B	C	D
1	Source Table			
2	Name	Designation	Joining Date	Salary
3	Riya	Analyst	Friday, July 20, 2018	Rs. 180,705.00
4	Raju	Manager	Wednesday, November 08, 2017	Rs. 82,371.00
5	Ramesh	Analyst	Saturday, February 27, 2016	Rs. 105,347.00
6	Rahul	Asst. Manage	Tuesday, September 04, 2018	Rs. 180,347.00
7	Rahul	Sr. Analyst	Saturday, August 26, 2017	Rs. 116,931.00

You can use a single VLOOKUP formula to do this, but a companion column will make your life much simpler.

You create a helper column in the table that concatenates Name & Designation, then utilize it as a lookup column.

I4 =VLOOKUP(G4&H4,C3:E7,3,0)

	A	B	C	D	E	F	G	H	I
1	Source Table								
2	Name	Designation	Helper	Joining Date	Salary				
3	Riya	Analyst	RiyaAnalyst	Friday, July 20, 2018	Rs. 180,705.00		Name	Designation	Salary
4	Raju	Manager	RajuManager	Wednesday, November 08, 2017	Rs. 82,371.00		Rahul	Sr. Analyst	116931
5	Ramesh	Analyst	RameshAnal	Saturday, February 27, 2016	Rs. 105,347.00				
6	Rahul	Asst. Manage	RahulAsst. M	Tuesday, September 04, 2018	Rs. 180,347.00				
7	Rahul	Sr. Analyst	RahulSr. Ana	Saturday, August 26, 2017	Rs. 116,931.00				
8									
9			=CONCATENATE(A3,B3)						

Excel charts often use "Helper Columns" to include additional features.

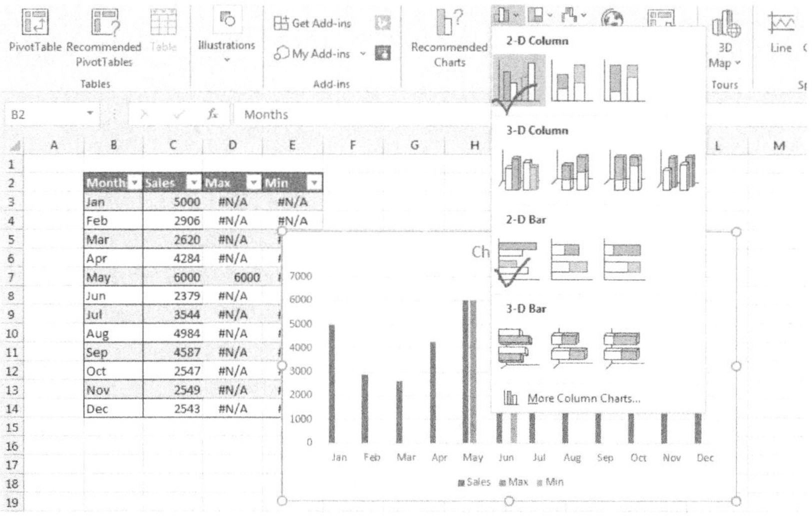

These are some examples of charts with additional columns to provide context.

11.3 WORKSHEET PROTECTION

Excel's sheet-level protection is not a reliable security measure. A password-protected worksheet's data is not meant to be hidden from prying eyes. Why? Worksheets in Microsoft Excel can be protected with a basic encryption algorithm. A password-protected Excel worksheet is still very vulnerable to being cracked.

In Excel 2010 and later, you may rest certain that your password is completely secure, but in older versions, it makes no difference how lengthy or complexes your password is. An individual with even a rudimentary understanding of VBA can break it in a matter of minutes (here is an illustration of the VBA code that quickly cracks passwords throughout Excel 2010 & lower versions).

Even though more advanced techniques of sheet security are used in Excel 2016, 2019, and 2021, these versions are still insecure and may be unlocked with or without a password. If someone is determined to see a password-protected document, they will succeed.

Do we conclude that protecting Excel sheets is completely unnecessary? That's not the case! Locking Excel sheets makes sense since it prevents accidental changes to the sheet's contents. Locking formula cells is a popular practice to avoid the accidental deletion or alteration of formulae.

Simply said, never save sensitive information on Excel sheets and always lock them to prevent unauthorized users from making changes.

Following all these steps will provide the highest level of security for any Excel files you can provide.

- It's recommended that you upgrade to a more recent version of Excel (versions 2010 through 2023, including improved data encryption techniques).
- Password-protecting your sheets using a mix of alphanumeric and special characters is the best way to ensure their safety.
- In any case, it's recommended that you use a random password generator to ensure the security of your accounts.
- Prevent unauthorized changes to your sheets by locking the workbook to stop anyone from inserting, renaming, removing, or unhiding them.
- Protect the workbook from unauthorized access and changes by encrypting it with two separate passcodes.

- If feasible, keep your Excel files containing confidential data in a safe place, such as an encrypted hard drive.

How can you protect your Excel sheet

Following are instructions for protecting a spreadsheet with a password in Excel 2016, Excel 2019, & Excel 2023.

- Right-click a spreadsheet tab at the bottom of the screen and choose Protect Sheet from the context menu.
- Choose the Protect Sheet option under the Changes group of the Review tab.

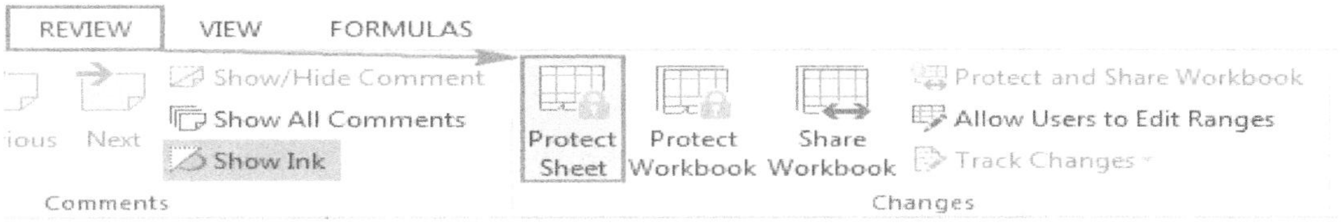

Here's what you should do within Protect Sheet dialogue box:

- Fill the password area to make your Excel sheet secure from prying eyes.
- For future usage, you'll need to be able to unprotect the document, so make sure you either remember or write down the password.
- If protecting the worksheet is only a precaution against the contents being changed by mistake by you or your local team members, you may not want to take the time to memorize the password and may leave it blank. In this situation, you may unprotect the sheet by clicking the corresponding button on the ribbon or by using the right-click menu that appears when you mouse over the sheet tab.
- Decide which user interactions are available and set permissions accordingly.

The default settings favor selecting both locked & unlocked cells. Leave just these two options checked, and your sheet's users, including yourselves, will be limited to selecting cells using the cell selection tools (both locked & unlocked).

In addition to sorting, formatting cells, filtering, removing, and adding columns and rows, you may enable these features by checking the appropriate boxes.

When you share an Excel sheet with others, they can see its contents if you don't choose any actions.

Follow the on-screen instructions by selecting the OK button.

For security reasons, Excel will urge you to retype your password in the Confirm Password dialogue box if you enter it incorrectly the first time. Reenter the password and choose OK to confirm. Done!

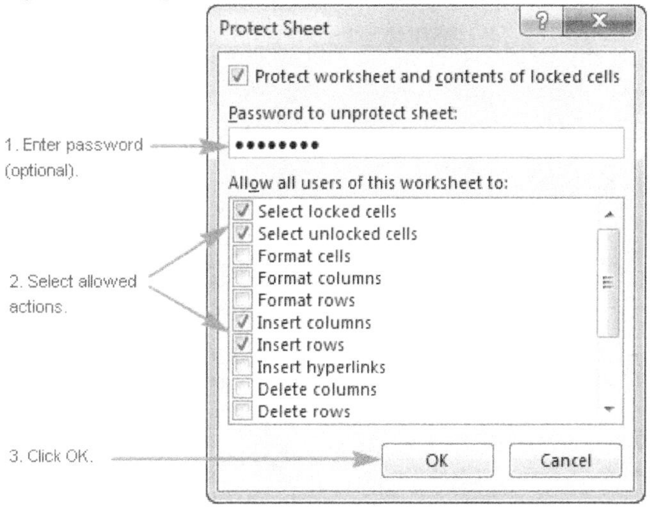

11.4 DATA VALIDATION

Excel's data validation tool restricts what kind of information may be entered into a cell. It's like having your little rulebook that everyone must follow. Additionally, a user-defined error message may be shown if incorrect information is submitted.

Data Validation into Excel?

Excel's data validation tool helps prevent accidental data changes by users. It's a common method for controlling the number of subscribers.

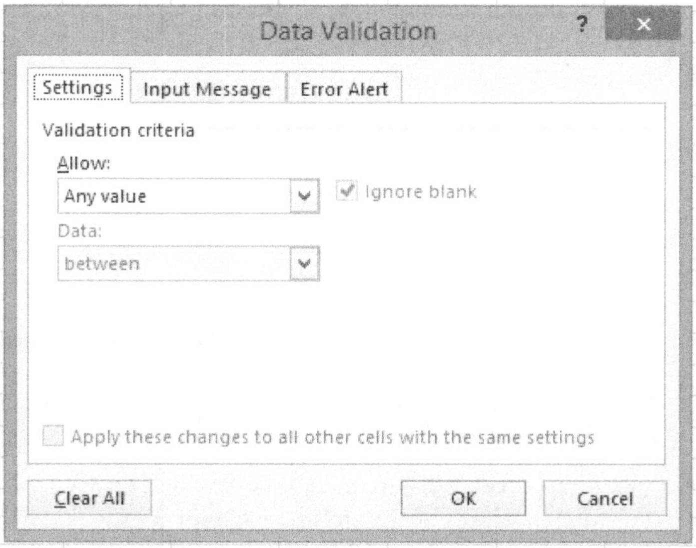

Settings Tab

The validation criteria are entered in the settings tab. User input may be validated in eight diverse ways:

- Every Possible Number - It nullifies all previous data checking.
- No fractions or decimals are accepted. You may require the user to input a number between 0 and 30 if you want.
- Decimal - A value with decimal places is required.
- List - The users were asked to generate a list of options.
- Date - The user must specify the date format.
- The user must enter the time.
- The width of the submitted text is checked for accuracy.
- The unique formula ensures that the user's input is correct.

Input Message Tab

You may customize the cell's input message to specify the acceptable data. You may skip this tab if you'd like. Set the cell to reveal its input message whenever the cell is chosen.

Put in the title here.

Type in input here.

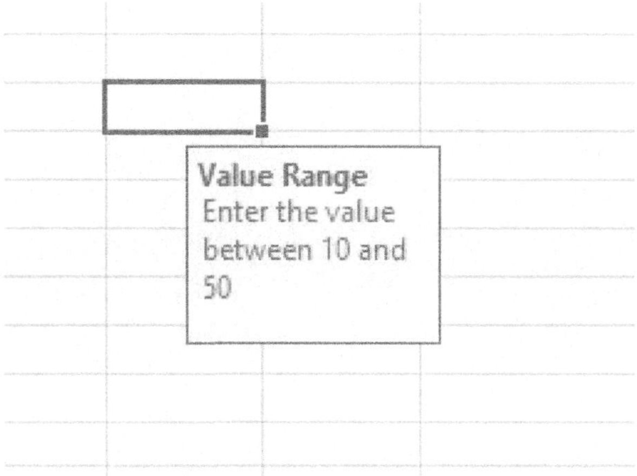

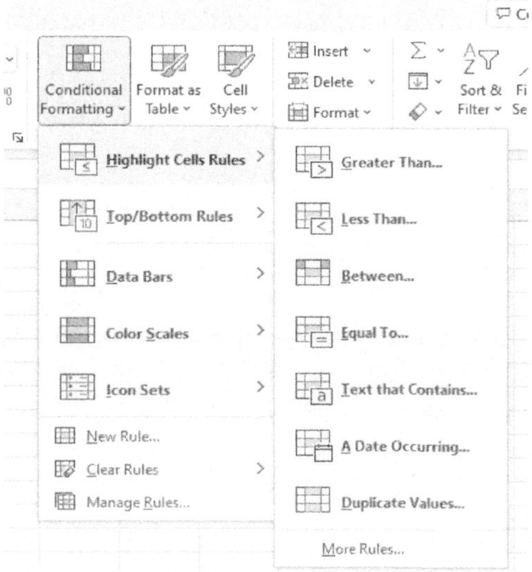

Error Alert Tabs

You may display the error message if the user attempts to input the incorrect data.

In the fault section:

- Choose the corresponding box to display an error message once an incorrect entry has been made.
- Put in the title here.
- Type in the mistake that occurred.

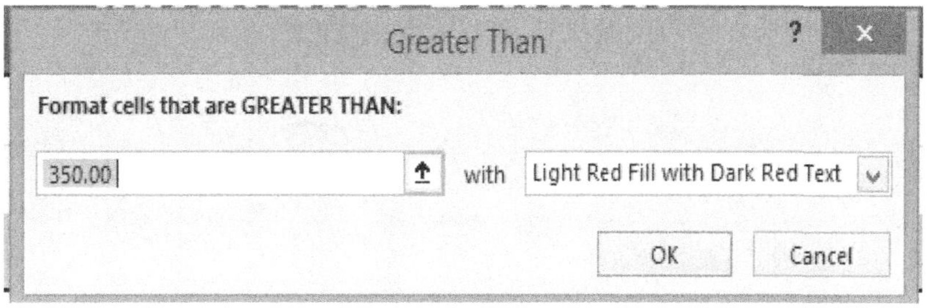

A warning message will show if you try to enter a number beyond the acceptable range.

Now that you have a strong grasp of the principles, let's look at a systematic process for applying data verifications in Excel.

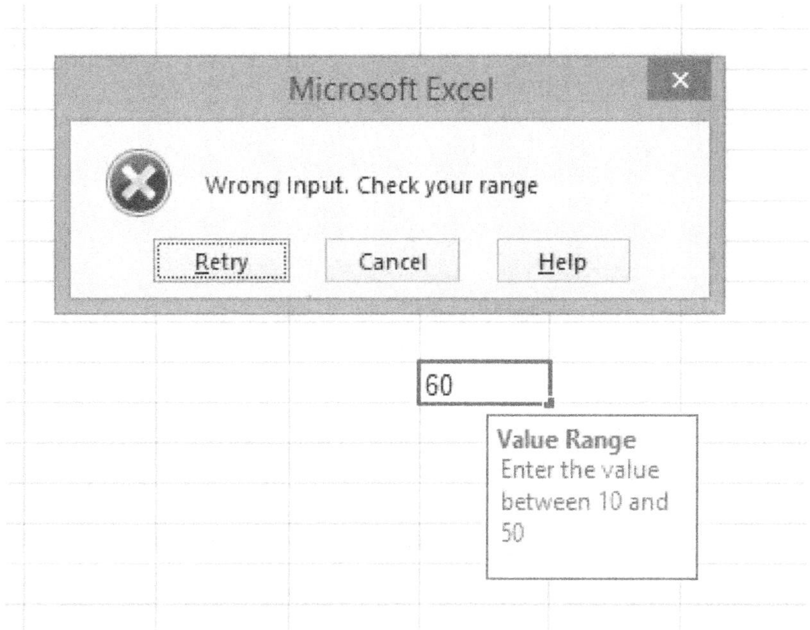

Validating Data using Excel?

First, find the cell you need to check. Select the Data Validation option under the Data menu's Data Tools section.

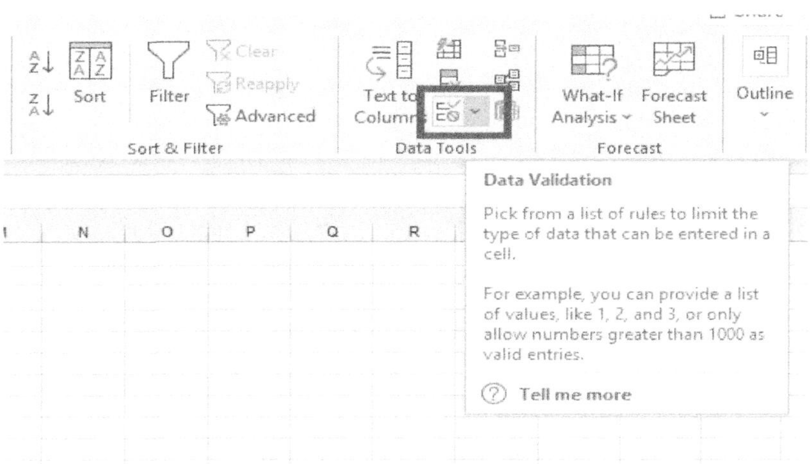

There will be a data validation dialogue box with three sections: Settings, Input Messages, & Error Alerts.

To define your criterion for validation, go to the options tab.

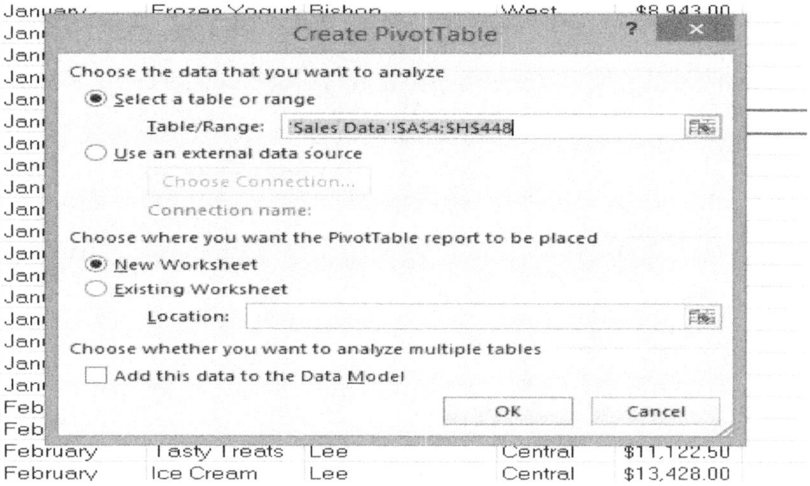

There is an optional third step where you may enter the input message. That is not required.

As an additional option, you may personalize the error message shown. That is not required.

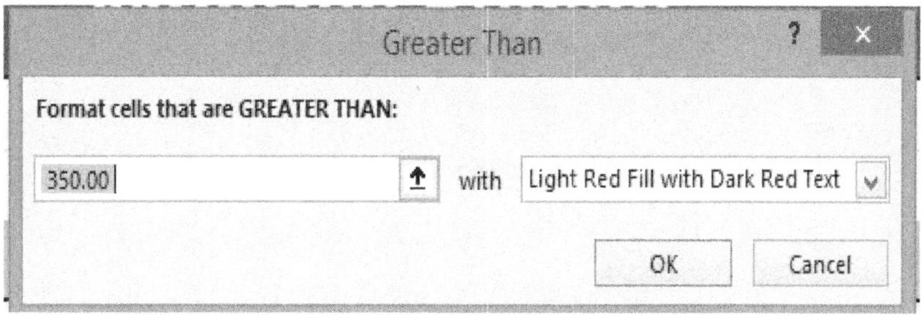

Proceed to next by selecting OK. This will now cause an error if you attempt to input a number that is not between 10 and 50.

Excel Data Validations List (Drop-Down)

The steps to include the drop-down menu are as follows:

- Start up the data checker by opening the dialogue box.
- Choose the list under the Settings menu.
- Use commas to separate items on your validation list and put them into the source field.

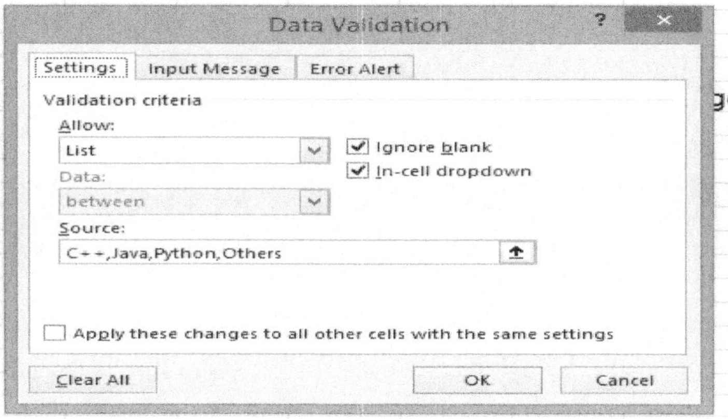

This is the end effect you may expect.

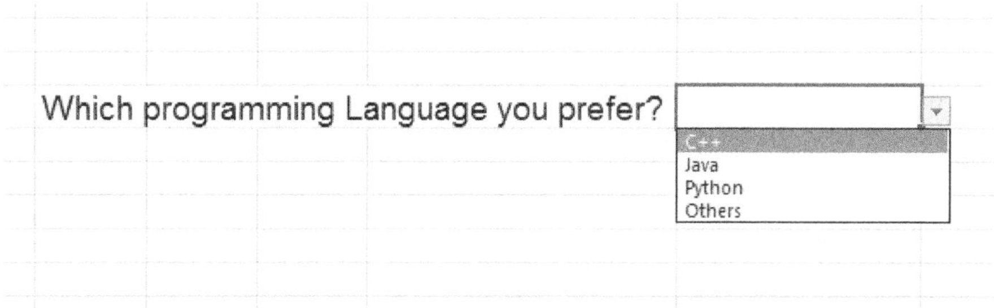

Data Validation

The Excel date validation may be customized. Choose the appropriate criteria and the date to allow.

Date validation may be put up in a few simple ways:

- Identify the cells that will get the data validation and click on them.
- The date must be chosen from the available dropdown calendar.
- Choose between in the Data menu.
- Select the cell (O10) where the Launch Date is entered by clicking in the corresponding box.
- To make the cell reference absolute ($O$10), press the F4 key.
- Select the cell (O11) containing the End Date by clicking on the corresponding End Date box.
- If you want to make the cell reference an absolute reference, like $O$11, press the F4 key.
- Close a Validation window by clicking the OK button.

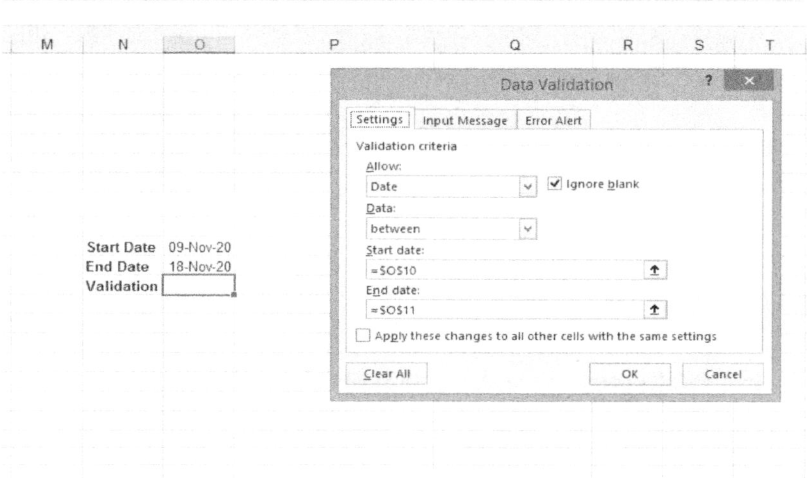

The dates 9 November 2020 through 18 November 2020 are valid for the above validation.

Excel helps ensure that users enter only correct information through its data validation features. This leads to the consistent recording of information and comprehensive reporting.

11.5 ERROR DELETION FROM CELLS

In case of a calculation error, equations display error messages instead of the real number. Let's examine a certain real-world example where the formulas and calculations failed.

Errors in Excel

In this chapter, error-prone cell formulae are explained. Knowing the meaning of each code (#VALUE!, #DIV/0!, #NAME!, #NULL!, #NUM!, # N/A!, #REF!) will help you detect and eliminate the formula errors.

Removing div/0?

When dividing into an empty cell, the software considers it a division by 0. #DIV/0 Hint shows this.

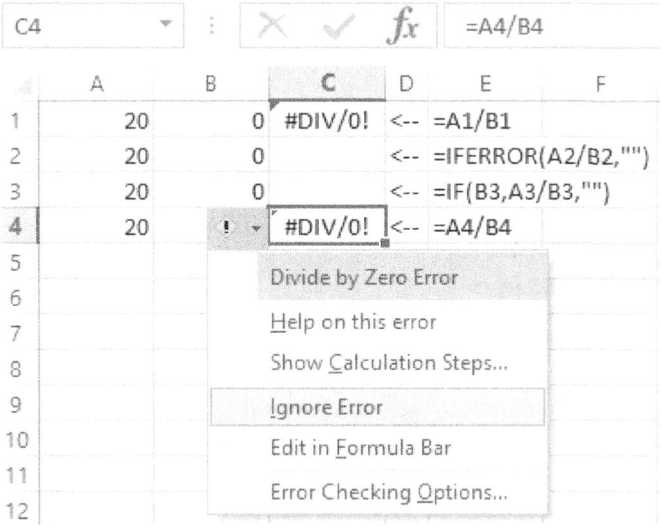

Empty cells are 0 in multiplication, addition, and subtraction. Note how =IFERROR (A 2/B 2,"") or =IF (B 3, A 3/B 3,"") deletes the error.

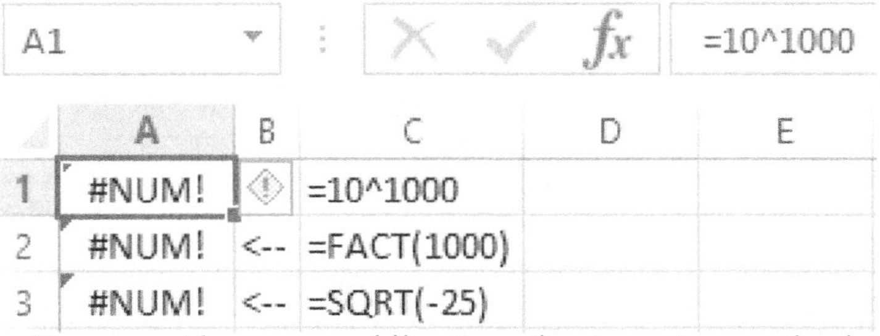

The erroneous calculation is num

#NUM! is a formula mistake that prevents calculation.

Few examples:

When a number is too big or little, #NUM! Happens. Also occurs while attempting to root a negative integer. =SQRT (-25).

- A1(101000) has too many numbers. Excel can't manage big numbers. In A2 with huge numerals. Excel can't manage 1.000's factorial FACT (1000) since it's too huge.
- The square root in cell A3 cannot be a negative value; thus, the software showed this error.

Removing NA

Unavailable value: #N/A! - Formula cannot access the value.

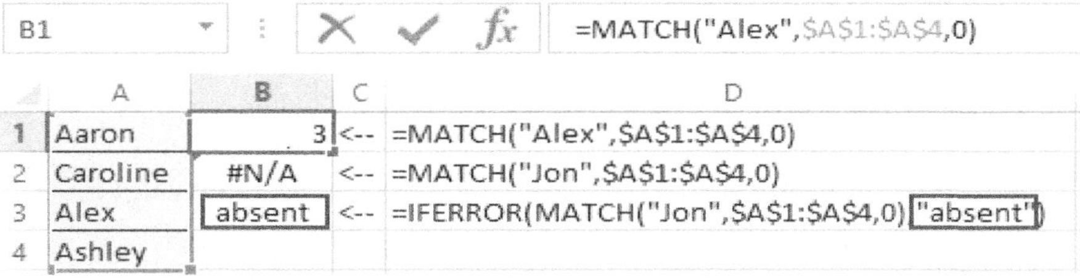

=MATCH («Alex», A 1: A 4, 0) looks for "Alex" in cells A1: A4. Cell A3-2 contains the material. The method yields 3. The second formula seeks for "Jon" =MATCH ("Jon," $A$1: $A$4,0), but A1:A4 has no such values. The function returns #N/A. (no data). Formula: =IFERROR (MATCH ("Jon," $A$1: $A$4,0),"absent"

ERROR NAME

It's about writing mistakes. Incorrect name: #NAME! means Excel didn't recognize formula text. The function name syntax problem caused this. Ex:

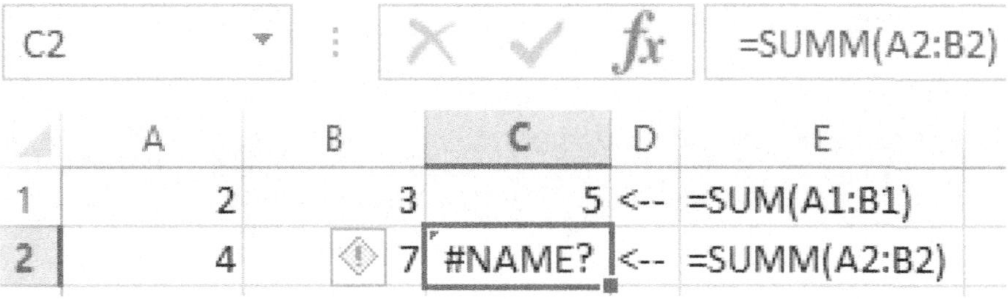

ERROR NULL

Empty set: #NULL! - intersection operator faults. Excel has set intersection.

It swiftly retrieves data from big tables by searching the intersection of vertical and horizontal cells.

If the ranges don't overlap, #NULL is shown. Single space intersects sets. It divides the function's vertical and horizontal ranges.

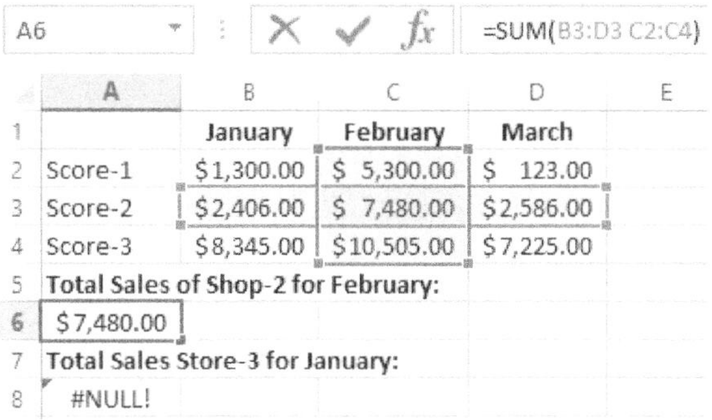

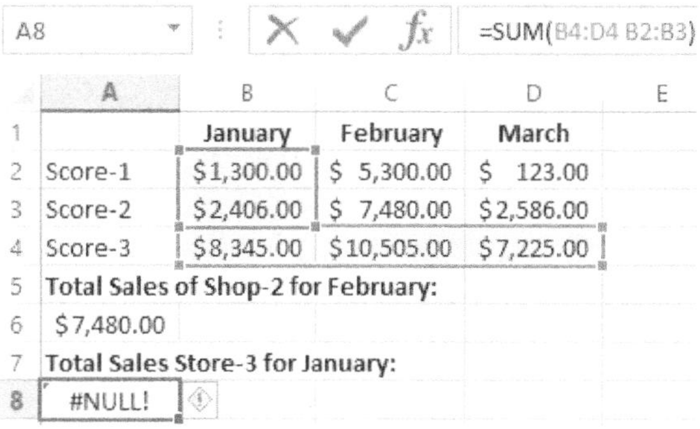

The intersection of a range is cell C 3, and the method returns its value.

= SUM (B4: D4 B2: B3) does not overlap. The method returns #NULL!

REF - THE ERROR LINKS

#REF! signifies the formula's parameters point to a wrong address. Usually a non-existent cell.

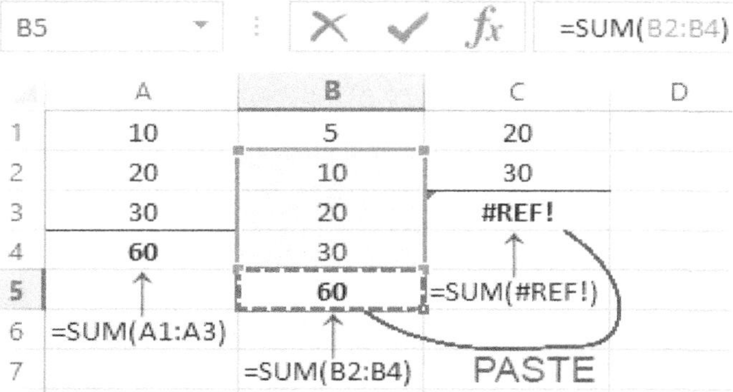

The formula was duplicated wrongly in this example. A1:A3, B1:B4, and C1:C2 are cell ranges.

In cell A4's first range, enter =SUM (A1:A3).
Then you copy the same formula to B5. The formula sums cells B2:B4, skipping B1.

When transferred to the 3rd range, function cell C3 returns #REF! Only 2 cells may be above C3, not 3.

When your sheet name is erroneously supplied in three-dimensional link addresses, #REFERENCE! Happens.

CORRECT the VALUE

Meaning error: #VALUE! Excel may give the #VALUE! Error if we add one number & a word. Using the =SUM() method, if you sum two cells where the first is a number & the 2nd is text, there is no error & text will equal 0. Ex:

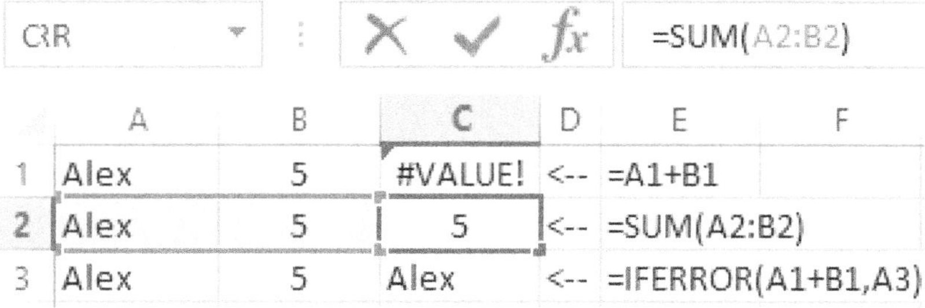

SHARP ###

The mistake is not the quantity of sharps symbols in cell ######. Your column is just too thin to show the cell's contents effectively. Expand the column. Double-click this cell's column headings to select them.

So, grids (######) have negative dates instead of cell values. You're attempting to create a brand-new date from old. Because of the computation, «Date» (not «General») is set as the cell format.

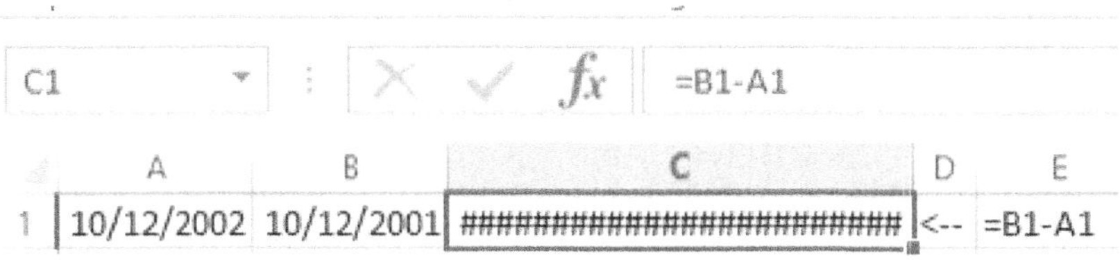

Incorrect cell formatting may also show lattice symbols (######).

CHAPTER 12

BONUS 2 TIPS AND TRICKS

A few tips and tricks are discussed in details to make you work faster in a short time.

12.1 SORT DATA QUICKLY

Sorting worksheet data lets you rapidly discover values. One or even more columns may sort a data table or range. First, sort personnel by department, then last name.

Sorting with Excel

Select the data you want to sort

Select tabular data, including A1: L5 or C1: C80 (single column). The range might contain column headers.

Jan	Feb	Mar	Apr	May	Jun	Jul	Aug	Sep	Oct	Nov	Dec
40	38	44	46	51	56	67	72	70	59	45	41
34	33	38	41	45	48	51	55	54	45	41	38
61	69	79	83	95	97	100	101	94	87	72	66
0	2	9	24	28	32	36	39	35	21	12	4

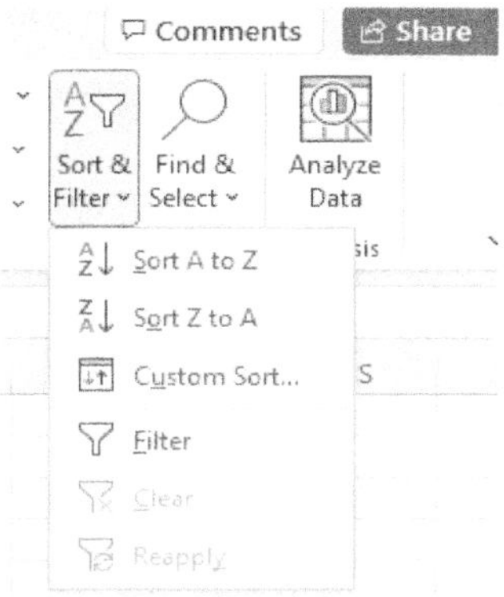

Easy sorting

Sort a single column cell.

Sort ascending on the Data tab's Sort & Filter group.

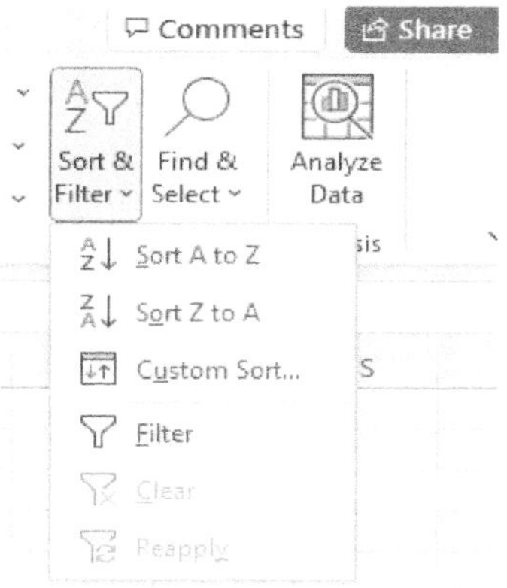

Criteria-based sorting

This method lets you sort by font, column, or cell color.

Choose a cell in the range to sort.

On the Data tab, under Sort & Filter category, click Sort.

Select the first column from the Sort by dropdown list.

Choose Values, Font Color, Cell Color, and Cell Icon.

In the Order list, pick whether to sort alphabetically, numerically, ascending, or descending (A-Z (or Z-A) for text, lower-higher, or higher-lower for numbers).

12.2 COPY AND DRAG INSTEAD OF RETYPING

Move or duplicate cell content with Cut, Copy, & Paste. Or copy cell contents and properties. Copy a formula's result without the formula or only the result.

When you copy or move a cell, the spreadsheet copies or moves its formulae, values, formats, or comments.

Move Excel cells by dragging or using Cut & Paste.

Move cell by drag & dropping

Select cells you want to work with to duplicate or move a range of cells. The boundary of the selection can be indicated by pointing. Drag the cell or selection of cells when the pointer changes to a move pointer.

Moving cells by Cut & Paste

Choose a single cell or a range of cells.

Go to Home > Cut (or use Ctrl + X on your keyboard) to cut something. The data can be moved to another cell if you choose.

Choose Edit > Paste, or use the shortcut Ctrl + V.

Copy cell by Copy & Paste

Pick the cells to work with.

A copy can be made by using the menu option or the shortcut Ctrl + C.

Choose Paste or Ctrl + V to paste.

12.3 QUICK FORMATTING

Do you format Excel data often?

If so, AutoFormat may help you format faster. It lets you easily format a data collection using a header row and column.

It lets you easily format a data collection using a header row and column.

So, you get the following result:

	Q1	Q2	Q3	Q4
Item A	3089	5519	4909	4541
Item B	7869	3195	7446	3934
Item C	3624	5364	5969	5277
Item D	2162	6359	2445	5780

→

	Q1	Q2	Q3	Q4
Item A	£3,089.00	£5,519.00	£4,909.00	£4,541.00
Item B	7,869.00	3,195.00	7,446.00	3,934.00
Item C	3,624.00	5,364.00	5,969.00	5,277.00
Item D	2,162.00	6,359.00	2,445.00	5,780.00

AutoFormat using Excel

AutoFormat isn't on Excel's ribbon or Quick Access Toolbar (QAT).

- You must add it manually.
- How to add AutoFormat to QAT:
- Right-click QAT icons.
- Choose 'Customize Quick Access Toolbar'

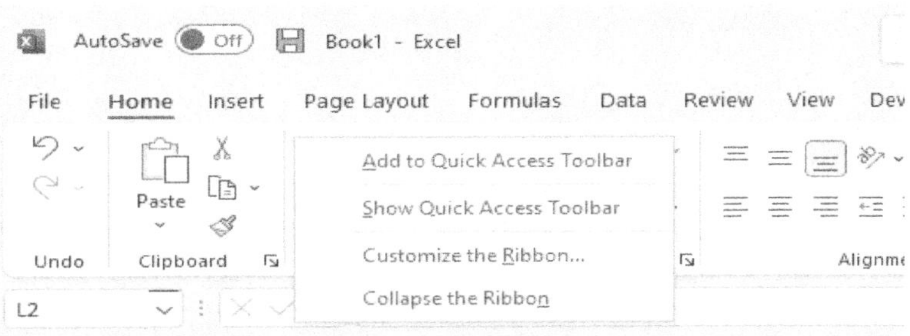

Within the Excel Options dropdown, choose All Commands.

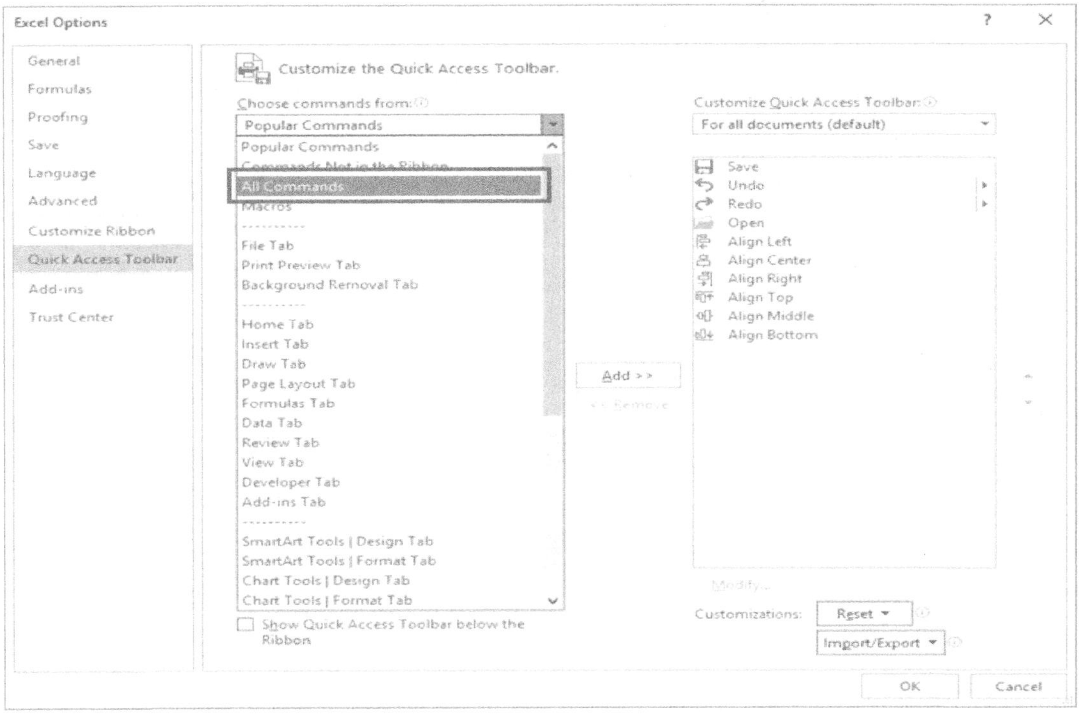

Select AutoFormat from the command list.

Press Add. This adds AutoFormat to QAT's icons.

Ok.

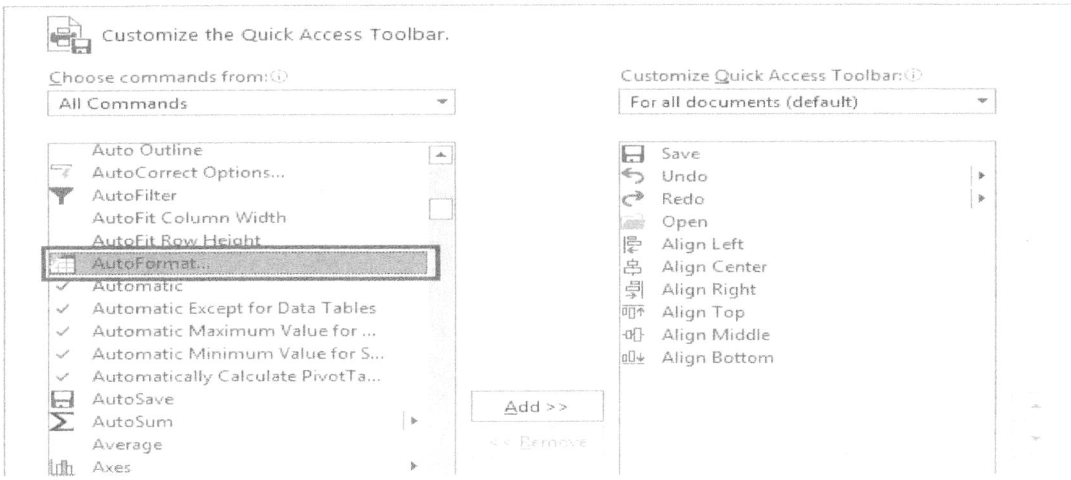

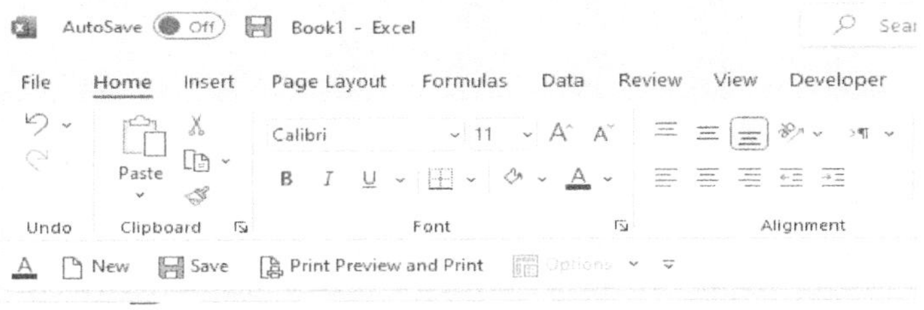

The preceding procedures introduce AutoFormat to the QAT.

Quickly Format Data Using AutoFormat

AutoFormat works for data with column and row headings.

Below:

	A	B	C	D	E
1		Q1	Q2	Q3	Q4
2	Item A	3089	5519	4909	4541
3	Item B	7869	3195	7446	3934
4	Item C	3624	5364	5969	5277
5	Item D	2162	6359	2445	5780

Here are the AutoFormat steps:

- Choose all data.
- Quick Access Toolbar AutoFormat icon.

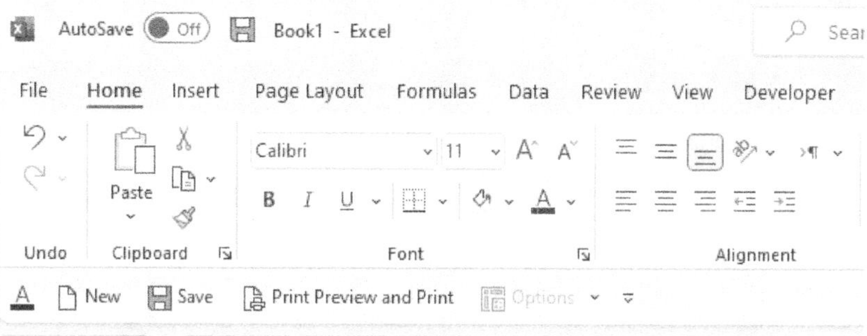

The dialogue box has 16 formatting designs. Choose one.

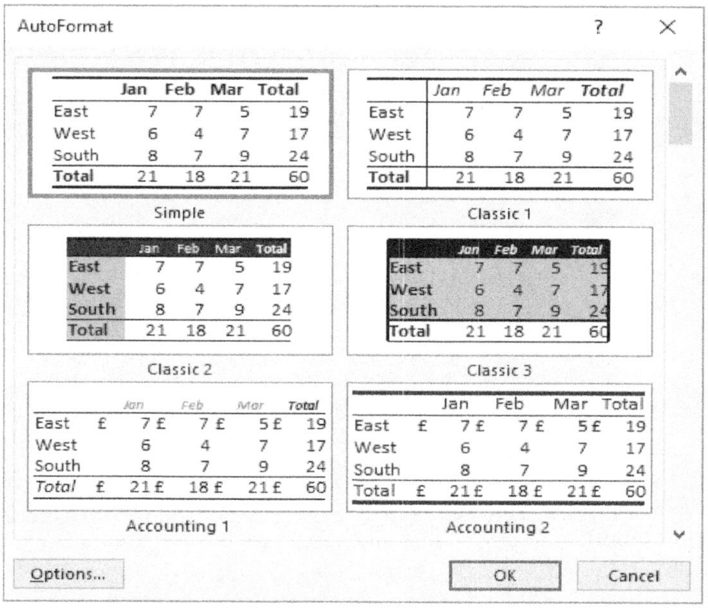

Click on OK.

This quickly formats the dataset.

AutoFormat formatting may be changed. Changing the header color is easy.

Also, any dataset formatting will be overwritten. Choosing a format with such a blue header will override red headers & apply blue to the cells.

Modifying the Design using AutoFormat

AutoFormat has restricted formatting design adjustments.

AutoFormat's six formats are as follows:

- Width/Height
- Border
- Patterns
- Alignment
- Font
- Number Formatting

AutoFormat format changes are as follows:

Click AutoFormat in QAT.

Click 'Options' in the dialogue window.

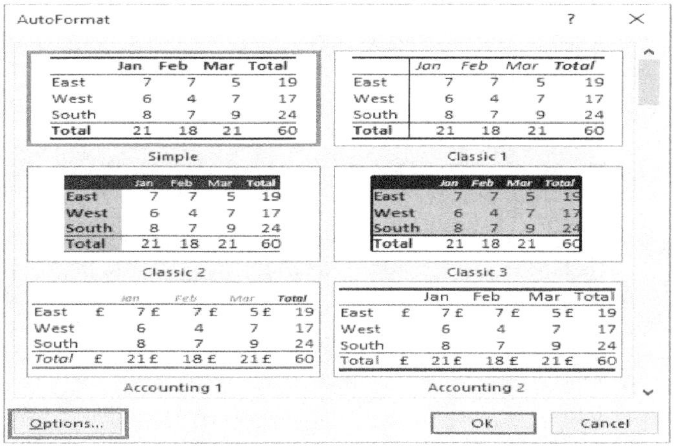

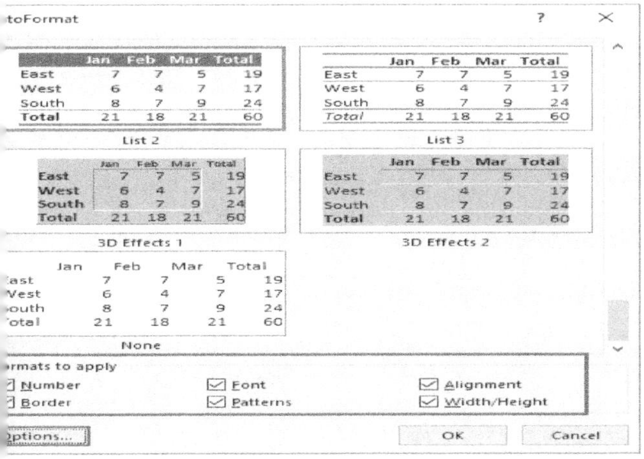

Select/deselect data set formatting choices. When you select/deselect any option, the live preview of all designs in the dialogue box appears.

Click OK once done.

Removing any Formatting, you're your Dataset

AutoFormat lets you delete formatting effortlessly.

Two ways:

- Using built-in options, remove components. To eliminate borders, utilize the boundaries option.
- Unformat everything. Select the final design in Autoformat.

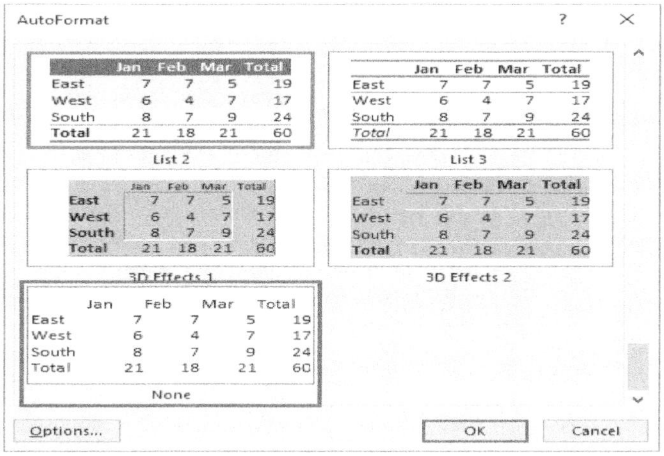

Limitations of Your AutoFormat Option

This feature has been there for a while, but its usefulness has waned as Excel's ribbon has added additional table formatting/design choices. I only suggest it for structured data. Use separate formatting choices if your data isn't arranged this way.

AutoFormat can't adjust formatting options. You can't thicken or dash the border.

12.4 EXCEL SHORTCUT KEYS

Here are most of Microsoft Excel's shortcut keys & key combinations.

Shortcut	Description
Tab	Move to the next cell, to the right of the currently selected cell.
Ctrl+A	Select all contents of a worksheet.
Ctrl+B	Bold all cells in the highlighted section.
Ctrl+C	Copy all cells in the highlighted section.
Ctrl+D	Fill down. Fills the cell beneath with the contents of the selected cell. To fill more than one cell, select the source cell and press Ctrl+Shift+Down arrow to select multiple cells. Then press Ctrl+D to fill them with the contents of the original cell.
Ctrl+F	Search current sheet.
Ctrl+G	Go to a certain area.
Ctrl+H	Find and replace.
Ctrl+I	Puts italics on all cells in the highlighted section.
Ctrl+K	Inserts a hyperlink.
Ctrl+L	Opens the Create Table dialog box.
Ctrl+N	Creates a new workbook.
Ctrl+O	Opens a workbook.
Ctrl+P	Print the current sheet.
Ctrl+R	Fill right. Fills the cell to the right with the contents of the selected cell. To fill more than one cell, select the source cell and press Ctrl+Shift+Right arrow to select multiple cells. Then press Ctrl+R to fill them with the contents of the original cell.
Ctrl+S	Saves the open worksheet.
Ctrl+T	Open the Create Table dialog box.
Ctrl+U	Underlines all cells in the highlighted section.
Ctrl+V	Pastes everything copied onto the clipboard.
Ctrl+W	Closes the current workbook.
Ctrl+X	Cuts all cells in the highlighted section.
Ctrl+Y	Repeats the last entry (redo).
Ctrl+Z	Undo the last action.
Ctrl+1	Changes the format of the selected cells.
Ctrl+2	Bolds all cells in the highlighted section.
Ctrl+3	Puts italics all cells in the highlighted section.
Ctrl+4	Underlines all cells in highlighted section.
Ctrl+5	Puts a strikethrough all cells in the highlighted section.
Ctrl+6	Shows or hides objects.
Ctrl+7	Shows or hides the toolbar.
Ctrl+8	Toggles the outline symbols.
Ctrl+9	Hides rows.
Ctrl+0	Hides columns.
Ctrl+Shift+:	Enters the current time.
Ctrl+;	Enters the current date.
Ctrl+`	Changes between displaying cell values or formulas in the worksheet.

Ctrl+'	Copies a formula from the cell above.
Ctrl+Shift+"	Copies value from cell above.
Ctrl+-	Deletes the selected column or row.
Ctrl+Shift+=	Inserts a new column or row.
Ctrl+Shift+~	Switches between showing Excel formulas or their values in cells.
Ctrl+Shift+@	Applies time formatting.
Ctrl+Shift+!	Applies comma formatting.
Ctrl+Shift+$	Applies currency formatting.
Ctrl+Shift+#	Applies date formatting.
Ctrl+Shift+%	Applies percentage formatting.
Ctrl+Shift+^	Applies exponential formatting.
Ctrl+Shift+*	Selects the current region around the active cell.
Ctrl+Shift+&	Places border around selected cells.
Ctrl+Shift+_	Removes a border.
Ctrl++	Insert.
Ctrl+-	Delete contents of the currently-active cell.
Ctrl+Shift+(	Unhide rows.
Ctrl+Shift+)	Unhide columns.
Ctrl+/	Selects the array containing the active cell.
Ctrl+\	Selects the cells with a static value or don't match the formula in the active cell.
Ctrl+[	Selects all cells referenced by formulas in the highlighted section.
Ctrl+]	Selects cells that contain formulas that reference the active cell.
Ctrl+Shift+{	Selects all cells directly or indirectly referenced by formulas in the highlighted section.

Ctrl+Shift+}	Selects cells which contain formulas that directly or indirectly reference the active cell.
Ctrl+Shift+| (pipe)	Selects the cells within a column that don't match the formula or static value in the active cell.
Ctrl+Enter	Fills the selected cells with the current entry.
Ctrl+Spacebar	Selects the entire column.
Ctrl+Shift+Spacebar	Selects the entire worksheet.
Ctrl+Home	Move to cell A1.
Ctrl+End	Move to last cell with text on the worksheet.
Ctrl+Tab	Move between Two or more open Excel files.
Ctrl+Shift+Tab	Activates the previous workbook.
Ctrl+Shift+A	Inserts argument names into a formula.
Ctrl+Shift+F	Opens the drop-down menu for fonts.
Ctrl+Shift+O	Selects all of the cells that contain comments.
Ctrl+Shift+P	Opens the drop-down menu for point size.
Shift+Insert	Pastes what is stored on the clipboard.
Shift+Page Up	In a single column, highlights all cells above that are selected.
Shift+Page Down	In a single column, highlights all cells above that are selected.
Shift+Home	Highlights all text to the left of the cursor.
Shift+End	Highlights all text to the right of the cursor.
Shift+Up Arrow	Extends the highlighted area up one cell.
Shift+Down Arrow	Extends the highlighted area down one cell.
Shift+Left Arrow	Extends the highlighted area left one character.
Shift+Right Arrow	Extends the highlighted area right one character.
Alt+Tab	Cycles through applications.
Alt+Spacebar	Opens the system menu.
Alt+Backspace	Undo.
Alt+Enter	While typing text in a cell, pressing Alt+Enter moves to the next line, allowing for multiple lines of text in one cell.
Alt+=	Creates a formula to sum all of the above cells.
Alt+'	Allows formatting on a dialog box.
F1	Opens the help menu.

F2	Edits the selected cell.
F3	After a name is created, F3 pastes names.
F4	Repeats last action. For example, if you changed the color of text in another cell, pressing F4 changes the text in cell to the same color.
F5	Goes to a specific cell. For example, C6.
F6	Move to the next pane.
F7	Spell check selected text or document.
F8	Enters Extend Mode.
F9	Recalculates every workbook.
F10	Activates the menu bar.
F11	Creates a chart from selected data.
F12	Save As option.
Shift+F1	Opens the "What's This?" window.
Shift+F2	Allows the user to edit a cell comment.
Shift+F3	Opens the Excel formula window.
Shift+F5	Brings up a search box.
Shift+F6	Move to previous pane.
Shift+F8	Add to selection.
Shift+F9	Performs calculate function on active sheet.
Ctrl+F3	Open Excel Name Manager.
Ctrl+F4	Closes current window.
Ctrl+F5	Restores window size.
Ctrl+F6	Next workbook.

Ctrl+Shift+F6	Previous workbook.
Ctrl+F7	Moves the window.
Ctrl+F8	Resizes the window.
Ctrl+F9	Minimize current window.
Ctrl+F10	Maximize currently selected window.
Ctrl+F11	Inserts a macro sheet.
Ctrl+F12	Opens a file.
Ctrl+Shift+F3	Creates names using those of either row or column labels.
Ctrl+Shift+F6	Moves to the previous worksheet window.
Ctrl+Shift+F12	Prints the current worksheet.
Alt+F1	Inserts a chart.
Alt+F2	Save As option.
Alt+F4	Exits Excel.
Alt+F8	Opens the macro dialog box.
Alt+F11	Opens the Visual Basic editor.
Alt+Shift+F1	Creates a new worksheet.
Alt+Shift+F2	Saves the current worksheet.

CHAPTER 13

FINAL TEST

1. To disable the worksheet gridlines, you'll need to select which option from the ribbon.

- View
- Formulas
- Developer
- Review

2. A corporation projected $180,000 in revenue between 2014 and 2018. To see 2016 revenue, if it was over budget or 0 otherwise, what formula must be inserted in cell E6?

	A	B	C	D	E	F	G
1	USD $000's		2014A	2015A	2016A	2017A	2018A
2	Revenue		150,000	165,000	181,500	199,650	219,615
3							
4	Exceeded Budget?						
5	If < 180,000	180,000	150,000	165,000	0	0	0
6	If >= 180,000	180,000	0	0	181,500	199,650	219,615
7							

- =IF (E 2 < $B$6, E 2, 0)
- =IF (E 2 > $B$6, E 2, 0)
- =IF (E 2 > $B$6,0, E 2)
- =IF (E 2 < $B$6,0, E 2)

3. To the extent that more than one option applies, please check all that apply: Which options can't be accessed from the Data tab?

- PivotTable
- Text to Column
- What-If Analysis
- Data Validation

4. Where on the ribbon do you find the option to switch to Page Break Preview for your Workbook?

- View
- Page Layout
- Review
- Data

5. Let's pretend that "12000.7789" is showing up in cell A1. How do You round this to the nearest integer?

- =MROUND (A1, 10)
- =ROUND (A1, 1)
- =ROUND (A1, 0)
- =MROUND (A1, 100)

6. Which one of the below Excel tools lets you highlight all formula-containing cells for easy selection?

- Find
- Go To Special
- Replace
- Go To

7. In the example below, cell C8 should include the weighted mean scores calculated using one of the following formulas.

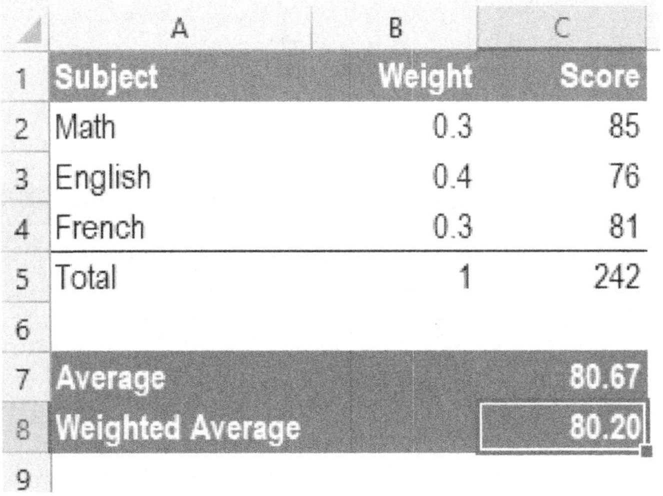

	A	B	C
1	Subject	Weight	Score
2	Math	0.3	85
3	English	0.4	76
4	French	0.3	81
5	Total	1	242
6			
7	Average		80.67
8	Weighted Average		80.20
9			

- =SUMPRODUCT (C 2: C 4, B 2: B 4)
- =AVERAGE (C 2: C 4)
- =SUMPRODUCT (C 2: C 5,B 2: B 5)
- =AVERAGE (B 2: B 4)

8. How can You insert a table using the keyboard shortcuts?

- ALT+N +R
- ALT+N+C
- ALT+N+V
- ALT+N+T

9. How can You quickly access the Find & Replace dialogue box using its shortcuts?

- ALT+H+FD+R
- CTRL+FD
- ALT+H+R
- ALT+H+FD

10. To quickly access more decimal places, Shortcut is:

- ALT+H+D
- ALT+H+P
- ALT+H+9
- ALT+H+0

11. How do You change a formula inside a cell using the keyboard?

- CTRL+1
- F2
- F4
- CTRL+F

12. When working with an Excel spreadsheet, what keys do you use to quickly add a new row?

- ALT+H+I+C
- ALT+H+I+R
- ALT+H+I+S
- ALT+H+I+I

You will find the answers key to the test before the conclusion

CHAPTER 14

BONUS 3 CUSTOMIZE YOUR TEMPLATE

Here, you'll find information about making changes to your Excel template.

14.1 BUILDING A FINANCIAL PLAN IN EXCEL

Attempting to find a little more individuality in your spending plan? You may create a new Excel budgeting spreadsheet to further your budgeting abilities.

The following is an in-depth explanation of how to make a budget in Excel from scratch, along with suggestions for making the program work better for you.

Open the Blank Workbook

Create a budget that starts with zero and includes all your income and outgoings. It's a fantastic method for keeping tabs on your finances since it's precise.

I don't believe you'll ever use another budgeting method after trying this one. Launch Excel and choose "Blank Workbook" from the File menu to start. You may now begin working with a blank slate.

Set Up the Income Tab

Once you have a clean spreadsheet, set aside a section of columns to serve as a monthly header, select the top two rows within columns A-G, then go to the "Home" tab and choose "Merge and Center." That makes the entire thing A1; you may name it any way you choose from here on out.

Click "Merge and Middle," then pick cells A3:A11, and type "Income" in the center of the page. Make use of various typefaces and color schemes if you're feeling artistic.

Then, combine B3 and C3 or name them "Source" to show how your money comes in, whether from a regular job, a side hustle, or any other means. Similarly, rows B and C should be merged up to and including row 11. The date this payment was received may be noted by typing "Date" into field D3. If your monthly revenue comes from various sources, it may be good to include a dates section. If your salary is consistent, it might not be worth it.

Next, designate E3 as either "Planned" or "Budgeted." Income projections are as follows. The "Actual" column in Section F3 displays the actual sum of money deposited into the bank account, which should be more than the "Estimate" column. Finally, G3's "Difference" column would keep records of the variance between your forecasted and actual revenue streams automatically.

	A	B	C	D	E	F	G	H	I	J	K
1											
2				August							
3		Source		Date	Planned	Actual	Difference				
4											
5											
6											
7	Income										
8											
9											
10											
11											
12											
13											
14											
15											
16											
17											
18											
19											
20											

Add Formulas for Automation

Choose the full area to make the Excel budget seem more organized. Then, choose "All Borders" from the borders tool (it looks like a square cut into four parts) on the "Home" tab of the workbook. It would be much simpler on the eyes if you shaded certain sections.

When satisfied with the budget spreadsheet layout, you can enter the formulae that will do the heavy lifting for you. Here's how to fill up cell B11 by writing "Total" in it, as seen in the sample below. You may tack it onto the end of as many income streams as you want.

Once you've assigned a name to everything that adds up to "Total," you can use the "AutoSum" function to add up the items in the "Planned" column to obtain a monthly total. The alternative is to choose the last line of that column using the formula =SUM (E4:E10). You should, of course, substitute the desired range of cells for the E4 through E10 notations. Simply switch the values in the "Actual" & "Difference" columns back and forth.

Put the formula =SUM (F 4: E 4) at the end of each row to have Excel automatically determine the disparity between your "Planned" & "Actual" revenue. Similarly, in cells F4 & E4, enter the values for "Actual" with "Planned." Simply keep doing this for every row that has money coming in.

G11 fx =SUM(F11-E11)

	A	B	C	D	E	F	G	H	I
1									
2				August					
3		Source		Date	Planned	Actual	Difference		
4		Ralph's Main		5-Aug, 19-Au	$3,000	$3,100	$100		
5		Gina's Main		10-Aug, 24-A	$4,000	$3,000	($1,000)		
6		Side business 1		15-Aug	$500	$500	$0		
7	Income	Side business 2		20-Aug	$450	$550	$100		
8									
9									
10									
11		Total			$7,950	$7,150	($800)		
12									

Add The Expenses

After determining your revenue, you may go on to the next stage and determine your expenditures. This may be done on the current sheet or a new sheet created. Create a new space beneath the "Income" part and format it as needed to maintain your spending on the same page as your income. Use the same column titles as before (Due Date, Actual, Planned, and Difference). Produce the formulae as you did before, but with one key change. The formula "=SUM (Actual Number-Planned Number)" in the "Difference" column must be inverted. To determine how much you went over budget, apply the formula =SUM (Planned Number-Actual Number).

If you want to maintain a second document to record your expenditures, just click the + sign next to "Sheet 1" to create a new sheet. At this point, you may rename any sheets by right-clicking on them and selecting the option to do so.

You may arrange the categories for your budget report as you choose. Change the level of specificity to suit your needs. Simple monitoring of frequent expenditures is essential. Utility bills may be broken down into natural gas, garbage, and electricity, but some individuals prefer to keep track of them all under one umbrella term. Your decision is final.

	Total		$7,950	$7,150	($800)
	Category	Due Date	Planned	Actual	Difference
	Mortgage	1-Aug	$1,500	$1,500	$0
	Groceries		$450	$600	($150)
	Utilities		$300	$290	$10
	Loans		$700	$700	$0
	Childcare		$1,000	$1,000	$0
	Car Insurance		$250	$250	$0
	Health Insurance		$500	$500	$0
	Gas		$250	$350	($100)
	Car Payment	15-Aug	$500	$500	$0
Expenses					
	Total		$5,450	$5,690	($240)

Add a few More Sections

The good times are finally here! The Excel budget may include as many categories and sheets as you want. Also included new headings labeled "Funds" & "Savings" within an illustration. Since you aren't worried about overspending, eliminate the "Difference" column from these tables. You may leave them in if you want to track how much money you saved over and above your original budget.

	Total		$5,450	$5,690	($240)
	Account	Planned		Actual	
	Emergency Fund	$500		$300	
Funds	Home Maintenance	$100		$25	
	Holidays	$50		$0	
	Total	$650		$325	
	Account	Planned		Actual	
	Retirement	$1,000		$500	
	College	$500		$500	
Savings	Total	$1,500		$1,000	

Your Final Balance

When you've set up all the segments you wish to monitor, you should constantly be aware of your running equilibrium. Thank goodness Excel has automated tracking features so you can put the calculator away.

Having everything on one document makes this a breeze. Make a new column in the document's footer. Next, write "Total Expenditures" in one column and "Balance" in another. It's simple to keep tabs on your spending and see how it stacks up against your budget. You can find your total planned budget by plugging in the formula "=SUM (Planned Fund Total, Planned Expense Total, Planned Saving Total)". Then, to get your projected balance, apply the formula = SUM (Total Planned Expenditures: Total Planned Income). Make the same adjustments to the sections labeled "Actual Expenses" and "Balance" using the true amounts.

To determine an exact balance, one must always subtract one's income from expenditures. Below is a made-up example showing a budget overrun of $115. Using a spreadsheet, we could easily observe where the family spent too much and didn't make enough money. The main objective is to facilitate simple financial monitoring so that you can keep tabs on every penny.

31						
32						
33						
34						
35		Total		$5,700	$5,940	($240)
36		Account	Planned		Actual	
37		Emergency Fund	$500		$300	
38	Funds	Home Maintenance	$100		$25	
39		Holidays	$50		$0	
40						
41		Total	$650		$325	
42		Account	Planned		Actual	
43		Retirement	$1,000		$500	
44		College	$600		$500	
45						
46	Savings	Total	$1,600		$1,000	
47			Planned		Actual	
48		Total Spending	$7,950		$7,265	
49		Final Balance	$0		($115)	
50						

Totaling the Numbers from some Other Sheets

If you've divided your finances into many tabs, such as savings, spending, and so on, choose the tab you'd want the total to appear on. There are two options: add the sum to the first page or make a separate sheet for the grand totals.

B2 fx =SUM(Expenses!E24,Funds!D6,Savings!D5)

	A	B	C	D	E	F	G
1		Planned		Actual			
2	Spending	$7,950		$7,265			
3	Final	$0		$115			
4							
5							
6							
7							
8							
9							
10							
11							

You used labels and included a final totals sheet for the illustration above. The totals for both the budgeted and actual balances, as well as any adjustments, will be calculated on the final page.

Simply choose the cell in which you'd want the sum to display, then type =SUM (Sheet Name! Cell, Sheet Name! Cell, Sheet Name! Cell) into the formula bar. This formula might look like this: =SUM (Expenses! E 24, Funds! D 6, Savings!D 5). Switch out the target and achieve sums.

Select a cell wherever you like the balance to appear after subtracting your income from your total expenses. Type = SUM (Sheet Name! Cell-Spending Cell) into the resulting cell. For example, which would be "=SUM (Income! F 11-D 2)". A negative amount will appear in this column if your expenses exceed your income.

Insert the Graph (It's Optional)

You don't have to include a graph in the spreadsheet budget, although doing so may help you see your spending patterns more clearly.

You will need to make a column for % before making a bar graph or pie chart to show your expenditures.

A	Category	Due Date	Planned	Actual	Difference	Percentage
	Mortgage	1-Aug	$1,500	$1,500	$0	25%
	Groceries		$450	$600	($150)	10%
	Utilities		$300	$290	$10	5%
	Loans		$700	$700	$0	12%
	Childcare		$1,000	$1,000	$0	17%
	Car Insurance		$250	$250	$0	4%
	Health Insurance		$500	$500	$0	8%
	Gas		$250	$350	($100)	6%
	Car Payment	15-Aug	$500	$500	$0	8%
	Phone/Internet		$250	$250	$0	4%
Expenses						

You can find that by simply inserting another column in the sample data.

Plug in "= Category Total Cell / Actual Total Cell" to have the percentages add up automatically. Using this case, the formula would look like this: = F 2/F 24.

You may use this formula to get a percentage for every category. To rapidly switch from decimal to percentage format, choose the column you want to convert and click the " percent " icon. Your percentages must sum up to 100.

B11 fx Phone/Internet

A	Category	Due Date	Planned	Actual	Difference	Percentage
	Mortgage	1-Aug	$1,500	$1,500	$0	25%
	Groceries		$450	$600	($150)	10%
	Utilities		$300	$290	$10	5%
	Loans		$700	$700	$0	12%
	Childcare		$1,000	$1,000	$0	17%
	Car Insurance		$250	$250	$0	4%
	Health Insurance		$500	$500	$0	8%
	Gas		$250	$350	($100)	6%
	Car Payment	15-Aug	$500	$500	$0	8%
	Phone/Internet		$250	$250	$0	4%
Expenses						

Afterward, concurrently choose the column containing the category headings and the percentage column. Once you have both selected, click "Insert" and choose the kind of graph you need. You can always right-click your graph and choose "Change Chart Type" if you decide you don't really like the style you first selected. The donut chart depicted below is one of the favorites because of the clear separation of costs into parts.

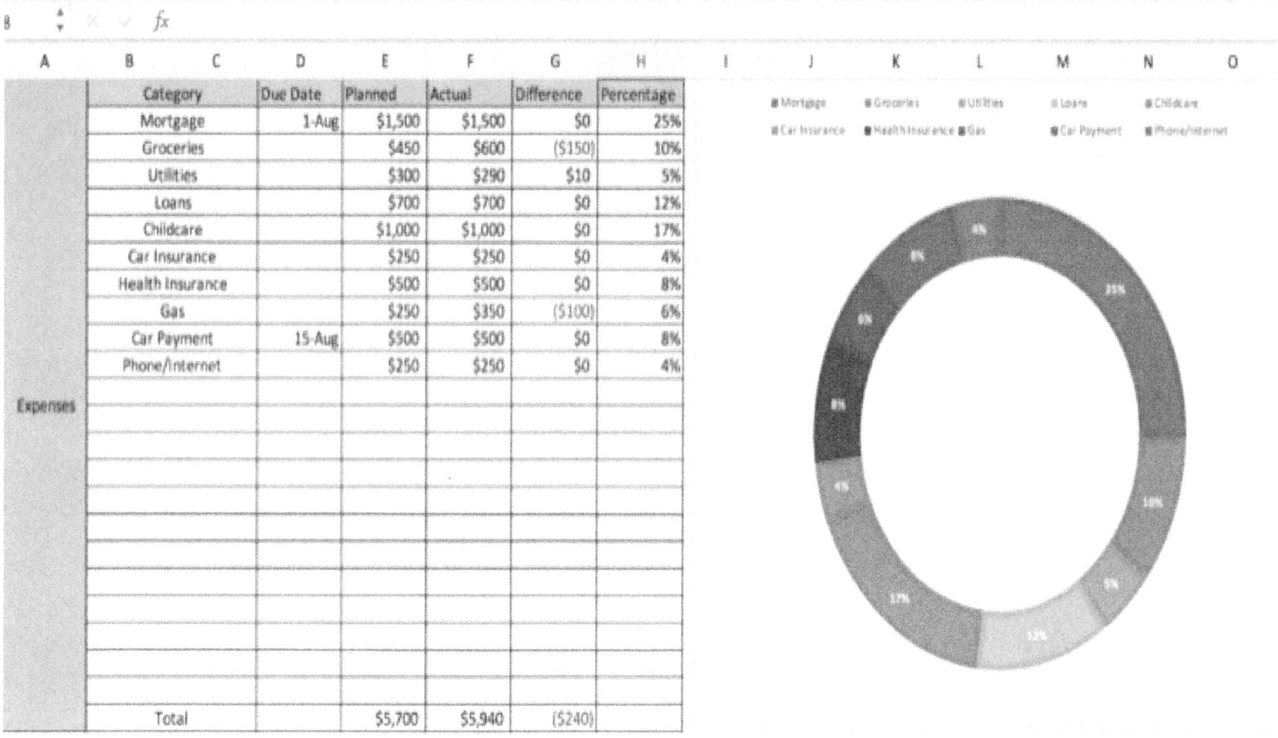

	Category	Due Date	Planned	Actual	Difference	Percentage
Expenses	Mortgage	1-Aug	$1,500	$1,500	$0	25%
	Groceries		$450	$600	($150)	10%
	Utilities		$300	$290	$10	5%
	Loans		$700	$700	$0	12%
	Childcare		$1,000	$1,000	$0	17%
	Car Insurance		$250	$250	$0	4%
	Health Insurance		$500	$500	$0	8%
	Gas		$250	$350	($100)	6%
	Car Payment	15-Aug	$500	$500	$0	8%
	Phone/Internet		$250	$250	$0	4%
	Total		$5,700	$5,940	($240)	

Before we conclude, here are the answers to the test in Chapter 13:

Answer Key:

1: A - 2: A - 3: A & D - 4: B - 5: B - 6: B - 7: B - 8: D - 9: C - 10: D - 11: B - 12: B

BONUS: VIDEO LECTURES & TEMPLATES READY-TO-USE

Excel is an essential program; knowing how to use it can make a difference.

However, learning it can be stressful, especially if you don't have time and need good guidance.

I wrote this mastery with the goal of helping those who need to learn the many features Excel offers in a short time. However, many people prefer the video course, having difficulty learning this program through the book alone. If you also prefer video lessons, don't worry. I have thought of that too.

I have included ***+ 140 Video Lectures*** that you can access right now so that you will no longer have any doubts and will become an Excel master.

Scan the QR Code for each section or click on the appropriate link;

Microsoft Excel Beginner's Tutorials

http://bit.ly/3GENuCa

Excel Tutorial for beginners

https://bit.ly/3GCoDyv

Basic Excel Proficiency Test

http://bit.ly/3WJ8Rar

100+ Templates Ready-To-Use

https://bit.ly/3ADg56P

CONCLUSION

Excel is the industry standard for database applications, often used for data input, financial planning, and money management, among other similar tasks. MS Excel, like every other piece of software, has certain flaws that need to be fixed. After you have purchased the certificate, you will need to consider both the advantages and the downsides of using Excel to determine whether it is the right choice for you. One of the most fundamental uses for Microsoft Excel is data collecting and organizing, which is also one of its most prevalent applications. The information may be easily organized into clean columns and rows and can then be classified according to the data.

Users can produce displays in which the data has been analyzed and inserted into graphs, charts, or tables to make visualization and analysis easier. This is made possible by the program's resources, which allow users to produce displays in which the data has been presented in its raw form. Excel's power to transform massive amounts of data into understandable, well-organized spreadsheets and graphs is one of the program's most useful and indispensable capabilities. When the data is organized, it is much easier to analyze and manage, especially when it is utilized to make charts and other visual representations of data interpretations. Excel does calculations on numbers in a fraction of a second, making it far easier to perform bulk computations using Excel than using a calculator. Depending on one's familiarity with Excel and level of expertise working with the program, formulas and computations may be utilized to efficiently calculate simple and complex equations using huge volumes of data. Excel may be accessed in several forms, including on mobile devices such as phones and tablets. Most alternative spreadsheet programs can import Excel sheets and operate with them.

The advantages are not limited to what has been discussed here; begin using Microsoft Excel and educate yourself.

This is the conclusion of Excel 2023.

Learning this software can help you manage your private with the use of templates for various needs and, of course, to increase your work skills and get higher roles or salaries.

If this book was helpful to you, please leave an honest review.

Thank you

Thomas Harrett

Printed in Great Britain
by Amazon

25845600R00093